SAP GRC AC
FOR
BEGINNERS

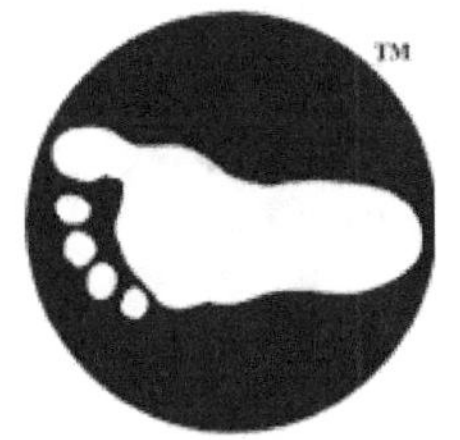

SAP GRC AC

FOR BEGINNERS

Premraj Kaushik

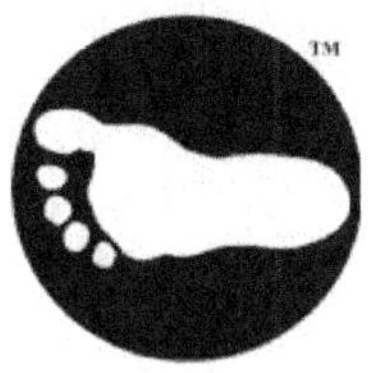

Bigfoot Publications

Because, there's a writer in everyone.

SAP GRC AC For Beginners
Author : Premraj Kaushik

First Published by
Bigfoot06 Publications (OPC) Pvt. Ltd.
B- 10,12 Shree Shyam Palace,
Sector 4,5 Chowk, Old Railway Road,
Gurugram, Haryana (122001)
Website: www.bigfootpublications.in
Email: info@bigfootpublications.in

First Edition : March 2023
© Premraj Kaushik

ISBN Print Book - **978-81-961461-9-1**

Although the author and publisher have made every effort to ensure the accuracy and completeness of information contained in this book, we assume no responsibility for errors, inaccuracies, omissions, or any inconsistencies herein. Any slights on people, places, or organizations are unintentional.

Printed in India

ACKNOWLEDGEMENT

Writing is a long and difficult process which cannot be accomplished without the help and support of some extraordinary and important people around you. I too have been lucky enough to have such people around me, who helped me through this process in every way they could.

First and most importantly I would like to thank my parents and my family whose support and motivation helped me in achieving my goal of writing this book.

Secondly, I would like to extend my gratitude to my IBM colleagues – "Tushar Tandon, Sushil Shah, Atit Upadhyay, Sanjay Gupta and Ramesh Deshmukh.

Above all, I express my special gratitude to Lord Ganesha for making me the person that I am, for always guiding me to the right path and providing me with strength to succeed in every endeavor of my life. I am nothing without his grace. His blessings made everything happen. *'Om Ganeshay Namah.'*

Premraj Kaushik

Table Of Content

EAM– Emergency Access Management	89 to 122
ARM - Access Request Management	123 to 149
MSMP WorkFlow	150 to 170
BRF (Business Rule Framework)	181 to 198
Template Management	199 to 202
Process Id Configuration	203 to 223
SOD Risk Review	224 to 241
User Access Review	242 to 259
BRM– Business Role Management	260 to 288
END USER LOGON CONFIGURATION	289 to 291
SAP S/4 Hana Fiori Rule set in GRC	292 to 298

<u>SAP GRC OVERVIEW</u>

GOVERNANCE : Is Communication of corporate control, key policies, regulatory and evaluating business performance through balanced scorecards, risk scorecards and operational dashboards. A governance process integrates all these elements into a logical process to drive corporate governance.

RISK : Enables an organization to evaluate all relevant business and regulatory risks and controls and monitor mitigation actions in a structured manner

COMPLIANCE : Ensures that an organization has the processes and internal controls to meet the requirements imposed by governmental bodies, regulators, industry mandates or internal policies.

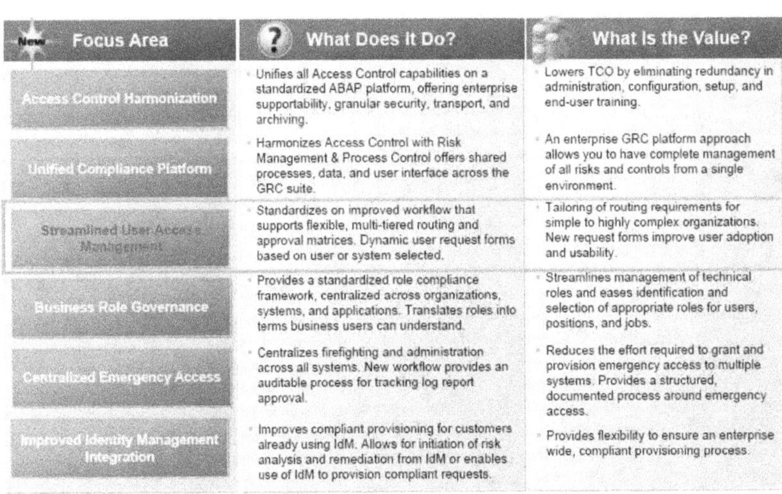

Focus Area	What Does It Do?	What Is the Value?
Access Control Harmonization	Unifies all Access Control capabilities on a standardized ABAP platform, offering enterprise supportability, granular security, transport, and archiving.	Lowers TCO by eliminating redundancy in administration, configuration, setup, and end-user training.
Unified Compliance Platform	Harmonizes Access Control with Risk Management & Process Control offers shared processes, data, and user interface across the GRC suite.	An enterprise GRC platform approach allows you to have complete management of all risks and controls from a single environment.
Streamlined User Access Management	Standardizes on improved workflow that supports flexible, multi-tiered routing and approval matrices. Dynamic user request forms based on user or system selected.	Tailoring of routing requirements for simple to highly complex organizations. New request forms improve user adoption and usability.
Business Role Governance	Provides a standardized role compliance framework, centralized across organizations, systems, and applications. Translates roles into terms business users can understand.	Streamlines management of technical roles and eases identification and selection of appropriate roles for users, positions, and jobs.
Centralized Emergency Access	Centralizes firefighting and administration across all systems. New workflow provides an auditable process for tracking log report approval.	Reduces the effort required to grant and provision emergency access to multiple systems. Provides a structured, documented process around emergency access.
Improved Identity Management Integration	Improves compliant provisioning for customers already using IdM. Allows for initiation of risk analysis and remediation from IdM or enables use of IdM to provision compliant requests.	Provides flexibility to ensure an enterprise wide, compliant provisioning process.

<u>SAP GRC SUITE OVERVIEW AND</u>
<u>COMPONENTS</u>

SAP GRC provides end-to-end automation for documenting, detecting, remediating, mitigating, and preventing risks enterprise-wide, resulting in proper segregation of duties (SoDs), proper operation of configuration and inherent controls, and oversight over transactions where necessary beyond proper configurations. SAP GRC does so at lower cost, at reduced risk, and with better business performance.

The SAP GRC suite contains the following components to address compliance management.

- *SAP Access Control*

- *SAP Process Control*

- *SAP Risk Management*

- *SAP Global Trade Services (SAP GTS)*

- *SAP Nota Fiscal Electronica (SAP NFE)*

SAP ACCESS CONTROL OVERVIEW

- Who are our users?

- What do they have access to?

- How did they get that access, who approved, and why?

- Are the extra access privileges provided to handle some extreme situations still available?

- Why is the active user ID available in the system even though the user left the company months ago?

SAP Access Control module helps in answering all the above questions and deriving solutions for them. It provides all mechanisms to simplify and streamline access provisioning and keeps the IT environment clean and risk free.

ACCESS CONTROL VERSIONS

VIRSA	GRC Access Control 5.X	GRC Access Control 10.0	GRC Acess Control 12.0
Access Enforcer (AE)	Compliant User Provisioning (CUP)	Access Request Management (ARM)	Access Request Management (ARM)
Compliance Calibrator (CC)	Risk Analysis and Remediation (RAR)	Access Risk Analysis (ARA)	Access Risk Analysis (ARA)
Fire Fighter (FF)	Super User Privilege Management (SPM)	Emergency Access Management (EAM)	Emergency Access Management (EAM)
Role Expert (RE)	Enterprise Role Management (ERM)	Business Role Management (BRM)	Business Role Management (BRM)

<u>FEATURES OF 12.X VERSION</u>
<u>COMPARATIVE STUDY</u>

- From a technical perspective, SAP has moved from Java programming language (VIRSA 5.X) to the Advanced

- Business Application Programming (ABAP) platform.

- This standardization allows centralized support across all components new platform improves change management processes by leveraging SAP's standard transport system, and background job scheduling and archiving features.

- SAP has standardized the look and feel of each GRC solution component and further simplified the

- User experience by creating a single-entry point.

- Due to moving to the new ABAP platform is the ability to incorporate multistage and multipath (MSMP) workflow configuration into approval routings.

- Centralized Emergency Access Management from a single system

- Use of BRF+ to bring flexibility in Workflow paths for Access Request.

FEATURES OF 12.X VERSION

COMPARATIVE STUDY

- GRC Persona-based launchpad simplifies navigation to convert GRC Work Centre to Fiori Links.

- Access Risk analysis for SAP Fiori apps in SAP S/4HANA (Including Services and Web Dynpro).

- SAP Identity Management for centralized provisioning and business role management.

- SAP SuccessFactors Employee Central Payroll. (Out of the box Integration capability with SAP SuccessFactors Employee Central)

- Repository sync optimization.

- Mass role methodology update.

- GRC 12.X Support SAP HANA database for User Provisioning and Risk Analysis.

- Simplify firefighter owner/controller maintenance.

- GRC 12 can be Integrated with SAP Cloud Identity Access Governance bridge to have Interface with cloud applications like Ariba, Fieldglass, SAC etc.

- Support Web-based applications.

- Business role integration with SAP Identity Management.

- Support PFCG menu hierarchy.

SOD – SEGREGATION OF DUTIES

A single person should not be able to complete two or more contradictory business actions. This is referred to as Segregation of Duties.

In general, the approval function, the accounting/ reconciling function, and the asset custody function should be separated among employees. When these functions cannot be separated, a detailed supervisory review of related activities is required as a compensating control activity. Segregation of duties is a deterrent to fraud because it requires collusion with another person to perpetrate a fraudulent act. Specific examples of segregation of duties are as follows:

- The person who requisitions the purchase of goods or services should not be the person who approves the purchase.

- The person who approves the purchase of goods or services should not be the person who reconciles the monthly financial reports.

- The person who approves the purchase of goods or services should not be able to obtain custody of checks.

- The person who maintains and reconciles the accounting records should not be able to obtain custody of checks.

- The person who opens the mail and prepares a listing

of checks received should not be the person who makes the deposit.

- The person who opens the mail and prepares a listing of checks received should not be the person who maintains the accounts receivable accounting records.

<u>SOX – SARBANES-OXLEY ACT</u>

SOX (Sarbanes–Oxley Act of 2002) is an US Accounting law that deals with the financial accounting of the companies.

To comply with SOX requirements, it is required that there should be well documented IT Processes. Over each of the IT Processes there should be well designed and documented internal controls and these controls should be well implemented and tracked and monitored.

There should be effective controls over the key security and financial processes. There needs to be a proof that these processes are well followed and tracked. To comply with section 404 of SOX, we should:

- Identify and document processes and SoD controls across key IT Security and financial processes.

- Design mitigating controls and document them, where appropriate SoD cannot be implemented.

- Design monitoring controls for critical processes and critical roles.

- Implement SoD and mitigating controls.

- Ensure continuous compliance by monitoring and tracking of controls.

<u>GRC TERMINOLOGIES</u>

- **Business Process :** A very high-level categorization which is used to group Access Rules e.g., Accounts Payable, HR & Payroll (Business process is a well-defined set of activities to be performed to handle a particular business scenario)

- **Action :** An activity that is performed in the system to fulfill a specific function (transaction code)

- **Permission :** Authorizations that allow a user to perform an activity in a system

- **Function :** A GRC Function identifies a medium-level business process and will have one or many transaction codes (GRC Actions) assigned, with additional permission level definitions where appropriate. Also, a transaction code may be assigned to several functions, if it has the implied business flexibility (Logical grouping of similar functionality Tcodes)

- **Risk :** An opportunity for physical loss, fraud, process disruption, or productivity loss that occurs when individuals exploit a specific condition. A GRC Access Risk is a description of a unique situation – a Critical Action /Role or a Segregation of Duties (SOD) breakdown. SOD Risk is comprised of two or more conflicting functions and Critical Action Risk is made of a single function which is critical for the system. e.g., SOD Risk H0164 is the combination of Function HR03 Modify Employee Payroll Data AND Function HR14 Enter time data

- **Access Rule :** A system-generated object with a single pair of tcodes & related permissions, based on the combination of GRC Functions which were defined as the Access Risk. Each Access Risk has one or more Access Rules generated for it.

- **Rule Set:** A pre-defined set of Access Risks and assigned Function combinations, against which a User or Role can be checked for potential SOD breakdown issues.

- **Action Level:** Term for analysis of risks at the SAP transaction code level, without looking at additional permissions (R/3 authorizations) which could otherwise eliminate the risk.

- **Permission Level :** This involves running the access reports taking account of the permissions a user has for a particular action as this helps in reducing the no of Risks.

- **Critical Action/Role/Profile :** Roles, Profiles and Transaction Codes (GRC Actions / Permissions) can be tagged as "critical" to ensure inclusion in access reviews (compliance and technical).

SOD RISK MANAGEMENT PROCESS OVERVIEW

SAP has developed a three-phase approach to risk management. By applying this method, it is possible to implement a process for segregation of duties (SoD) risk management. The process begins by defining the risks and building and validating rules.

Phase 1   **Phase 2**   **Phase 3**

1. RISK RECOGNITION :

The first phase of the SoD Risk Management process begins with identifying risks in your business processes and then classifying those risks

- *Identify authorization risks*

- *Approve exceptions*

- *Clarify and classify risk as high, medium, or low*

- *Identify new risks and conditions for future monitoring*

2. RULE BUILDING AND VALIDATION:

After risk recognition, the second step in Phase One of the SoD Risk Management process is Rule Building and Validation.

Rules include risks, functions, and business processes. Access Control automatically generates the rules as permutations of the different actions and permissions derived from the combined functions.

Actions and permissions combine to form functions. Functions in certain combinations result in a risk. Risks are associated with business processes and all the components come together to form rules. Rules are collected in a rule set.

3. RISK ANALYSIS:

During Risk Analysis, perform a security analysis to identify risks for Single Roles, Composite Roles and Users.

- *Run analytical reports*

- *Estimate cleanup efforts*

- *Analyze roles and users*

- *Modify rules based on analysis*

- *Set alerts to distinguish executed risks*

4. RISK REMEDIATION:

The purpose of the remediation phase is to determine alternatives for eliminating issues in roles.

- *Determine alternatives for eliminating risks*

- *Present analysis and select corrective actions*

- *Document approval of corrective actions*

- *Modify or create roles or user assignments*

5. RISK MITIGATION:

The purpose of the mitigation phase is to determine what mitigation controls are needed for those duties that cannot be segregated. Mitigation controls are required when it is not possible to segregate duties within the business process. For example, in a small office, one person must take over two roles within the business process, which causes a SoD conflict.

- *Determine alternative controls to mitigate risk*

- *Educate management about conflict approval and monitoring*

- *Document a process to monitor mitigation controls*

- *Implement controls*

TYPES OF MITIGATION CONTROLS

1. ***Preventative Controls :*** minimize the likelihood or impact of a risk before it occurs

2. ***Detective Controls :*** alert when a risk materializes and enable the responsible person to initiate corrective measures.

6. CONTINUOUS COMPLIANCE

The purpose of this phase is to maintain ongoing compliance. Future changes in roles, user assignments and business processes will require attention in the way of simulations and possible mitigation controls

- Communicate changes in roles and user assignments

- Simulate changes to roles and users

- Implement alerts to monitor for selected risks

- Mitigate control testing

GRC 12.X SYSTEM LANDSCAPE

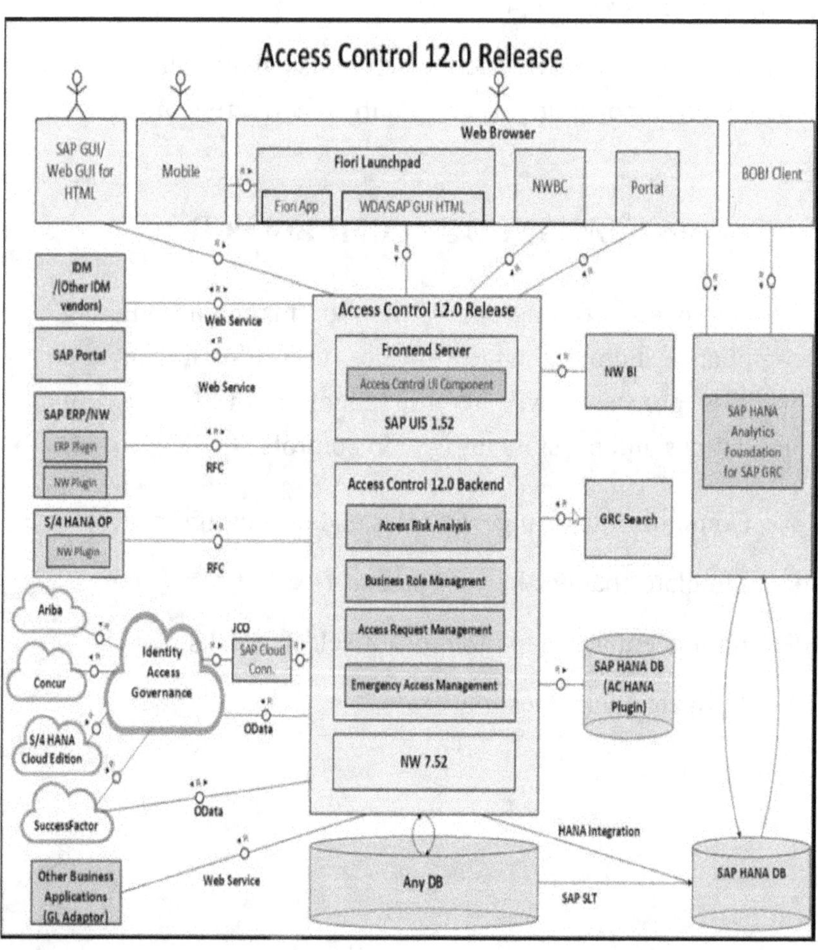

<u>GRC 12.X INSTALLATION</u>

Below are the pre-requisites for GRC 12 Setup:

- SAP NetWeaver 7.52 SP0x

- SAP UI Component 7.52 SP0x

- Adobe Flash 10 plug-in for GRC dashboards (for the browser and/or NWBC)

- SAP NWBC Client 4.0

- ABAP add-on "GRCFND_A" in GRC Box

- BACKEND plug-in GRCPIERP, (former HR RTA)

- BACKEND plug-in GRCPINW, (former non-HR RTA)

Installation of ABAP System along with GRC Component and Back End Plugin Systems are generally taken care by Basis Team. As a GRC Consultant, we need to verify that all these pre-requisites are maintained and then we can proceed with Post-Installation Activities.

POST INSTALLATION STEPS

1. *Client Copy*

2. *Creating the Initial User in the GRC ABAP System*

3. *Create Batch User*

4. *Create RFC connection GRC to Plug-In system*

5. *Activating Applications in Client*

6. *Check SAP ICF Services*

7. *Activate Profile of Roles Delivered by SAP*

1. CLIENT COPY

- Create a new client using SCC4

- Create & assigned Logical System using SALE

- Perform Client Copy using SCCL.

Display View "Clients": Overview

Client	Name	City	Crcy
000	SAP AG	Walldorf	EUR
001	SAP AG Konzern	Walldorf	EUR
066	EarlyWatch	Walldorf	EUR
100	GRC AC CLIENT	RSSGNR	INR
200	ERP BACKEND CLIENT	RSSGNR	INR

2. <u>CREATING THE INITIAL USER IN THE GRC ABAP SYSTEM</u>

- Create the Dialog User using SU01. This user Id is required to do Admin Task for GRC configuration.

- Assigned Below Roles.

  SAP_GRC_FN_BASE (General Role to all users)

  SAP_GRC_FN_ALL (Admin Role)

  SAP_GRC_FN_BUSINESS_USER (General Role to all users)

  SAP_GRC_NWBC (General Role to all users)

- Other Roles can be assigned based on the functionality required.

  GRAC Roles for Access Control

3. <u>CREATE BATCH USER</u>

- Create the Batch User using SU01 in ECC and GRC system. e.g.WF-BATCH. This Id is required for below Tasks:

  RFC Connections in ECC, Workflow Tasks, Background Jobs

- Roles Required:

  SAP_ALL and SAP_NEW may be assigned but based on client's

  IT policies, access can be restricted.

4. CREATE RFC CONNECTION GRC TO ECC/S4 HANA SYSTEM

- Maintain RFC (Remote Function Call)

- Connection from GRC to ECC System.

- Use SM59 to create RFC Destination.

- Batch Id in RFC connection should have

- Proper Authorizations assigned to it.

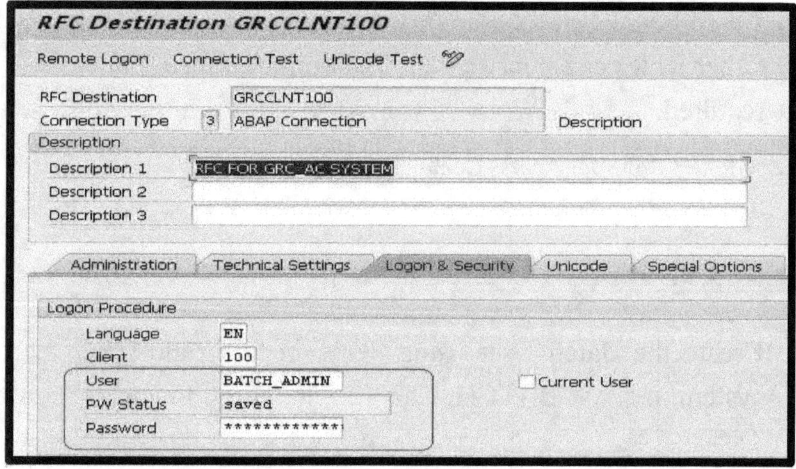

5. ACTIVATING APPLICATIONS IN CLIENT

- Call T-Code SPRO
- Choose SAP Ref IMG
- Expand the GRC
- General Settings node
- Choose Activate Applications in Client

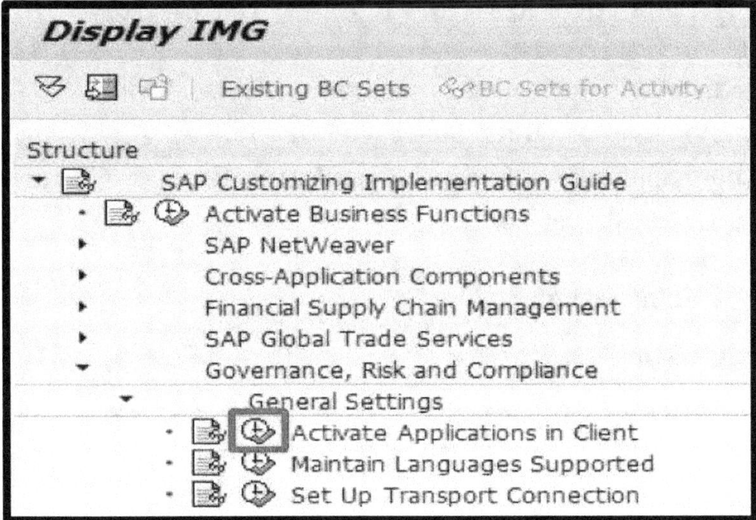

- Choose New Entries

- Click the first row and select the GRC solution(s) required for your project

- Then choose the Active checkbox

- Click Save

- Create the transport request if required.

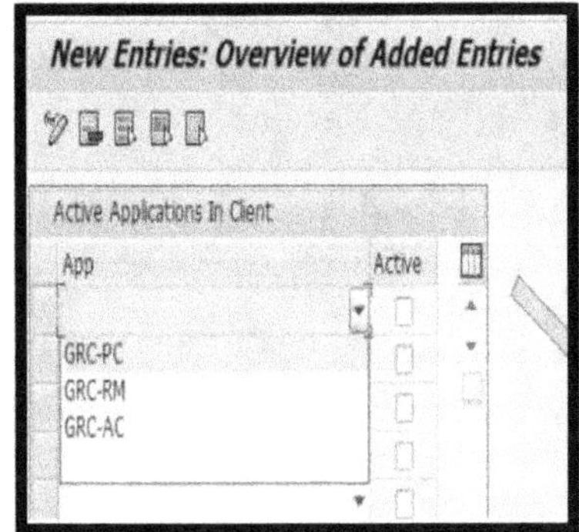

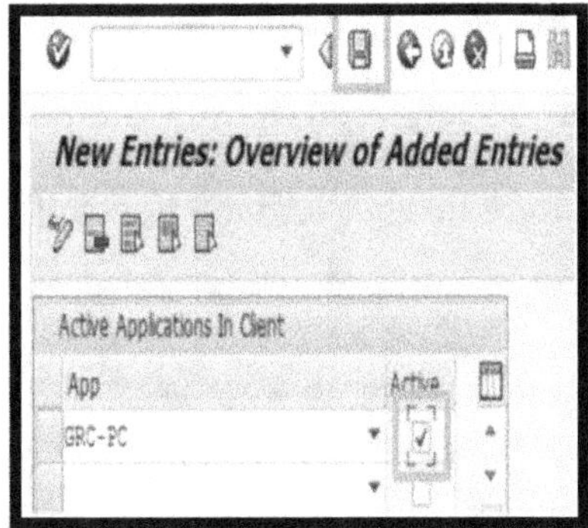

6. <u>ACTIVATING ICF SERVICES</u>

Internet Communication Framework (ICF) for all Web Dynpro services are required to view all ABAP Web Dynpro applications from SAP NetWeaver Business Client or SAP NetWeaver Portal

- Call transaction SICF

- Click the Execute icon

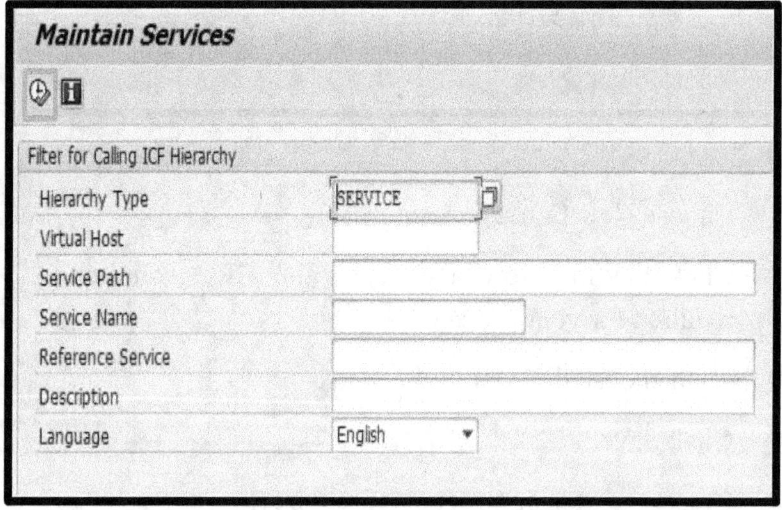

- Expand the node default_host-> sap -> public

- Right click public and choose Activate Service

- Choose Activate Service for all sub-nodes

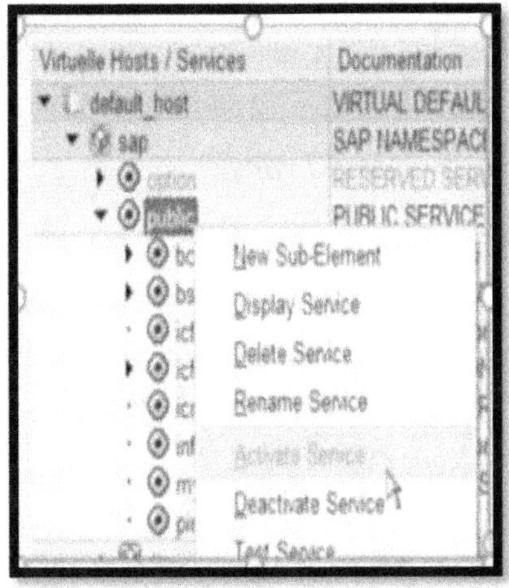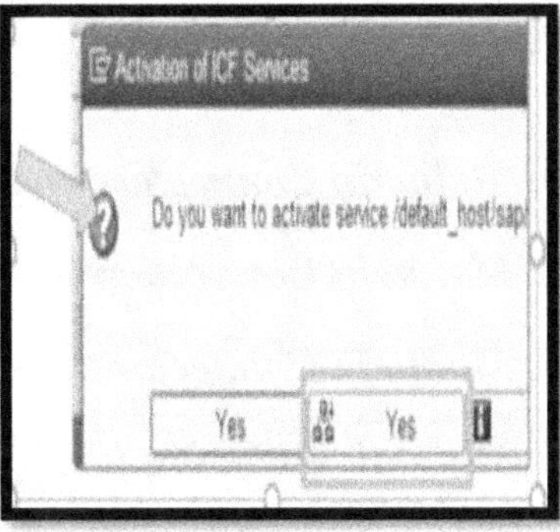

- Proceed likewise with the node default_host-> sap -> bc

- Activate all sub-nodes too

- Now activate the node default_host-> sap -> grc

- Also activate all sub-nodes

7. <u>ACTIVATE PROFILES FOR ROLES DELIVERED BY SAP</u>

- Activate profile of roles delivered by SAP via transaction PFCG if you want to use them directly

- Please use transaction "SUPC" for mass profile generation in case you want to generate profiles for multiple roles.

CONNECTOR CONFIGURATION

1. Maintain Connectors and Connection Types

2. Maintain Connection Settings (Integration Scenario)

3. Maintain Connector Settings

4. Maintain Mapping for Actions and Connector Groups

1. <u>MAINTAIN CONNECTORS AND CONNECTION TYPES</u>

Call SPRO --> SAP Reference IMG Governance, Risk and Compliance --> Common Component Settings --> Integration Framework --> Select Maintain Connectors and Connection Types

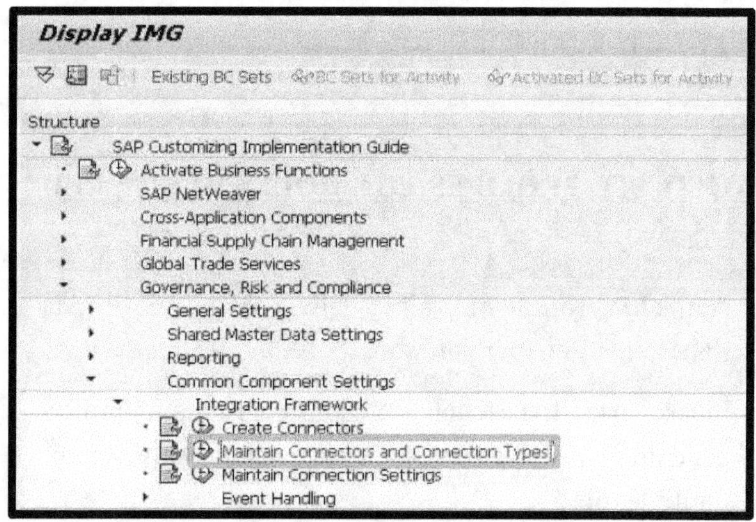

Select SAP (Connection Type) --> click on Define Connectors --> Go to new Entries --> Select Target Connector

Connection Type (SAP), Source Connector and Logical Port – Save

- Enter the RFC Connector Name for ECC System / Plug In system as Target System

- Logical Port will be same as Target Connector

- Source Connector would be RFC for GRC system. (Can be left Blank as well)

- For Every Plug-in system to be connected to GRC, this entry must be maintained.

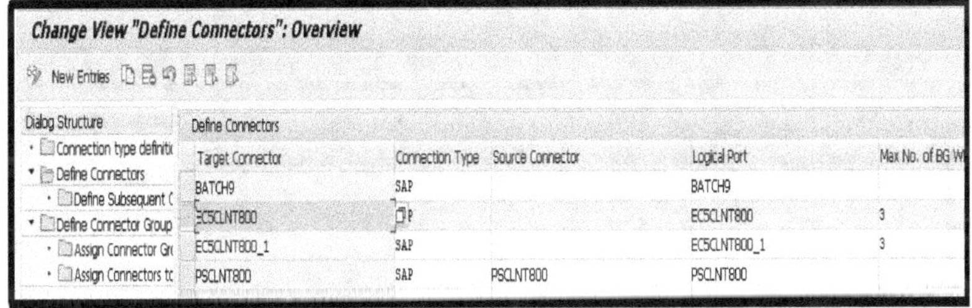

- Click on Define Connector Groups --> Select Connector Group (SAP_R3_LG) --> Select Logical Group --> Click on Assign Connectors to Connector Groups --> Enter Target Connector and Connection Type --> Click on Save.

- Please Note that SAP_R3_LG is the default connector Group for R3 Systems. You can create your own Connector Group if it is required to separate different systems in different groups. To create new Connector group, click on New Entries

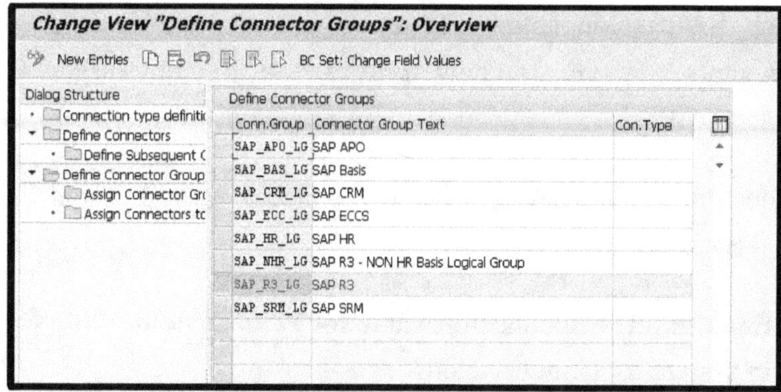

Select Connector Group –

✓ Click on Assign Connector Groups to Group Types --> Select Logical Group --> Click on Save

✓ Click on Assign Connectors to Connector Groups --> Enter Target Connector and Connection Type --> Click on Save.

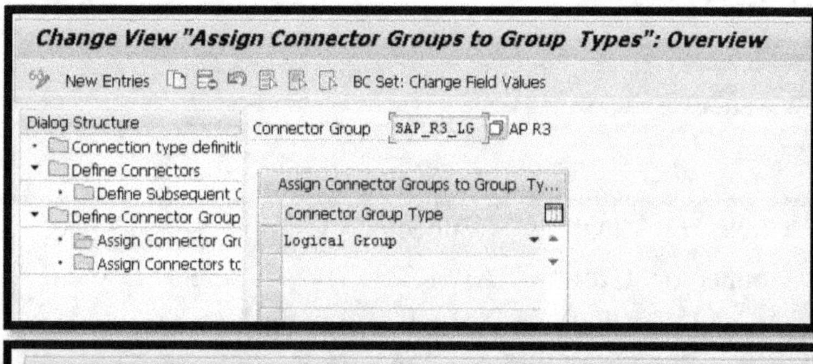

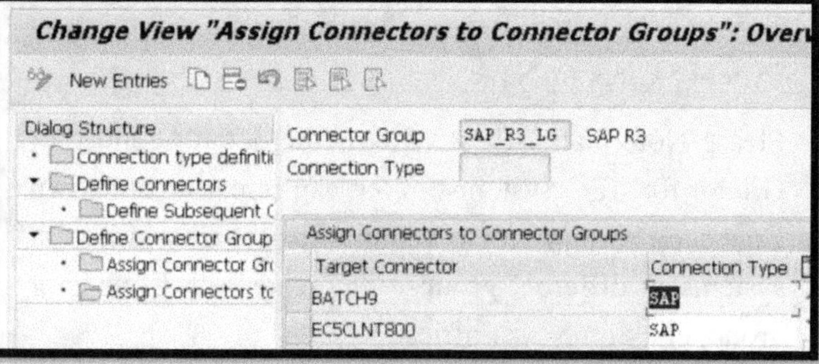

2. MAINTAIN CONNECTION SETTINGS (INTEGRATION SCENARIO)

Call SPRO -->SAP Reference IMG --> Governance, Risk and Compliance --> Common Component Settings --> Integration Framework --> Select Maintain Connection Settings.

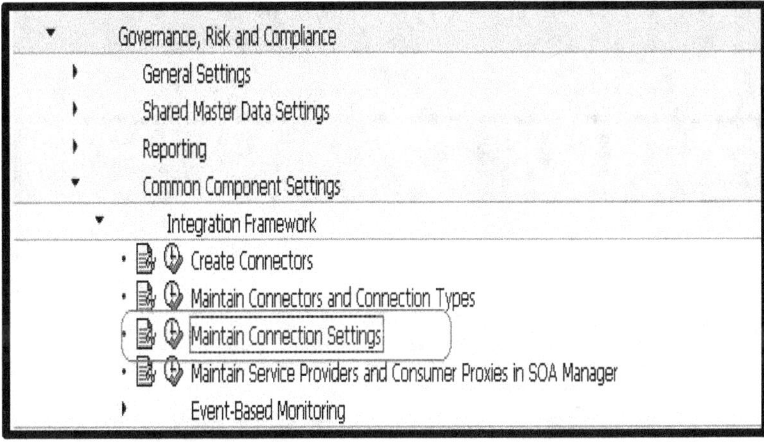

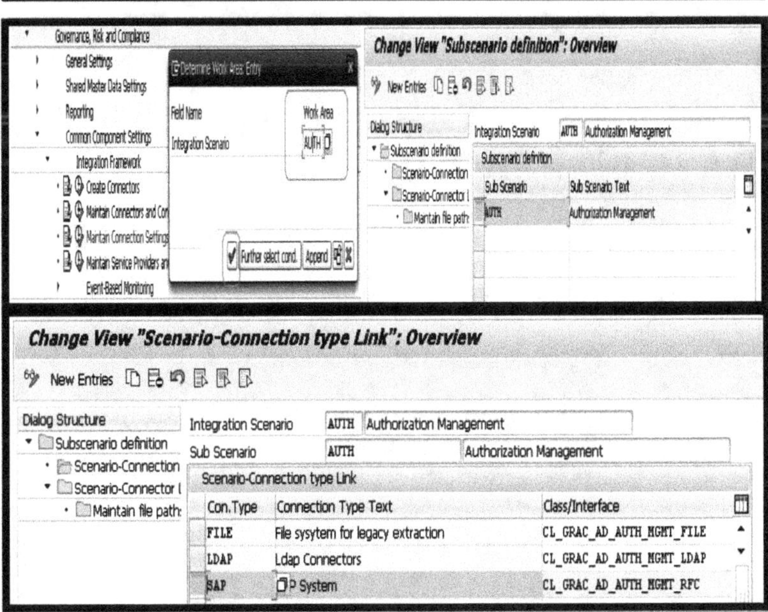

- For ARA, Select Integration Scenario AUTH —->
  Continue

- Select Sub Scenario (AUTH) - Double Click on
  Scenario-connection Type Link —-> Select SAP -->
  Save

Select SAP (Connection Type) - Double Click on Scenario
Connector Link - Select Target Connector and Connection
Type, then Save.

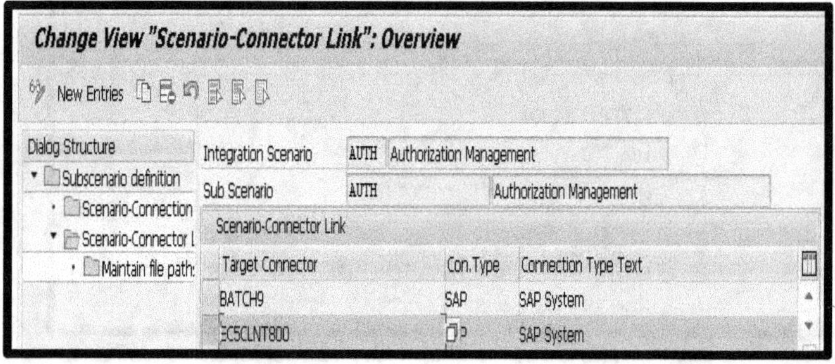

<u>REPEAT THE SAME STEPS FOR OTHER 3 INTEGRATION SCENARIO:</u>

- *PROV – This is for ARM Component*

- *ROLMG – This is for BRM Component*

- *SUPMG – This is for EAM Component*

3. <u>MAINTAIN CONNECTOR SETTINGS</u>

Call SPRO -->SAP Reference IMG --> Governance, Risk and Compliance --> Access Control --> Select Maintain Connector Settings

Click on New Entries --> Select Target Connector, Application Type as SAP, Environment (Dev, Test or Production)

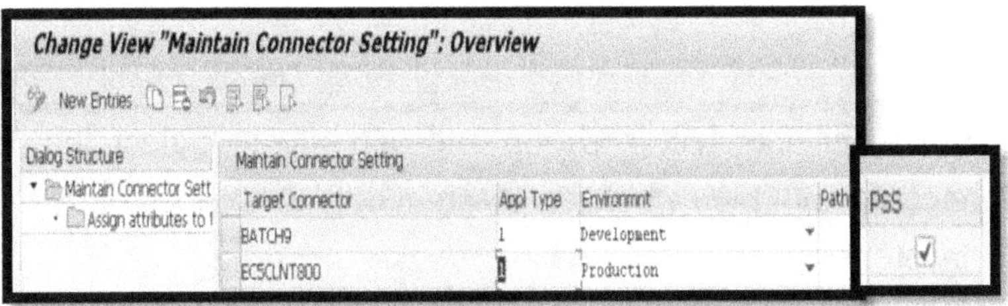

Enable PSS Checkbox if password self-service needs to be enabled for the system.

4. <u>MAINTAIN MAPPING FOR ACTIONS AND CONNECTOR GROUPS</u>

Call SPRO -->SAP Reference IMG --> Governance, Risk and Compliance --> Access Control --> Select Maintain Mapping for Actions and Connector Group

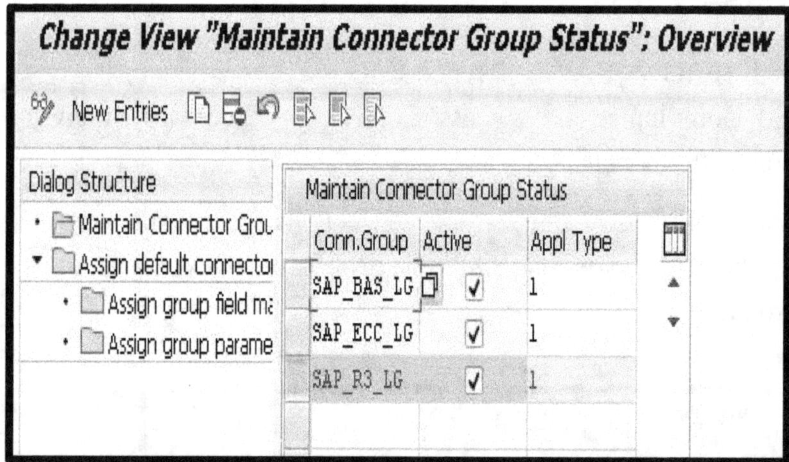

Maintain the Connector Group and activate it. Select the Connector and then click on Assign default connector to Connector Group.

Maintain the connector group and Target Connector combination for Action 0001, 0002, 0003 and 0004. For each action for the connector group, select one Target Connector as default.

This step is required so that GRC can identify the default system to be used for performing various actions in Access Control modules.

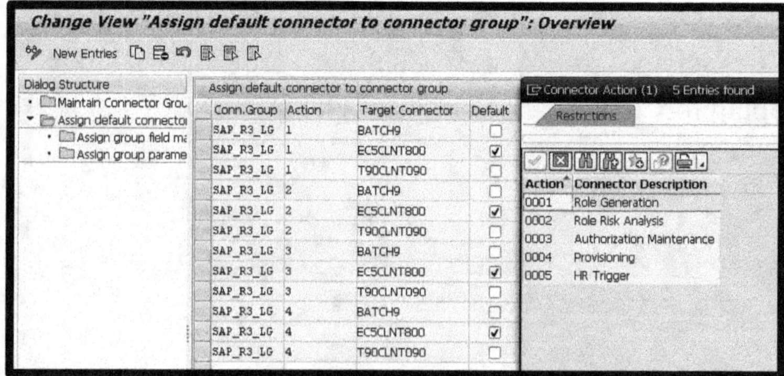

MAINTAIN CONFIGURATION SETTINGS

Call SPRO --> SAP Reference IMG --> Governance, Risk and Compliance --> Access Control --> Click on Maintain Configuration Settings --> Go to New Entries --> Select Param Group --> Select Param ID & Parameter Value

These settings are very important as it controls most of the access control functionalities.

Grp ID	Parameter Group Description	Grp ID	Parameter Group Description
01	Change Log	12	Access Request Role Selection
02	Mitigation	13	Access Request Default Roles
03	Risk Analysis	14	Access Request Role Mapping
04	Risk Analysis—Spool	15	SoD Review
05	Workflow	16	LDAP
06	Superuser Management	17	Assignment Expiry
07	UAR Review	18	Access Request Training Verification
08	Performance	19	Authorizations
09	Risk Analysis—Access Request	20	Access Request Business Role
10	Role Management	21	Management Dashboard Reports
11	Risk Analysis—Risk Terminator	22	Access Request Validations

1. <u>ARA SETTINGS</u>

Parameter 1023, 1024, 1025, 1026 and 1027 should always be maintained. All other parameters can be set based on Business Needs.

AC Configuration settings

Parm Group	Param ID	Parameter Value	Priority	Description
Risk Analysis	1023	02		Default report type for risk analysis
Risk Analysis	1024	*		Default risk level for risk analysis
Risk Analysis	1025	GLOBAL		Default rule set for risk analysis
Risk Analysis	1026	A		Default user type for risk analysis
Risk Analysis	1027	YES		Enable Offline Risk Analysis
Risk Analysis	1028	NO		Include Expired Users
Risk Analysis	1029	NO		Include Locked Users
Risk Analysis	1030	NO		Include Mitigated Risks
Risk Analysis	1031	NO		Ignore Critical Roles & Profiles
Risk Analysis	1032	YES		Include Reference user when doing user analysis
Risk Analysis	1033	YES		Include Role/Profile Mitigating Controls in Risk Analysis
Risk Analysis	1035	YES		Send email notification to the monitor of the updated mitigated object
Risk Analysis	1036	YES		Show All Objects in Risk Analysis
Risk Analysis	1037	YES		Use SoD Supplementary Table for Analysis.
Risk Analysis	1046	EC5CLNT800		Extended objects enabled connector

Configuration Parameter	Value	Description	Details
1034	5	Maximum number of objects in a package for parallel processing	The application uses this parameter in conjunction with the NUMBER OF TASKS specified in the customizing activity DISTRIBUTE JOBS FOR PARALLEL PROCESSING to determine the distribution of objects that are processed per job. Note: The RZ10 parameter RDISP/WP_NO_BTC overrides this configuration. Therefore, if the RZ10 parameter is set to 2, then the application ignores the parameter in this setting and uses the value 2 instead.

Configuration Parameter	Value	Description	Details
1021	No	Consider organization rules for other applications	Setting the value to YES automatically selects the CONSIDER ORG RULE checkbox on the RISK VIOLATIONS tab of the ACCESS REQUEST AND ROLE MAINTENANCE screens.
1023	2	Default report type for risk analysis	The risk analysis allows options such as analysis criteria, report options, and additional criteria. This parameter allows you to choose the type of report that is selected by default (02 = PERMISSION LEVEL). Note: This setting doesn't affect the RISK ANALYSIS TYPE fields on the BATCH RISK ANALYSIS screens; you must set these separately.

Configuration Parameter	Value	Description	Details
1024	3	Default risk level for risk analysis	Risk level that is selected by default (3 = CRITICAL).
1025	GLOBAL	Default rule set for risk analysis	This parameter allows you to choose the rule set that is selected by default.
1026	A	Default user type for risk analysis	This parameter allows you to choose the user type that is selected by default (A = DIALOG).
1027	NO	Enable offline risk analysis	Set the parameter value to YES to include offline data in risk analysis by default. On the RISK ANALYSIS screen, the OFFLINE DATA checkbox is selected automatically.
1028	NO	Include expired users	Set to YES to include expired users from plug-in systems for risk analysis.
1029	NO	Include locked users	Set to YES to include locked users from plug-in systems for risk analysis.
1030	YES	Include mitigated risks	Set the parameter value to YES to include mitigated risks in the risk analysis by default. The application displays the SoD violations, the mitigated risks, and the mitigating control assigned to it. On the RISK ANALYSIS screen, the INCLUDE MITIGATED RISKS checkbox is automatically selected.
1031	YES	Ignore critical roles and profiles	Set the value to YES to exclude critical roles and profiles for risk analysis.
1033	YES	Include role/profile mitigating controls in risk analysis	Set the value to YES to include the mitigating controls assigned to the user's roles and profiles for risk analysis.

2. <u>ARM SETTINGS</u>

Access Request Role Selection	2031	YES	Allow All Roles for Approver
Access Request Role Selection	2032	A	Approver Role Restriction Attribute
Access Request Role Selection	2033	YES	Allow All Roles for Requestor
Access Request Role Selection	2034	B	Requestor Role Restriction Attribute
Access Request Role Selection	2035	YES	Allow Role Comments
Access Request Role Selection	2036	NO	Role Comments Mandatory
Access Request Role Selection	2037	YES	Display expired roles for existing roles
Access Request Role Selection	2038	YES	Auto Approve Roles without Approvers
Access Request Default Roles	2009	YES	Consider Default Roles
Access Request Default Roles	2010	001	Request type for default roles
Access Request Default Roles	2011	REQUEST	Default Role Level
Access Request Default Roles	2013	SYSTEM	Request Attributes
Access Request Role Mapping	2014	YES	Enable Role Mapping
Access Request Role Mapping	2015	YES	Applicable to Role Removals

Risk Analysis - Access Requ...	1071	YES	Enable risk analysis on form submission
Risk Analysis - Access Requ...	1072	YES	Mitigation of critical risk required before approving the request

Along with above parameters, maintain parameters for Workflow and other Access related ones. Detailed description on the configuration parameters is available in the document below.

3. <u>EAM SETTINGS</u>

- Parameter ID 4000 determines whether you want to use the ID based or role-based firefighter application option.

- If you select the ID based firefighter application, then

you need to maintain parameter ID 4010 with the role name maintained in SAP ERP or any other target system to identify the firefighter ID.

- Also, you need to add another parameter 1113 with the WF-BATCH value as Access Control E-mail sender, which is part of the Workflow parameter group. This parameter setting is necessary to send email to the controller and owner about the emergency access activity with user and usage details.

Parm Group		Param Value	Description
Emergency Access Management	▼ 4000	1	Application type
Emergency Access Management	▼ 4001	15	Default Firefighter Validity Period (Days)
Emergency Access Management	▼ 4002	YES	Send Email Immediately
Emergency Access Management	▼ 4003	YES	Retrieve Change Log
Emergency Access Management	▼ 4004	YES	Retrieve System log
Emergency Access Management	▼ 4005	YES	Retrieve Audit log
Emergency Access Management	▼ 4006	YES	Retrieve OS Command log
Emergency Access Management	▼ 4007	NO	Send Log Report Execution Notification Immediately
Emergency Access Management	▼ 4008	YES	Send FirefightId Login Notification
Emergency Access Management	▼ 4009	NO	Log Report Execution Notification
Emergency Access Management	▼ 4010	SAP_GRAC_SPM_FFID	Firefighter ID role name

4. <u>BRM SETTINGS</u>

Parm Group	Param ID	Parameter Value	Priority	Description
Role Management	▼ 3000	BS00		Default Business Process
Role Management	▼ 3001	ADMIN		Default Subprocess
Role Management	▼ 3002	1		Default Critical Level
Role Management	▼ 3004	DEV		Default Role Status
Role Management	▼ 3005	NO		Reset Role Methodology when Changing Role Attributes
Role Management	▼ 3006	YES		Allow add functions to an authorization
Role Management	▼ 3007	YES		Allow editing organizational level values for derived roles
Role Management	▼ 3008	YES		A ticket number is required after authorization data changes
Role Management	▼ 3009	YES		Allow Role Deletion from Back-End
Role Management	▼ 3010	YES		Allow attaching files to the role definition
Role Management	▼ 3011	NO		Conduct Risk Analysis before Role Generation
Role Management	▼ 3012	YES		Allow Role Generation on Multiple Systems
Role Management	▼ 3013	YES		Use logged-on user credentials for role generation
Role Management	▼ 3014	YES		Allow role generation with Permission Level violations
Role Management	▼ 3015	YES		Allow role generation with Critical Permission violations
Role Management	▼ 3016	YES		Allow role generation with Action Level violations
Role Management	▼ 3017	YES		Allow role generation with Critical Action violations
Role Management	▼ 3018	YES		Allow role generation with Critical Role/Profile violations
Role Management	▼ 3019	YES		Overwrite individual role's Risk Analysis result during Mass Risk Analysis run
Role Management	▼ 3020	1		Role certification reminder notification

Configuration Parameter	Value	Description	Details
3000	<empty>	Business process	Default business process
3001	<empty>	Subprocess	Default subprocess
3002	<empty>	Criticality level	Default criticality level
3003	<empty>	Default project release	Maintains project release
3004	Dev	Default role status	Role status: development, test, or production
3005	NO	Reset role methodology	YES value resets the role methodology step to the initial, irrespective of the type of change carried out
3006	YES	Add functions to authorization	Enables adding new functions to authorization
3007	NO	Editing organization level value of derived roles	Enables editing organizational-level values for derived roles
3008	YES	Ticket for authorization data change	Requires a ticket number after authorization data changes
3009	YES	Role deletion	Enables deleting of roles from the plug-in system
3010	YES	Attaching files	Enables attaching files to the role definition
3011	YES	Risk analysis before role generation	Conducts risk analysis before role generation
3025	NO		Allows selection of organization value maps without leading organization
3026	YES		Saves role provisioning details while copying role

Configuration Parameter	Value	Description	Details
3012	NO	Role generation on multiple system	Enables role generation on multiple systems (useful for certain customers of global landscapes)
3013	NO		Uses logged-on user credentials for role generation
3014	NO		Allows role generation with permission level violations
3015	NO		Allows role generation with critical permission violations
3016	NO		Allows role generation with action level violations
3017	NO		Allows role generation with critical action violations
3018	NO		Allows role generation with critical role/profile violations
3019	NO		Overwrites individual role risk analysis results for mass risk analysis
3020	10		Provides role certification reminder notification in number of days
3021	<Empty>		Provides directory for mass role import server files
3022	21	Workflow	Provides request type for Role approval
3023	5	Workflow	Provides priority for role approval
3024	YES	Workflow	Enforces methodology process for derived roles during generation

BUSINESS CONFIGURATION SETS (BC SETS)

BC Sets are snapshots of customization settings or some master data that are captured by SAP and delivered as part of the software package. If you activate a BC Set, all relevant tables and table views are populated, and you can customize the configuration to suit your needs.

BC Set data are basically table entries that are populated in multiple tables and that can be extracted and repopulated in different systems directly from Transaction SCPR20.

To activate BC Sets, execute T-code SCPR20, Enter BC Set Name and click Activate.

- Access Control BC Sets starts with GRAC

- Process Control BC Sets starts with GRPC

- Risk Management BC Sets starts with GRRM

Enter GRAC* in BC Set Input box and press F4. You will get the list of all BC Sets available in Access Control. Select the BC Set and click on Activate Button.

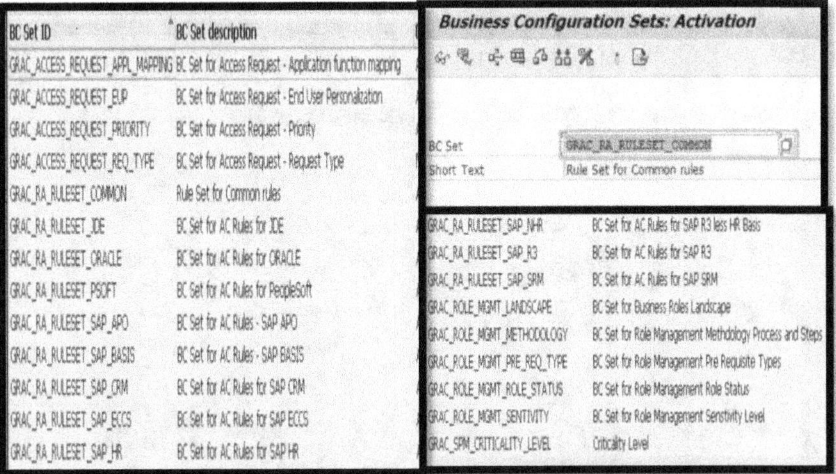

Once you click on Activate Button, it will ask for Transport request. Please enter the transport which can be moved to Quality and Production system later.

Activation Options screen will open. Select the options 'overwrite all data' and 'default mode(recommended)' to activate very first time. In case, you are familiar with BC Set activation you can use 'expert mode' for activation and any data you want to append with already existing data then use 'do not overwrite default values'

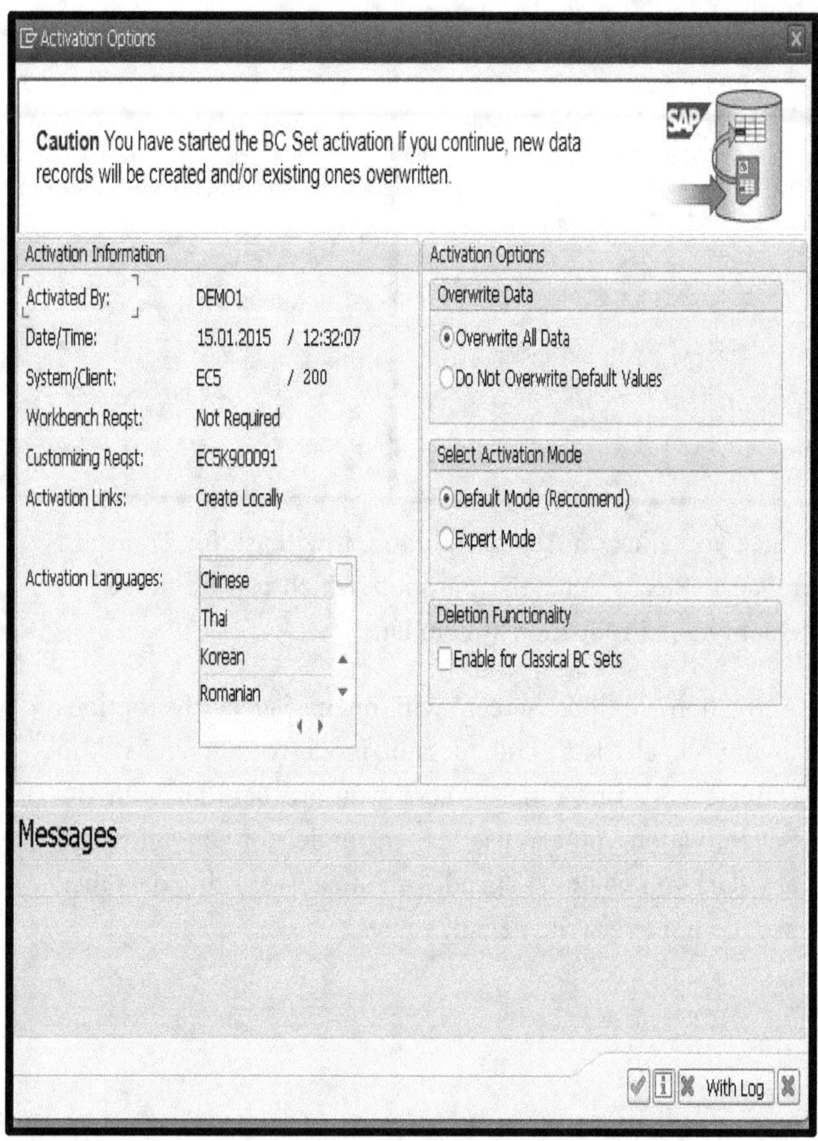

Activation Options

Caution You have started the BC Set activation If you continue, new data records will be created and/or existing ones overwritten.

SAP

Activation Information
Activated By: DEMO1
Date/Time: 15.01.2015 / 12:32:07
System/Client: EC5   / 200
Workbench Reqst: Not Required
Customizing Reqst: EC5K900091
Activation Links: Create Locally

Activation Languages:
Chinese
Thai
Korean
Romanian

Activation Options

Overwrite Data
Overwrite All Data
Do Not Overwrite Default Values

Select Activation Mode
Default Mode (Reccomend)
Expert Mode

Deletion Functionality
Enable for Classical BC Sets

Messages

With Log

LIST OF BC SETS :

- Common BC Set: GRAC_RA_RULESET_COMMON (This is required if we want to use the Rule set provided by SAP i.e., GLOBAL Ruleset)

- BC Set for R3 System Rule Set:

  GRAC_RA_ RULESET_SAP_R3 (This Rule Set applies to R3 System). This will insert the SAP provided Functions, Risks into corresponding table.

- If we are using any other backend system, respective BC set from Below list need to be activated. To use the enabled rule set, connectors need to be assigned to the respective logical group in IMG.

GRAC_RA_RULESET_JDE	BC Set for AC Rules for JDE
GRAC_RA_RULESET_ORACLE	BC Set for AC Rules for ORACLE
GRAC_RA_RULESET_PSOFT	BC Set for AC Rules for PeopleSoft
GRAC_RA_RULESET_SAP_APO	BC Set for AC Rules - SAP APO
GRAC_RA_RULESET_SAP_BASIS	BC Set for AC Rules - SAP BASIS
GRAC_RA_RULESET_SAP_CRM	BC Set for AC Rules for SAP CRM
GRAC_RA_RULESET_SAP_ECCS	BC Set for AC Rules for SAP ECCS
GRAC_RA_RULESET_SAP_HR	BC Set for AC Rules for SAP HR
GRAC_RA_RULESET_SAP_NHR	BC Set for AC Rules for SAP R3 less HR Basis
GRAC_RA_RULESET_SAP_R3	BC Set for AC Rules for SAP R3
GRAC_RA_RULESET_SAP_SRM	BC Set for AC Rules for SAP SRM

BC Sets for ARM: Below BC Sets needs to be activated for ARM Master Data

BC Set ID	BC Set description
GRAC_ACCESS_REQUEST_APPL_MAPPING	BC Set for Access Request - Application function mapping
GRAC_ACCESS_REQUEST_EUP	BC Set for Access Request - End User Personalization
GRAC_ACCESS_REQUEST_PRIORITY	BC Set for Access Request - Priority
GRAC_ACCESS_REQUEST_REQ_TYPE	BC Set for Access Request - Request Type

BC Set for EAM: GRAC_SPM_CRITICALITY_LEVEL

BC Sets for BRM: Below BC Sets needs to be activated for BRM Master Data

GRAC_ROLE_MGMT_LANDSCAPE	BC Set for Business Roles Landscape
GRAC_ROLE_MGMT_METHODOLOGY	BC Set for Role Management Methdology Process and Steps
GRAC_ROLE_MGMT_PRE_REQ_TYPE	BC Set for Role Management Pre Requisite Types
GRAC_ROLE_MGMT_ROLE_STATUS	BC Set for Role Management Role Status
GRAC_ROLE_MGMT_SENTIVITY	BC Set for Role Management Senstivity Level

ARA – ACCESS RISK ANALYSIS

1. ***Generate Rules***

2. ***Synchronization Jobs***

3. ***Batch Risk Analysis [For Offline Analysis]***

4. ***First Adhoc Risk Analysis***

5. ***Risk Simulation***

1. GENERATE RULES

Call SPRO --> SAP Reference IMG --> Governance, Risk and Compliance --> Access Control --> Access Risk Analysis --> SoD Rules --> Generate SoD Rules

Alternatively use the T-code GRAC_GENERATE_RULES to generate Rules.

Enter the Risk Id for which you need to generate the Rules or leave it blank to generate for all Risk Ids. For the first time keep it blank.

The activity generates SoD rules and inserts them into the corresponding tables GRACACTRULE and GRACSYSRULE.

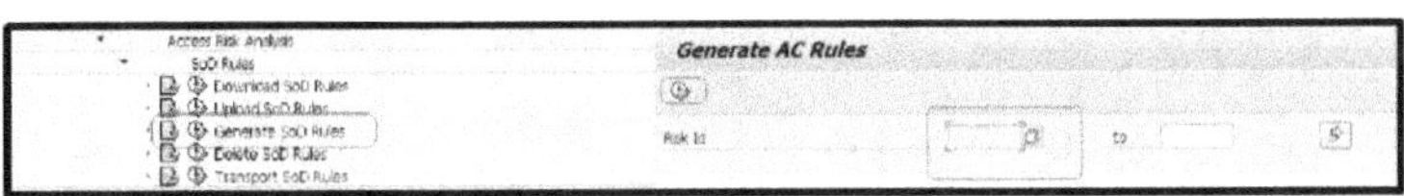

To check the available Risk IDs loaded from the BC Set, execute T-code NWBC. Business client will open in browser Window.

Navigate to Setup --> Access Rule Maintenance --> Access Risks.

Select a Risk Id and click on Open to view the details for the Risk.

Also, you can check the table GRACSODRISK to get list of Risk Ids.

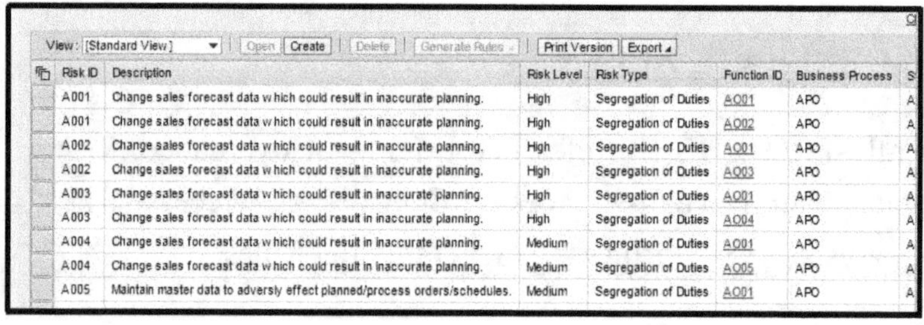

Risk ID	Description	Risk Level	Risk Type	Function ID	Business Process	S
A001	Change sales forecast data which could result in inaccurate planning.	High	Segregation of Duties	AQ01	APO	A
A001	Change sales forecast data which could result in inaccurate planning.	High	Segregation of Duties	AQ02	APO	A
A002	Change sales forecast data which could result in inaccurate planning.	High	Segregation of Duties	AQ01	APO	A
A002	Change sales forecast data which could result in inaccurate planning.	High	Segregation of Duties	AQ03	APO	A
A003	Change sales forecast data which could result in inaccurate planning.	High	Segregation of Duties	AQ01	APO	A
A003	Change sales forecast data which could result in inaccurate planning.	High	Segregation of Duties	AQ04	APO	A
A004	Change sales forecast data which could result in inaccurate planning.	Medium	Segregation of Duties	AQ01	APO	A
A004	Change sales forecast data which could result in inaccurate planning.	Medium	Segregation of Duties	AQ05	APO	A
A005	Maintain master data to adversly effect planned/process orders/schedules.	Medium	Segregation of Duties	AQ01	APO	A

2. <u>BACKGROUND JOBS</u>

We have Two Types of Synch jobs to synch backend Data.

● Authorization Synch

Program   GRAC_PFCG_AUTHORIZATION_SYNC   (T-code GRAC_AUTH_SYNC)

● Repository Object Synch

Program GRAC_REPOSITORY_OBJECT_SYNC (T-code

GRAC_REP_OBJ_SYNC)

AUTHORIZATION SYNC :

In this Customizing activity, we can synchronize the authorization master data from the back-end ERP systems and store it in the GRC AC repository.

Call SPRO -->SAP Reference IMG --> Governance, Risk and Compliance --> Access Control --> Access Risk Analysis --> Synchronization Jobs --> Click on Authorization Synch

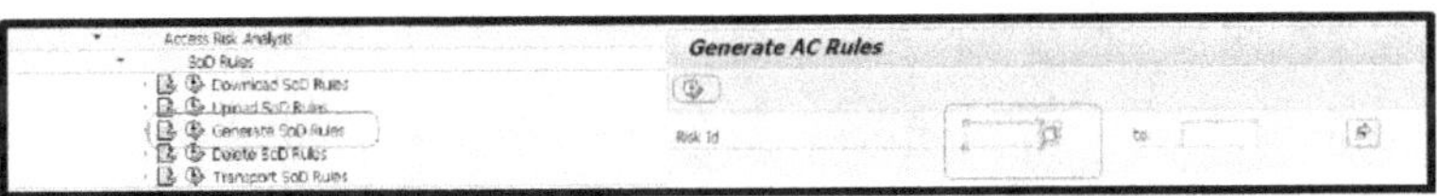

The Authorization synchronization updates the data for the following:

- **Resource Sync** - permissions, resources, and descriptions for authorization objects

- **Action Sync** - descriptions for actions, and permissions and resources for authorization objects

- **Resource Class Sync** - permissions and resources for authorization object classes and their relationships

- **Resource Extension** - organization level, activities, and descriptions for resource extensions

- **Default (SU24) Values Sync** - default authorization objects and field values for actions.

Mention the Target Connector and the language and schedule the job in background. Also schedule a periodic job for this sync for updating the recent changes.

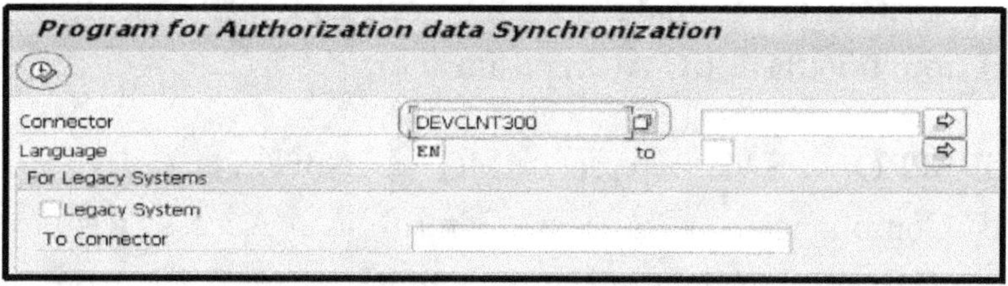

Repository Object Sync :

In this Customizing activity, we can synchronize the data for profiles, roles and users from the ERP back end and legacy systems and store it in the GRAC repository.

Call SPRO -->SAP Reference IMG --> Governance, Risk and Compliance --> Access Control --> Access Risk Analysis --> Synchronization Jobs --> Click on Repository Object Sync

The activity allows you to select from the following synchronization options:

- **Profile Synch** - This is required for the SoD Risk Analysis of Profiles.

- **Role Synch** - This is required for the SoD Risk Analysis of Roles.

• **User Synch** - This is required for the SoD Risk Analysis of Users.

Profile Synch :

• PD Profiles and descriptions

• PD Profiles Actions for legacy systems

• PD Profiles Permissions for legacy systems

• All related data for Deleted Profiles is deleted from the repository and violation tables

Role Synch :

• Roles and their descriptions

• Roles Org Levels relationship

• Role Actions for legacy systems

• Role Permissions for legacy systems

• All related data for Deleted Roles is deleted from the repository and violation tables

User Synch :

• Users and their descriptions

- Users and Profiles relationship

- Users and PD Profiles relationship

- Users and Roles relationship

- Users Org Levels relationship

- Users Actions and Permissions for legacy systems

Enter the Connector Name, select the Objects to be synched and specify the language(s) we wish to synchronize. First run should be done in Full Sync mode in background, then Incremental Sync can be scheduled with hourly or half hourly period to synchronize the near real-time changes from the plug-in system to the SAP Access Control system. Incremental Sync synchronize only the data changed since the last synchronization activity.

In addition to Authorization and Repository Object Sync, you need to schedule below jobs as well.

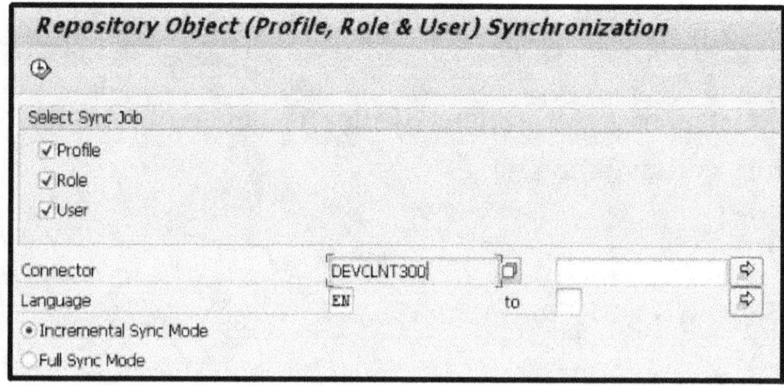

Action Usage Sync : This will synchronize the action usage data from the back-end system to the GRAC repository. Action usage data is the data related to the user executed transactions. This data is required for SoD Risk Analysis and Alert Generation.

Call SPRO -->SAP Reference IMG --> Governance, Risk and Compliance --> Access Control --> Access Risk Analysis --> Synchronization Jobs --> Click on Action Usage Sync

Enter the connector Name and user Ids and schedule it in background.

Role Usage Sync : This will synchronize the role usage data from the back-end system to the GRAC repository. Role usage data is the role related data that contain transactions executed by users.

Call SPRO -->SAP Reference IMG --> Governance, Risk and Compliance --> Access Control --> Access Risk Analysis --> Synchronization Jobs --> Click on Role Usage Sync

Enter the connector name and schedule the job in background.

3. <u>BATCH RISK ANALYSIS</u>

Call SPRO -->SAP Reference IMG --> Governance, Risk and Compliance --> Access Control --> Access Risk Analysis --> Batch Risk Analysis --> Execute Batch Risk Analysis

In this Customizing activity, we can schedule the Batch Risk Analysis. Batch Risk Analysis is required for Offline Risk Analysis and Management reports. The activity performs Access Risk Analysis for the selected objects based on the selection criteria. The violation data is updated into the respective violation tables for the selected types of reports.

Batch Risk Analysis can also be scheduled using transaction GRAC_BATCH_RA (OR)

<u>PROGRAM - GRAC BATCH RISK ANALYSIS</u>

You can monitor the batch risk analysis job with transaction GRACRABATCH_MONITOR

• In the Job Name field, enter the job name.

• In the System field, enter the name of the back-end system.

• In the Batch Mode Processing field, select Incremental or Full.

• In the Rule Set field, select the rule set.

- Under the Object Selection area, select from the following and enter the relevant information: User Analysis, Role Analysis, Profile Analysis and HR Object Analysis

- Under the Risk Analysis Type area, select the appropriate analysis type.

- Choose Execute in Background

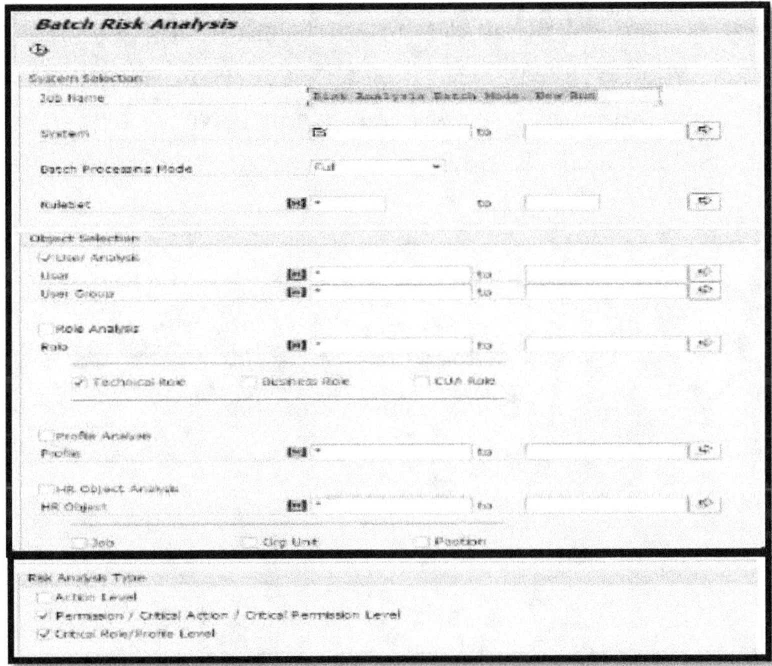

Batch Processing Mode field should be set to Full when you execute this batch risk analysis the first time to get a full scan of the system against all the users, roles, and profiles for the risks defined in the rule set.

For any subsequent scheduling, you can choose Incremental in the Batch Processing Mode field to reduce the load on the system for batch risk analysis; this will analyze only the changes to the user/role/ profile objects that happened after the previous batch risk analysis.

The best practice recommendation is to run batch risk analysis as a daily background job with incremental runs and then execute a full run once a month.

Now Execute NWBC go to the Reports and Analytics work center, choose Access Dashboard, and execute the Risk Violations report or User Analysis report to verify that all risks and risk analysis results.

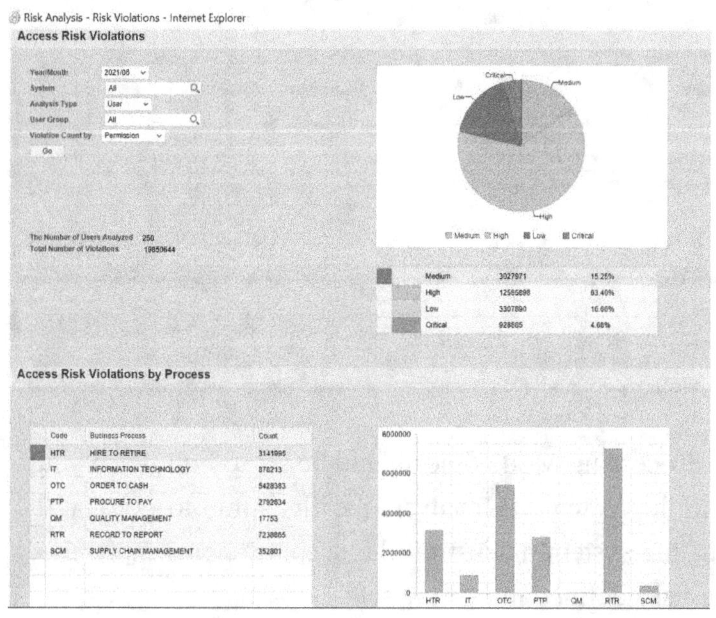

4. <u>RUNNING FIRST RISK ANALYSIS</u>

- Call NWBC --> Go to Access Management Work Center --> Click on Role Level

- Enter System, Role Type, Role, Risk Level and Rule Set. Select the Format and View

- Select Report type option: Access Risk Analysis and put tick mark on Action Level & Permission Level or Critical Action/Role/Profile/Permission as per the requirement.

- Click on Run in Foreground

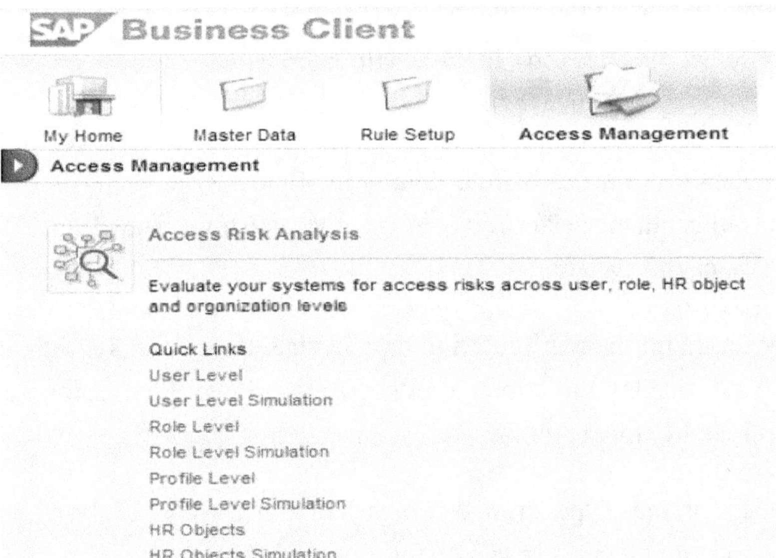

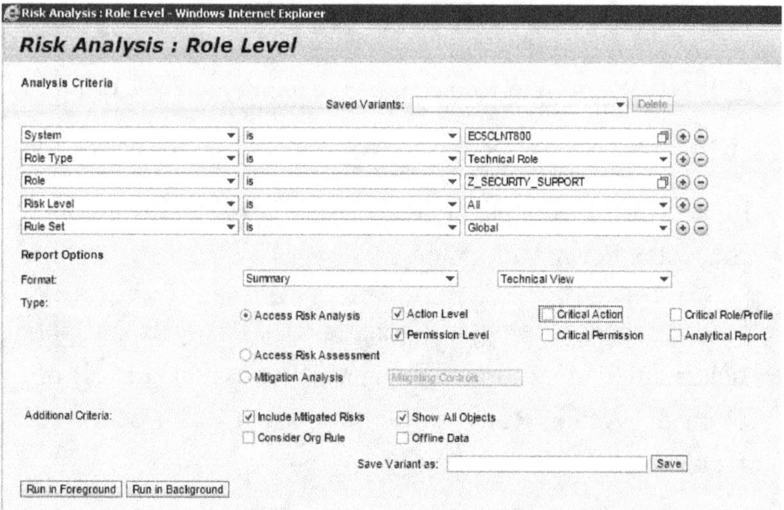

- If you need to include the mitigated Risks as well, please select the checkbox Include Mitigated Risk

- Enabling the Offline data checkbox will execute the Risk Analysis on the offline data from Batch Risk Analysis, rather than performing it on the existing data from Backend system.

- Based on the configuration parameter settings, the Report will display violations at either Action Level/Permission Level/Critical Action.

- From the Type drop down, select other Risk Analysis Result at Action Level/Permission Level/Critical Action.

Also, different summary are available in Format drop down like Summary, Detail, Management Summary and Executive Summary.

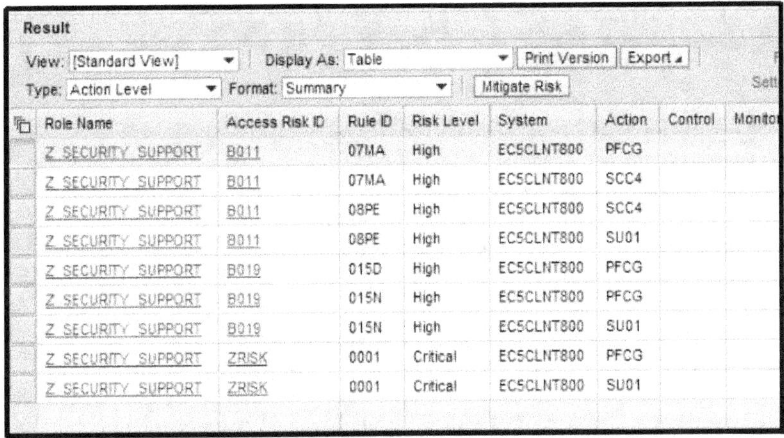

Similarly, we can run User Level Risk Analysis from User level Report under Access Management Work set.

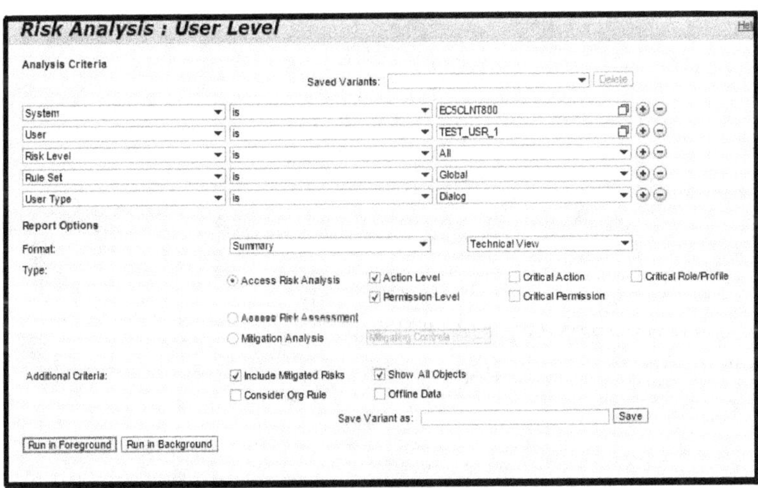

For running user analysis report for multiple users in one go, you can create a custom user group in GRC and add all users to the custom group. This custom group can be used in the criteria for user level risk analysis.

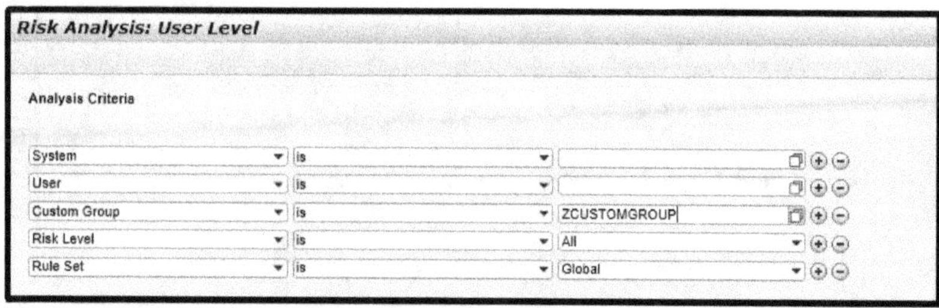

To create a custom User Group, follow below IMG path:

Call SPRO -->SAP Reference IMG --> Governance, Risk and Compliance --> Access Control --> Maintain Custom User Group

- Click on New Entries to create a User Group.

- Enter the Group Name and Description. Click on Save.

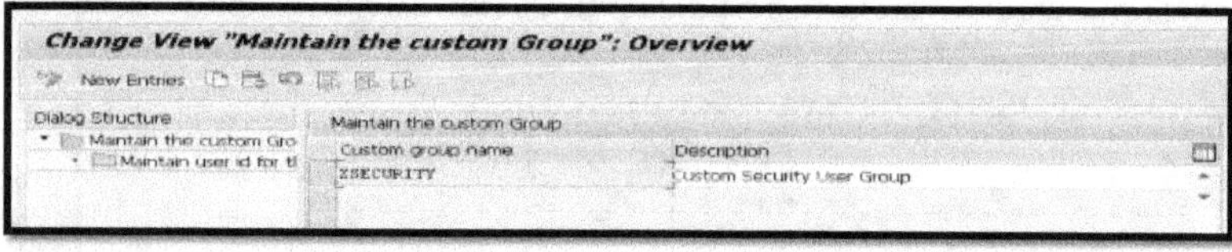

- Select the custom group created and Click on Maintain User Id for the group.

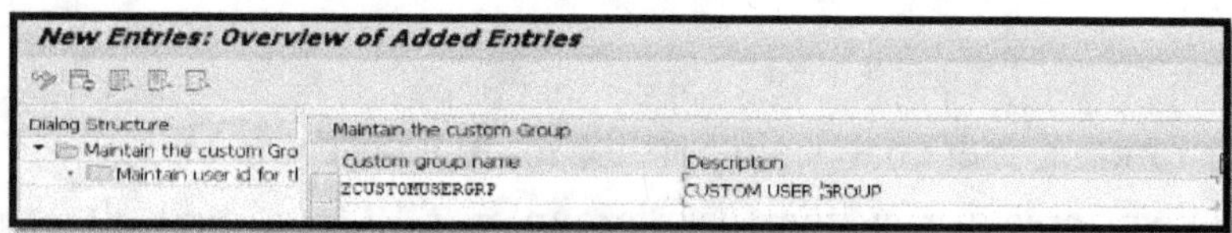

- In this screen, click on Add entries and provide the user Ids to be added to the group.

- Click on Save. Custom group is ready for Risk Analysis

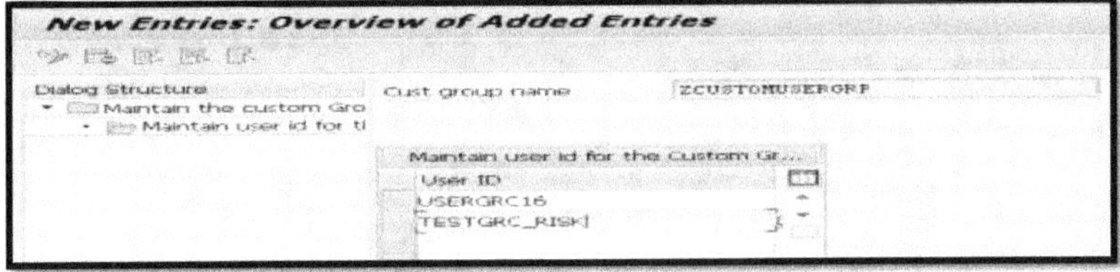

5. <u>RISK SIMULATION</u>

Simulation allows you to preview the result of changes to roles and user's actions to see if your changes create new risk situations before implementing them.

Role Level Simulation:

- Call NWBC --> Go to Access Management Work Center --> Click on Role Level Simulation

- Enter System, Role Type, Role, Risk Level and Rule Set

- Select the Format and View

- Select Report type option: Access Risk Analysis and put tick mark on Action Level & Permission Level

- Click on Next and enter the Simulation Values for Action and Permission.

- Click on Run in Foreground to get the simulation Results.

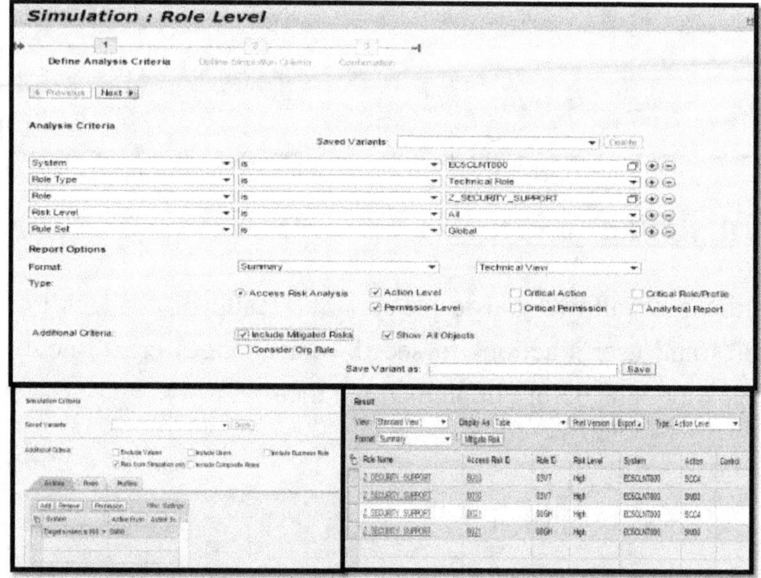

Additional Criteria in Simulation :

- **Include Users :** If we select the checkbox for Include users, Simulation will be performed taking account of the users to which the Role is assigned. All those user's current Roles will be checked for any conflicts for simulating object.

- **Include Composite Role :** If we select the checkbox for Include Composite Role, Simulation will be performed taking account of the Composite Roles to which the Single Role is Added. All those Composite Roles will be checked for any conflicts for simulating object.

- **Include Business Role :** If we select the checkbox for Include Business Role, Simulation will be performed taking account of the Business Roles to which the Single Role is Added in GRC. All those Business Roles will be checked for any conflicts for simulating object.

- **Risks from Simulation Only :** Enabling this checkbox will only show the Risks which are arising due to the simulating object. It will not show the Risk which are appearing due to existing T-codes and Permissions in the Role.

- **Exclude Values :** If you need to run a simulation to check the remaining Risks after an existing T-code or permission is removed from the Role, then you can check the Exclude Values checkbox and add that T-code for simulation. This will show only the Risks which are arising because of other T-codes/permissions in the Role. This feature is useful when you need to clean-up the Roles to remove Sod conflicts.

User Level Simulation:

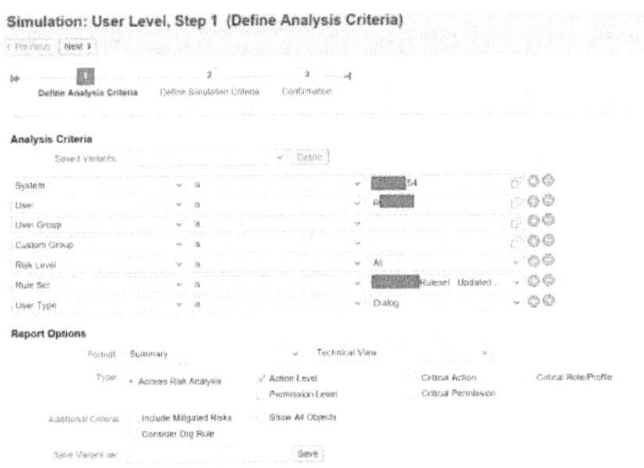

MITIGATION CONTROLS AND ASSIGNMENT

1. Root organization hierarchy

2. Mitigation Approver & Mitigation Monitor id`s

3. Maintain Access Control Owner

4. Owners Assignment in root hierarchy

5. Mitigation Controls Creation

6. Mitigation Control Assignment

1. ROOT ORGANIZATION HIERARCHY

Call SPRO --> IMG --> GRC --> Shared Master Data Settings --> Create Root Organization Hierarchy

In this activity, you need to maintain the root organization for the SAP GRC system. This value is mandatory to maintain the core structure and root organization to which

compliance and control reporting are made.

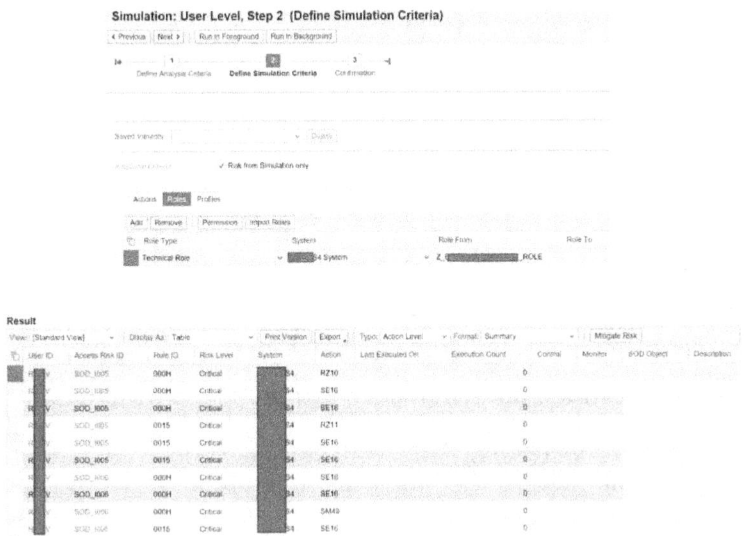

2. <u>MITIGATION APPROVER & MITIGATION MONITOR</u>

Mitigation Approvers are assigned to controls and are responsible for approving changes to the control definition and assignments when workflow is enabled. We need to maintain the below configuration settings in SPRO.

Create Mitigation Approver Id in GRC system with general Roles and Control Owner & Approver Role as shown below.

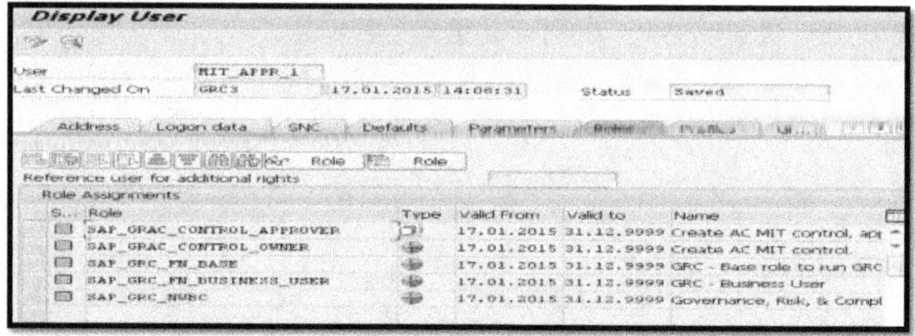

Mitigation monitor is the one who would be checking whether mitigation is being performed. This monitoring can be done either manually or alerts can be sent to the monitor. "Reports" which are maintained in reports tab of mitigating control, will trigger an e-mail to the Mitigation approver if control monitor does not run that report within the frequency mentioned.

Alerts can be set by executing the Tcode GRAC_ALERT_GENERATE.

Create Mitigation Monitor Id in GRC system with general Roles and Control Monitor.

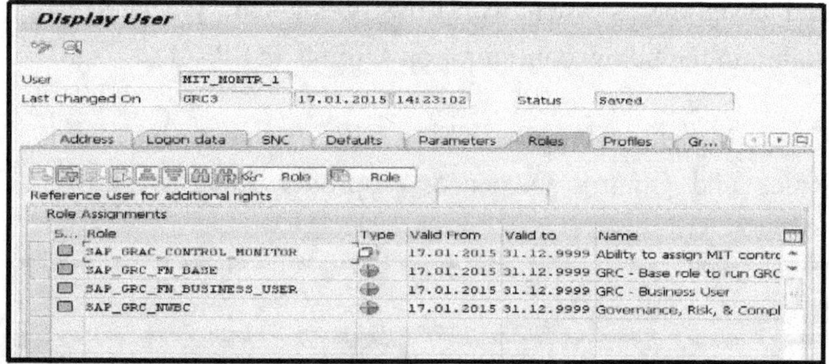

3. MAINTAIN ACCESS CONTROL OWNER

Open NWBC, go to Setup Work Center, then Click on Access Control Owners under Access Owners. In this activity, we will maintain the Approver and Monitor Ids created earlier in SU01 as Access Control Owner.

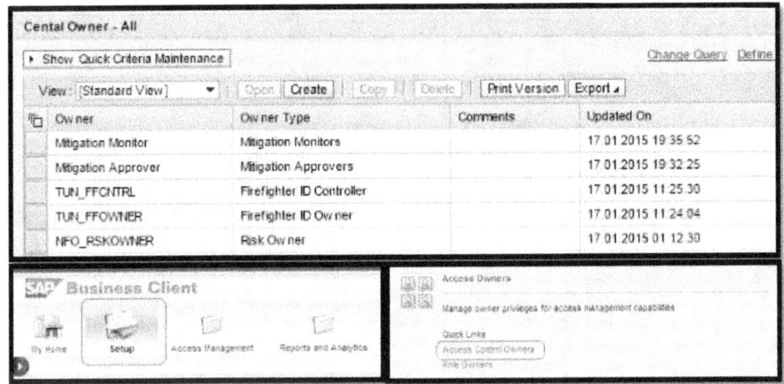

Click on Create Button to maintain Mitigation Approver and Monitor. Enter the Id in Owner field and select Owner Type and click on Save.

Group Type
- Owner
- Owner Group
- LDAP Group

Group Detail

Owner: * MIT_MONTR_1   Full Name: Mitigation Monitor
Distribution List Name: *
Distribution List Email: *
DL Connector:

Owner Type

Select All | Deselect All

Type	Description	Select
Firefighter ID Owner	Firefighter ID Owners are responsible for maintaining firefighter IDs and their assignments to firefighters	☐
Firefighter Role Owner	Firefighter Role Owners are responsible for maintaining firefighter roles and their assignments to firefighters	☐
Risk Owner	Risk Owners are assigned to risks and are commonly responsible for approving changes to risk definitions and violations of the risk. Risk Owners may also receive conflicting and critical action alerts	☐
Role Owner	Role owners are responsible for approving either role content or user-role assignment or both	☐
Mitigation Monitors	Mitigation Monitors are assigned to controls to monitor activity and may receive control monitor alerts	☑
Mitigation Approvers	Mitigation Approvers are assigned to controls and are responsible for approving changes to the control definition and assignments when workflow is enabled.	☐
Firefighter ID Controller	Firefighter ID Controllers are responsible for reviewing the log report generated during firefighter ID usage	☐
Firefighter Role Controller	Firefighter Role Controllers are responsible for reviewing the log report generated during firefighter role usage.	☐
Point of Contact	Point of Contact is an approver for a specific Functional	☐

Group Type
- Owner
- Owner Group
- LDAP Group

Group Detail

Owner: * MIT_APPR_1   Full Name: Mitigation Approver
Distribution List Name: *
Distribution List Email: *
DL Connector:

Owner Type

Select All | Deselect All

Type	Description	Select
Firefighter ID Owner	Firefighter ID Owners are responsible for maintaining firefighter IDs and their assignments to firefighters	☐
Firefighter Role Owner	Firefighter Role Owners are responsible for maintaining firefighter roles and their assignments to firefighters	☐
Risk Owner	Risk Owners are assigned to risks and are commonly responsible for approving changes to risk definitions and violations of the risk. Risk Owners may also receive conflicting and critical action alerts	☐
Role Owner	Role owners are responsible for approving either role content or user-role assignment or both	☐
Mitigation Monitors	Mitigation Monitors are assigned to controls to monitor activity and may receive control monitor alerts	☐
Mitigation Approvers	Mitigation Approvers are assigned to controls and are responsible for approving changes to the control definition and assignments when workflow is enabled.	☑
Firefighter ID Controller	Firefighter ID Controllers are responsible for reviewing the log report generated during firefighter ID usage	☐
Firefighter Role Controller	Firefighter Role Controllers are responsible for reviewing the log report generated during firefighter role usage.	☐
Point of Contact	Point of Contact is an approver for a specific Functional Area. Functional Area is an attribute used to categorize users and roles.	☐

4. <u>OWNERS ASSIGNMENT IN ROOT HIERARCHY</u>

Open NWBC, go to Setup Work Center, then Click on Organizations under Organizations. In this activity, we will maintain the Control Owner in Organization Hierarchy.

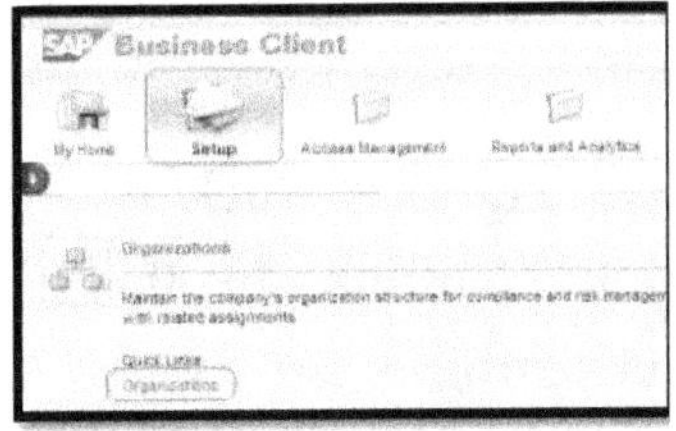

Select the Organization and click on Open and go to Owners tab.

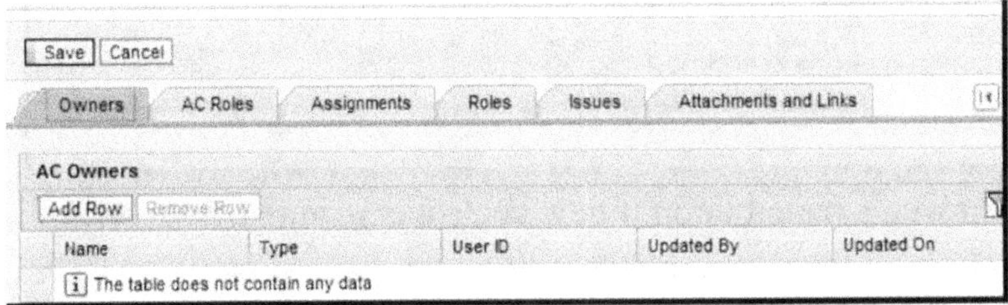

Click on Add Row and select the Control Approver created previously and click on Save. Similarly Add the Control Monitor as well.

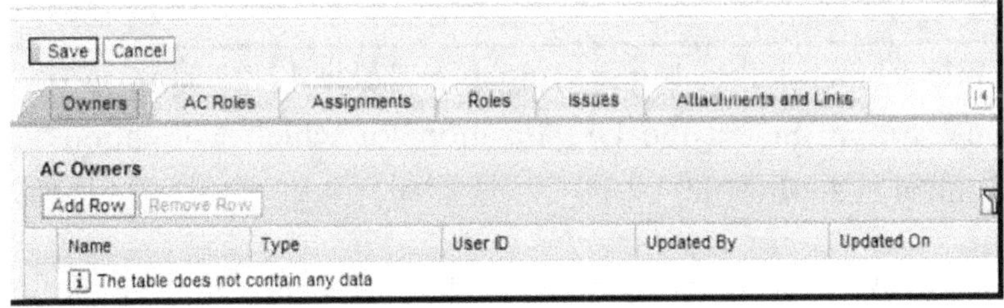

5. <u>Mitigation Control Creation</u>

Open NWBC, go to Setup Work Center, then Click on Mitigation Controls under Mitigation Controls. In this activity, we will create the Mitigation Control.

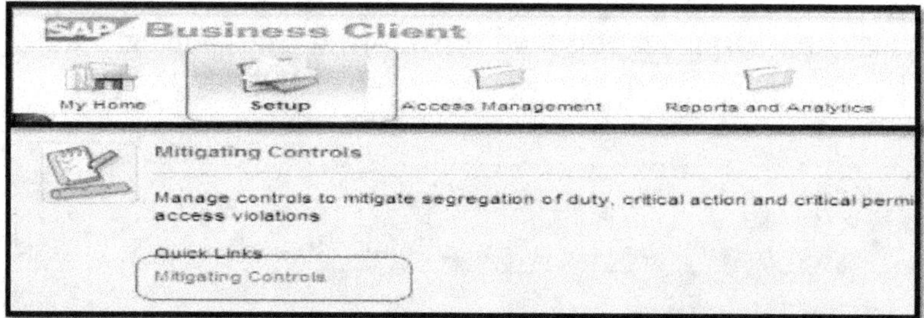

Click on Create button if new control is required. Else click open to modify existing Control.

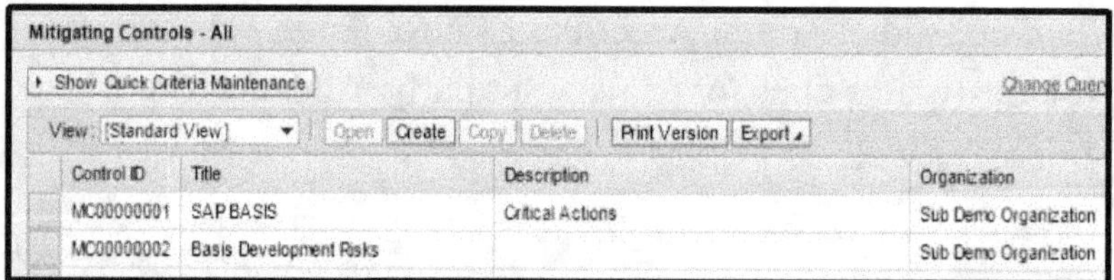

Under General Tab, Enter Mitigation Control Id, Name and Description. Select the Organization for which Mitigation Control is applicable.

Under Access Risks Tab, enter the Risk Ids for which control is valid. Under Owners Tab, Maintain Control Approver and Monitor Id. Under Reports Tab, specify the Action/T-codes to be executed by Monitor to follow the Mitigation process. Click on Save. If the Workflow parameter 1061 is set to Yes, you will see the Submit button and once clicked, it will send an Approval Request to Control Approver. Once Approved, Control will be saved.

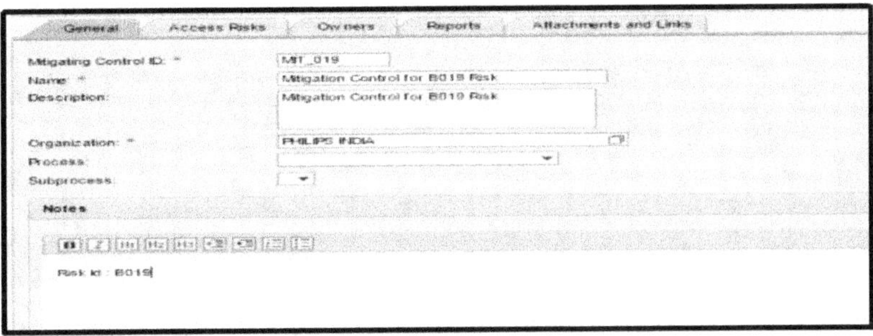

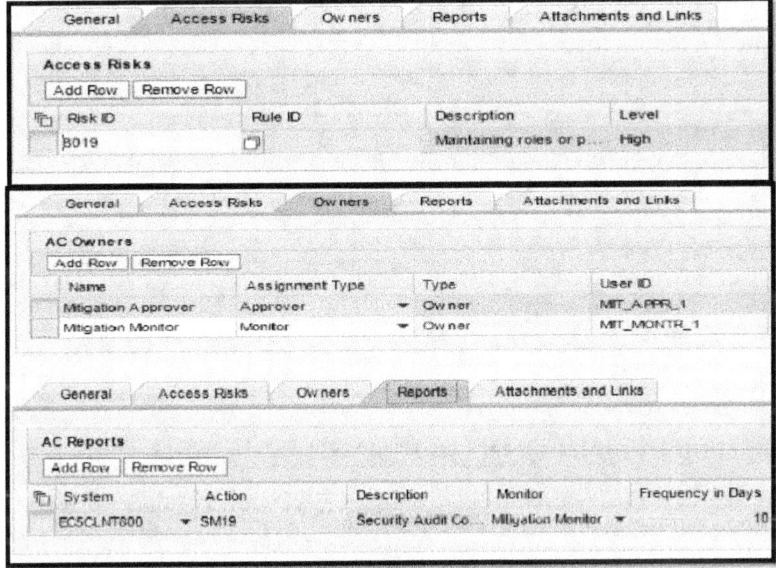

Login to NWBC with Mitigation Approver Id and click on Work Inbox from My Home Tab.

Click on the Workflow Item for Mitigation Control Creation. On the screen, which is opened, select whether to Approve or Reject and click on the respective button.

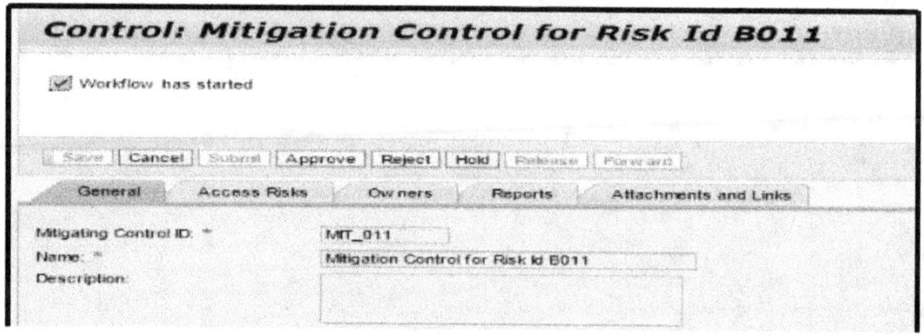

Once approved, new Mitigation control would be created. View the details from the Mitigation Control list under SetupWork Center.

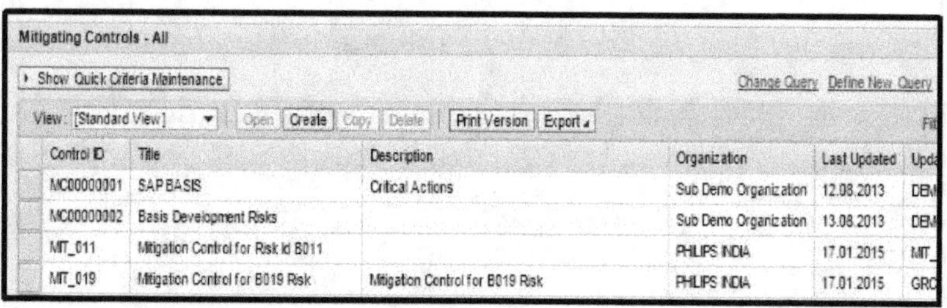

6. <u>MITIGATION CONTROL ASSIGNMENT</u>

Execute the Risk Analysis at Role Level or User Level. Select any Risk from the Result and click on Mitigate Risk.

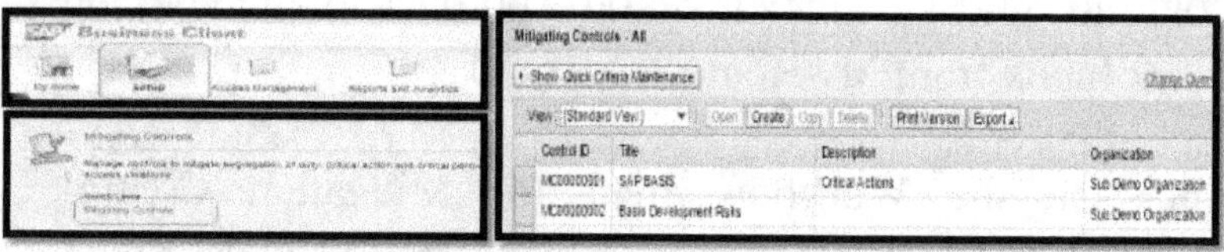

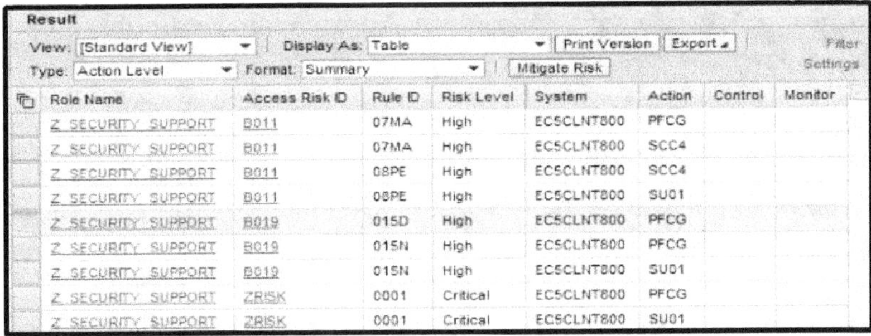

- In the Assign Mitigation Control Screen, one Control Id will be populated by default if any mitigation control is created for that Risk.

- In case there are multiple Control Ids, select the Control which is to be applied.

- If you want the mitigation to be applied to particular system, select the value in the system selection box.

- If you want the mitigation to be applied to particular Rule Id, select the value in the Rule Id selection box.

- Click on save to apply the Mitigation control.

- If the parameter 1062 under Workflow is set to Yes, submit button will appear instead of Save. Clicking on submit, system will send a workflow to Control Approver and once approved Mitigation will be assigned.

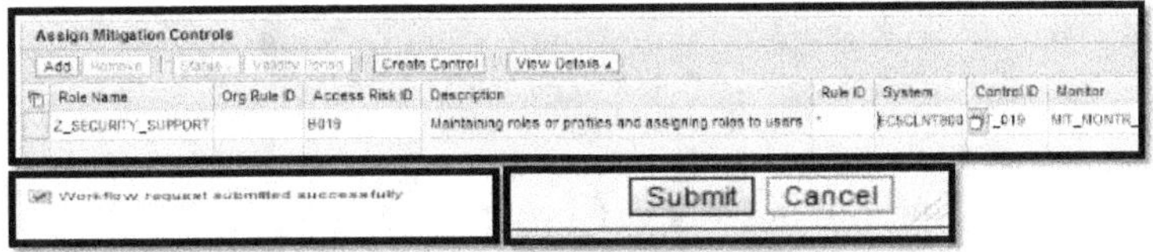

Login to NWBC with Mitigation Approver Id and click on Work Inbox from My Home Tab.

Click on the Workflow Item for Mitigation Approval. In the screen which is opened, select whether to Approve or Reject, and click on the respective button.

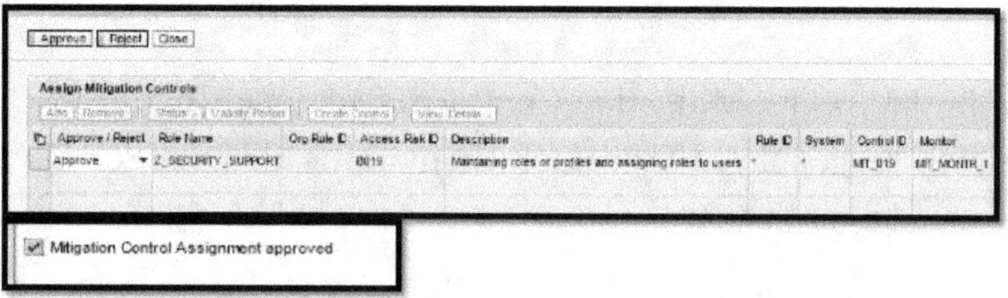

Run the Risk Analysis again by including Mitigated Risk to view if Mitigation is applied successfully.

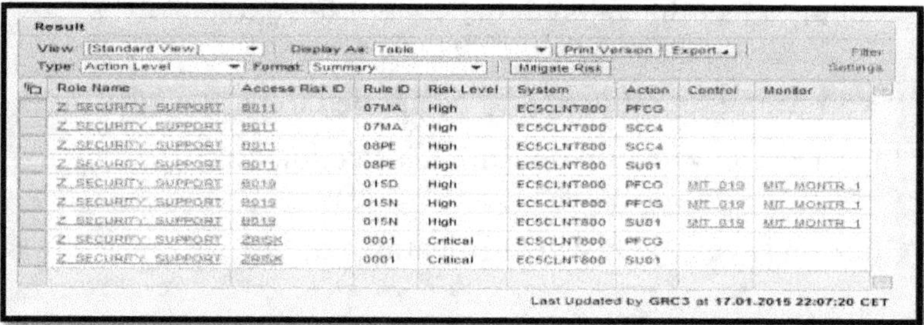

To view or Remove existing Mitigation Assignments, Go to

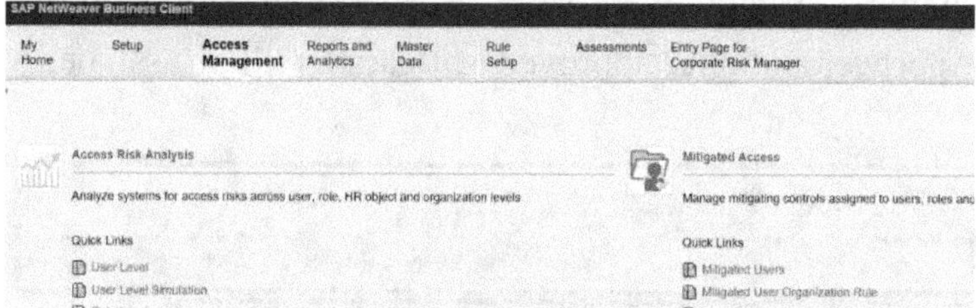

Access Management Work Center and select Mitigated Users/ Roles under Mitigated Access.

Select the Mitigation Assignment and click on Delete to remove the Mitigation. This will also initiate Workflow request if parameter 1062 is set to Yes You can also change the status to Inactive or update the validity for the Mitigation Assignment using this option.

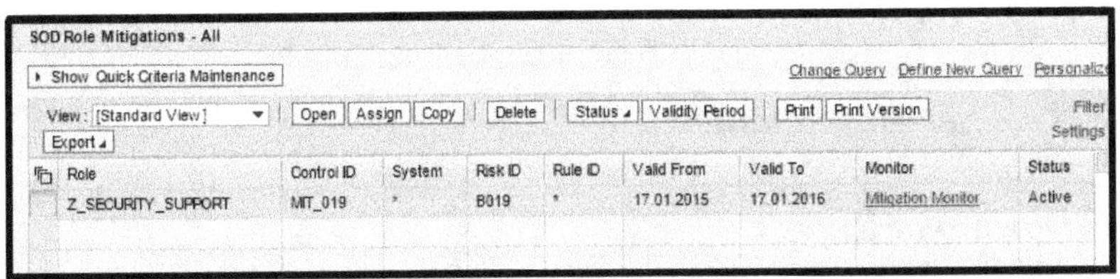

Using Assign button, new mitigation Assignment can be made. Select the Risk Id, Control Id, Add the systems and Role Name in respective field and click on Submit button. Workflow request would be initiated which once approved will assign Mitigation to the Risk.

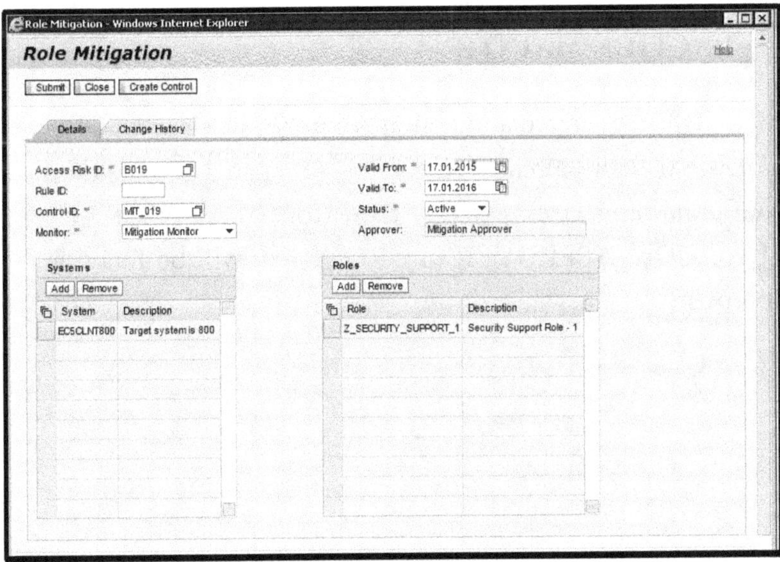

RULE SET MAINTENANCE

1. Function Maintenance

2. Risk Maintenance

3. Rule Set Maintenance

4. Download Rules

5. Upload Rules

6. Custom Rule Set creation

7. Critical Role and Profile Maintenance

1. FUNCTION MAINTENANCE

As a first Step, create a Function Approver in SU01 in GRC system if not already created. As part of standard configuration, Users with the Role SAP_ GRAC_ FUNCTION_APPROVER in GRC system will be function approver.

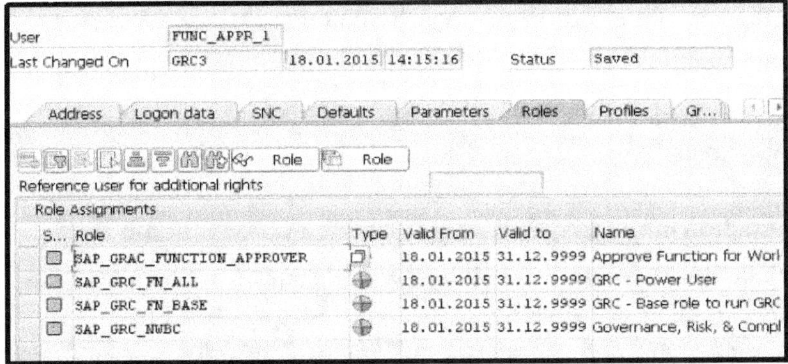

Open NWBC, go to Setup Work Center, then Click on Functions under Access Rule Maintenance.

Select a Function and click on Open to view and edit the function.

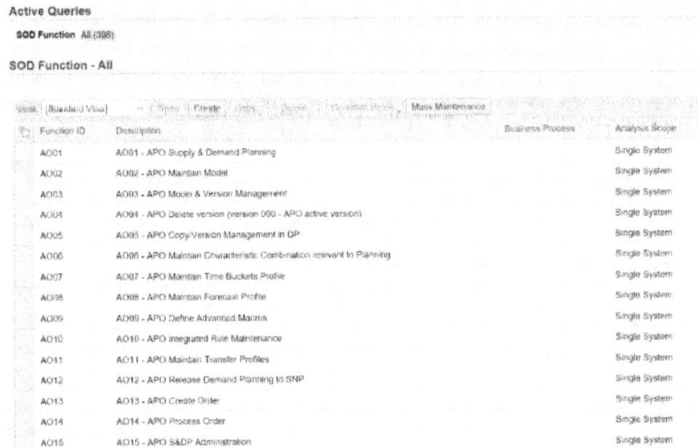

Update the Function by adding / Removing Action and Permission. Any Action or Permission can be activated or deactivated as well.

Click on Save button to save the changes. If the Workflow parameter 1064 is set to Yes, submit button will appear which will create a Workflow request for Function Approver.

Function approver will login to NWBC, My home work enter and in Work Inbox the approval request will appear.

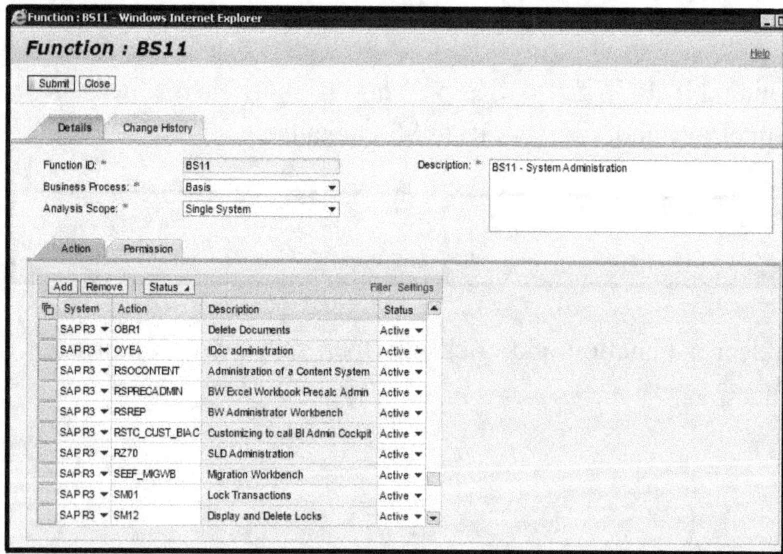

Once request is approved at all stages, changes would be updated to the function. Verify the changes and click on Generate Rules from NWBC or generate it from SPRO.

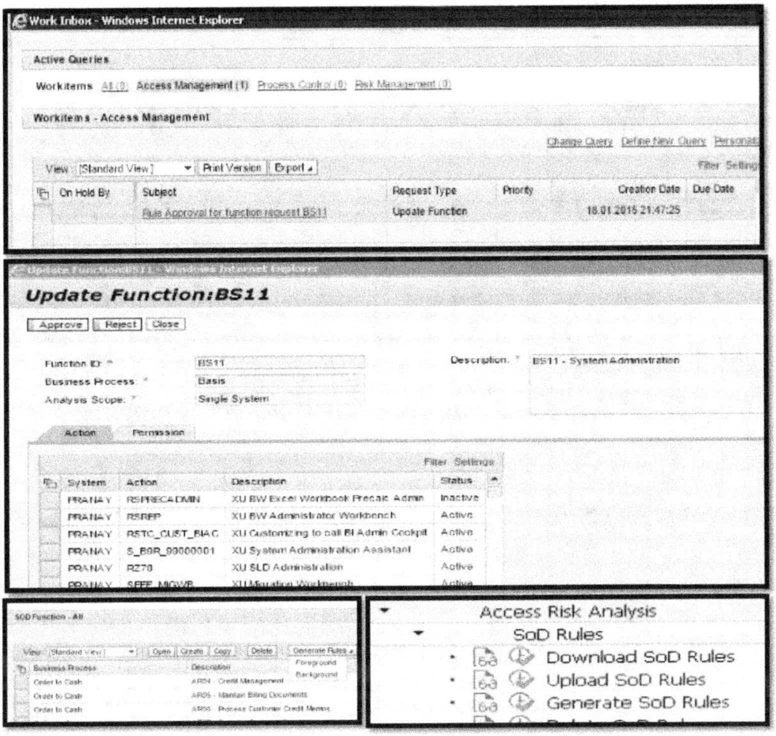

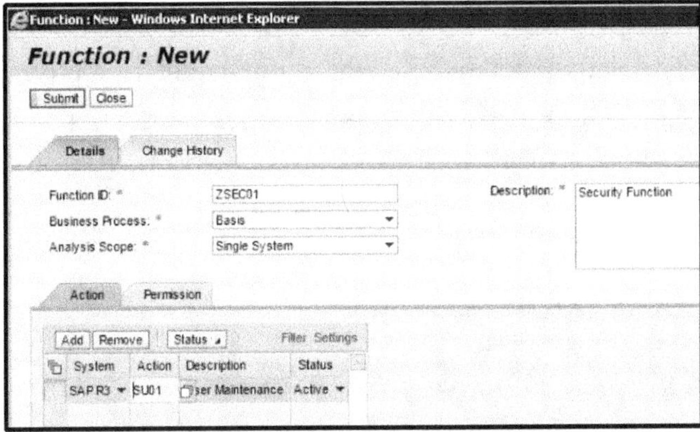

CREATE / DELETE FUNCTION

Similarly, A new function can be created using the Create Button from the initial function screen. To delete a function, select it and click on Delete.

FUNCTION MASS MAINTENANCE

We can maintain the functions in Mass using the Mass Maintenance button on functions screen.

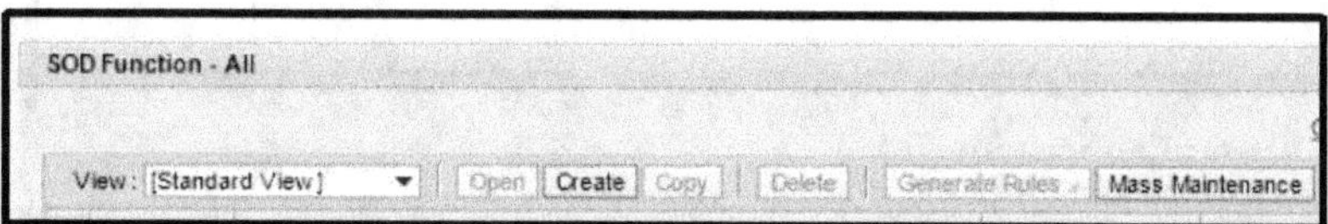

Add the functions which you need to mass Maintain in the first Step. Then click on Next and go to Maintenance Parameters.

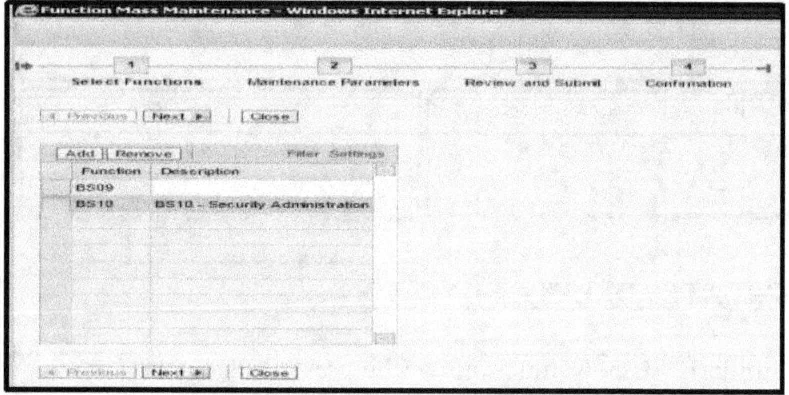

Select the Maintenance Type, Object Type (Action or Permission), Enter the system details and Action or Permission value details. Select if the value is Active or Inactive. Click on Next once details are mentioned.

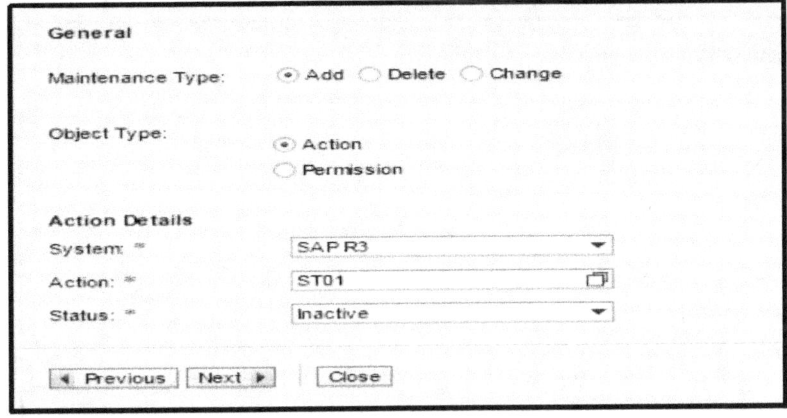

Review the request and click on Submit. Changes would be performed, and the result is shown on confirmation screen.

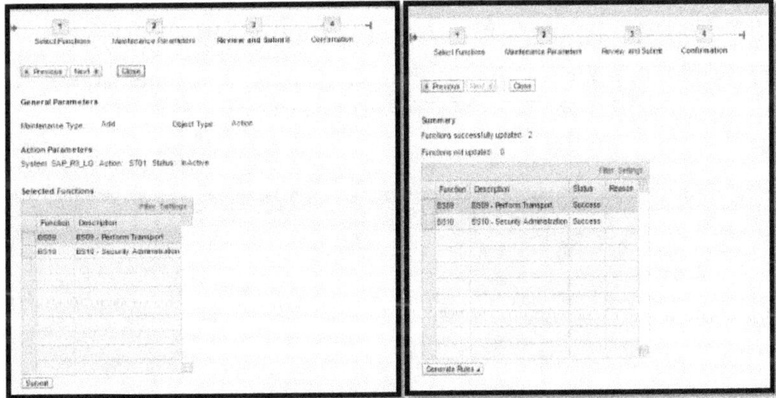

2. <u>RISK MAINTENANCE</u>

As a first Step, create a Risk Approver in SU01 in GRC system if not already created.

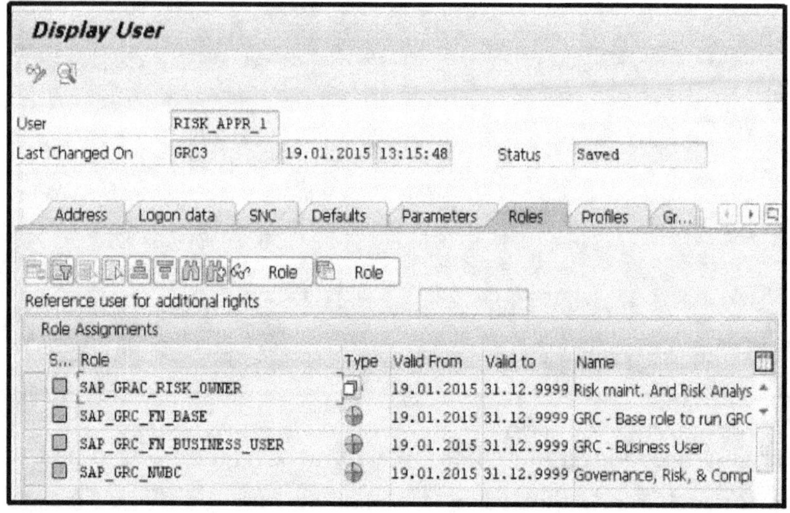

Add the Risk Approver to Access Control Owners. Select the user in Owner text box and check the Risk Owner check box. Save it.

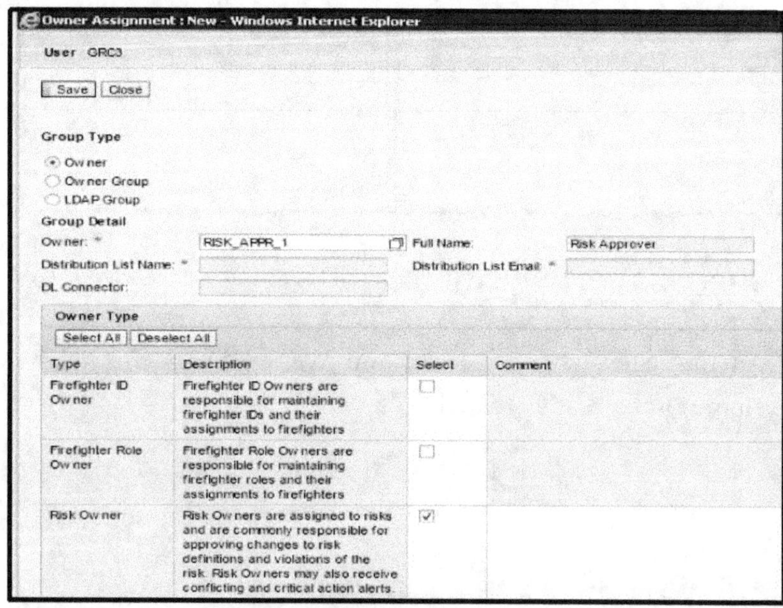

Open NWBC, go to Setup Work Center, then Click on Access Risks under Access Rule Maintenance.

Select a Risk and click on Open to view and edit the Risk.

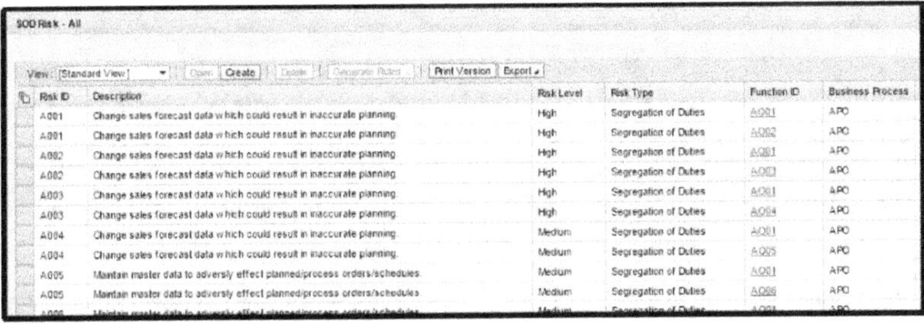

Update the Risk by adding / Removing Function. Also Rule sets and Risk Owners if required can be updated.

Click on Save button to save the changes. If the Workflow parameter 1063 is set to Yes, submit button will appear which will create a Workflow request for Risk Owner.

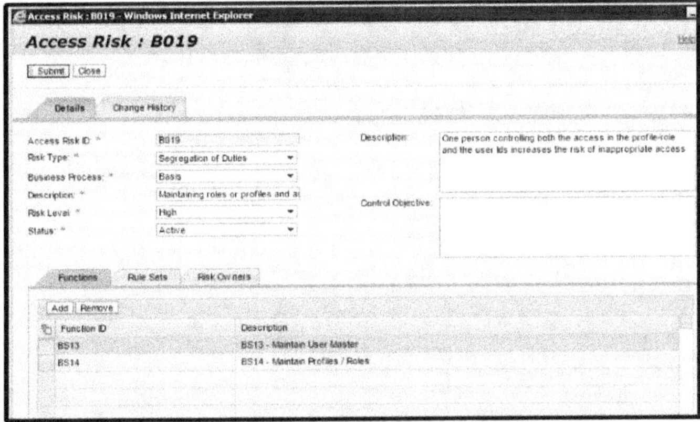

Risk Owner will login to NWBC, "My Home" work enter and in Work Inbox the approval request will appear.

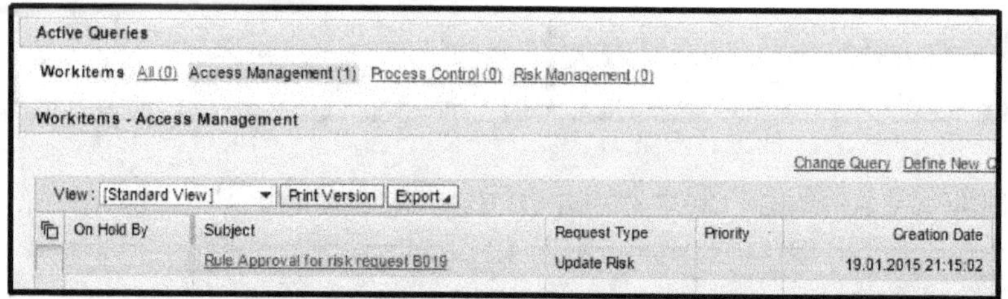

Once request is approved at all stages, changes would be updated to the Risk. Verify the changes and click on Generate Rules from NWBC or generate it from SPRO.

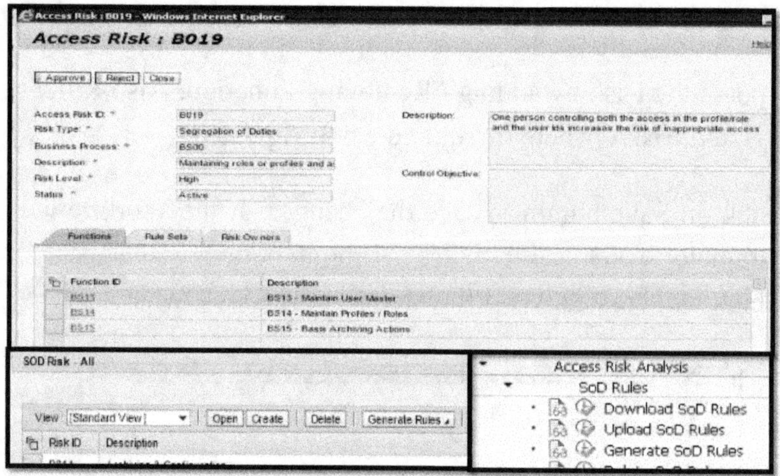

CREATE / DELETE RISK

Similarly, A new Risk can be created using the Create Button from the initial Risk screen. To delete a Risk, select it and click on Delete.

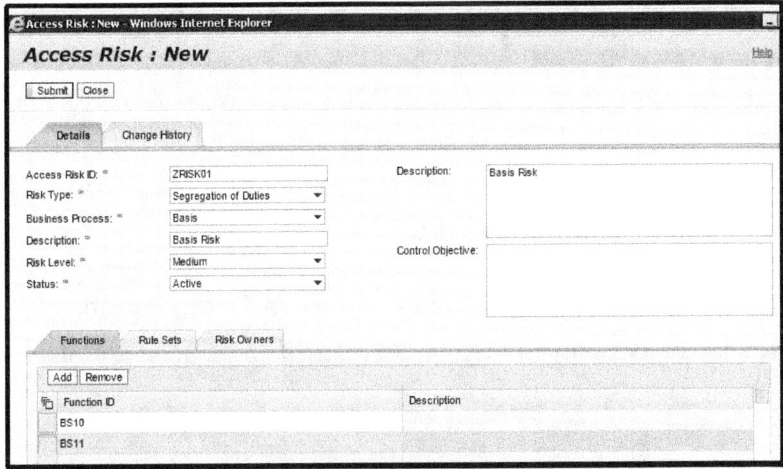

3. <u>RULESET MAINTENANCE</u>

Open NWBC, go to Setup Work Center, then Click on Rule Sets under Access Rule Maintenance.

To create a New Rule Set, click on Create. Provide Rule Set Id and Description and click on Save. To delete a Rule Set, select it and click on Delete.

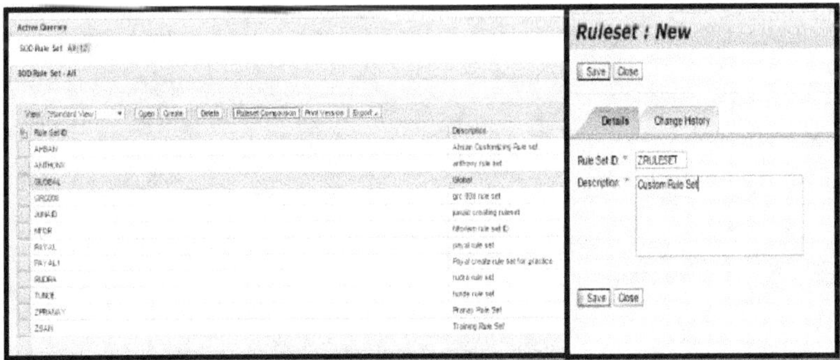

4. <u>DOWNLOAD RULES</u>

Call SPRO -->SAP Reference IMG --> Governance, Risk and Compliance --> Access Control --> Access Risk Analysis --> SoD Rules --> Download SoD Rules (T-code: GRAC_DOWNLOAD_RULES)

Select the system from which Rules to be downloaded. Connector Group can also be selected if there are multiple system.

Select the file location and file name where rules are to be downloaded. Mention a separate file for Business process, Function, Function Business Process, Actions, Permissions, Rule Se, Risks, Risk Description and Risk Rule Set Relationship.

Click on execute to download the Files.

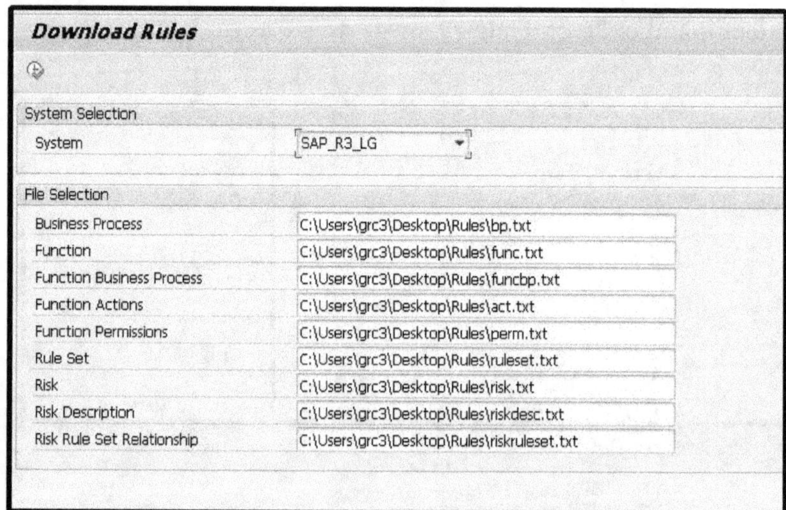

Download Rules

System Selection

System	SAP_R3_LG

File Selection

Business Process	C:\Users\grc3\Desktop\Rules\bp.txt
Function	C:\Users\grc3\Desktop\Rules\func.txt
Function Business Process	C:\Users\grc3\Desktop\Rules\funcbp.txt
Function Actions	C:\Users\grc3\Desktop\Rules\act.txt
Function Permissions	C:\Users\grc3\Desktop\Rules\perm.txt
Rule Set	P:\Users\grc3\Desktop\Rules\ruleset.txt
Risk	C:\Users\grc3\Desktop\Rules\risk.txt
Risk Description	C:\Users\grc3\Desktop\Rules\riskdesc.txt
Risk Rule Set Relationship	C:\Users\grc3\Desktop\Rules\riskruleset.txt

5. <u>UPLOAD RULES</u>

Call SPRO -->SAP Reference IMG --> Governance, Risk and Compliance --> Access Control --> Access Risk Analysis --> SoD Rules --> Upload SoD Rules (T-code: GRAC_UPLOAD_RULES)

Select the system/connector group to which Rules needs to be uploaded. Select the file location and file name where rules are to be uploaded.

Upload a separate file for Business process, Function, Function Business Process, Actions, Permissions, Rule Set, Risks, Risk Description and Risk Rule Set Relationship.

Select Append if existing data is to be kept as it is. To overwrite all data, select Overwrite. Click on execute to upload the Files.

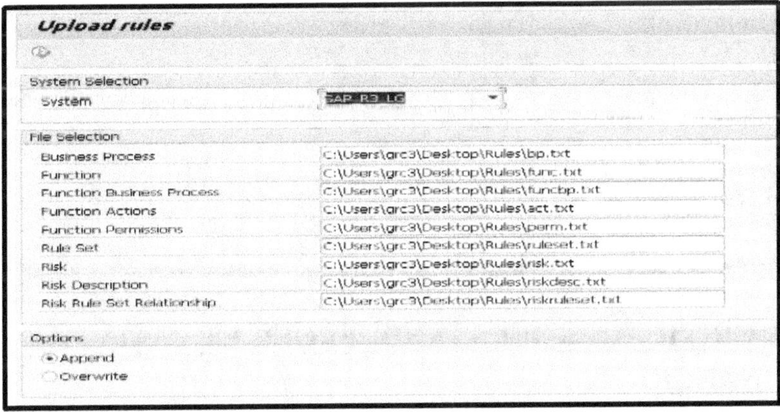

6. <u>CUSTOM RULE SET</u>

To create a custom Rule set, download the Rules. Update the files of rule set and risk rule set relationship file with the details of new custom rule set. Here in the below screens, we have added the custom rule set ZRULESET. Upload the files through the t-code GRAC_UPLOAD_RULES by selecting the system/connector group and use the option Append. If any changes are required in the functions or risk update the respective files and then upload accordingly.

```
File   Edit   Format   View   Help
A001        ZRULESET
A002        ZRULESET
A003        ZRULESET
A004        ZRULESET
A005        ZRULESET
A006        ZRULESET
A007        ZRULESET
A008        ZRULESET
A009        ZRULESET
```

```
GRC008   EN        grc 008 rule set
JUNAID   EN        junaid creating ruleset
NFOR     EN        Nforlem rule set ID
PAYAL    EN        payal rule set
PAYAL1   EN        Payal create rule set for practice
RUDRA    EN        rudra rule set
TUNDE    EN        tunde rule set
ZPRANAY  EN        Pranay Rule Set
ZSAN     EN        Training Rule Set
ZRULESET          EN        Custom Rule Set
```

7. <u>CRITICAL ROLES AND PROFILES MAINTE-NANCE</u>

Open NWBC, go to Setup Work Center, then Click on Critical Roles or Critical Profiles under Critical Access Rules.

To view a Critical Role Rule, select it and click on open. Any changes can be made through the same screen. Use Delete button to delete any critical access Rule. Status button can be used to change the status of Rule to active or inactive.

Click on create to enter a new critical Role Access Rule. Enter the Role Name, select system, provide the Risk level and Rule Set. Select Active dropdown in status to enable the Rule else select deactivate.

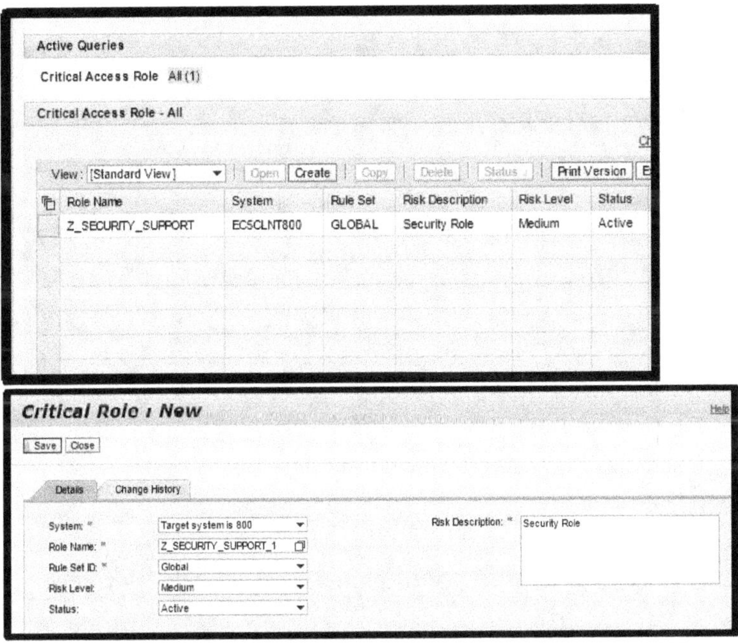

In similar way, new Critical Profile Rule can be created, modified or deleted.

These Rules would be referenced when Risk Analysis is performed at Critical Role/Profile level.

<u>AUDIT TRAIL</u>

All changes related to access rules can be tracked. The following components can have an audit trail:

1. Function

2. Risk

3. Org Rule

4. Supplementary Rule

5. Critical Role

6. Critical Profile

7. Rule set

<u>Benefits:</u>

- Quick access to the history of changes of the access rules.

- Administrators and power users can easily track who changed the different components of an access rule.

- This is useful when finding problems related to inconsistent rules.

- Comprehensive information about the changes to access rules including not only who made the change and when that change was made, but also information such as the old and new values.

- Higher visibility of changes, as the application can log information about every type of change to the rules, including changes to functions, rule sets, critical access rules and additional access rules.

- Auditors can have a detailed view of all changes in a single location

To enable the change log, below configuration parameter needs to be set:

New Entries: Overview of Added Entries

AC Configuration settings

Parm Group	Param ID	Parameter Value	Priority	Description
Change Log	1001	YES		Enable Function Change Log
Change Log	1002	YES		Enable Risk Change Log
Change Log	1003	YES		Enable Organization Rule Log
Change Log	1004	YES		Enable Supplementary Rule Log
Change Log	1005	YES		Enable Critical Role Log
Change Log	1006	YES		Enable Critical Profile Log
Change Log	1007	YES		Enable Rule Set Change Log
Change Log	1008	YES		Enable Role Change Log

To view the change logs for function, open the function and go to the tab Change History. The report will show the old and new values, who applied these changes, and the time of the operation.

Similarly change logs can be viewed for Risks, Rule Sets, Critical Role/Profile as well.

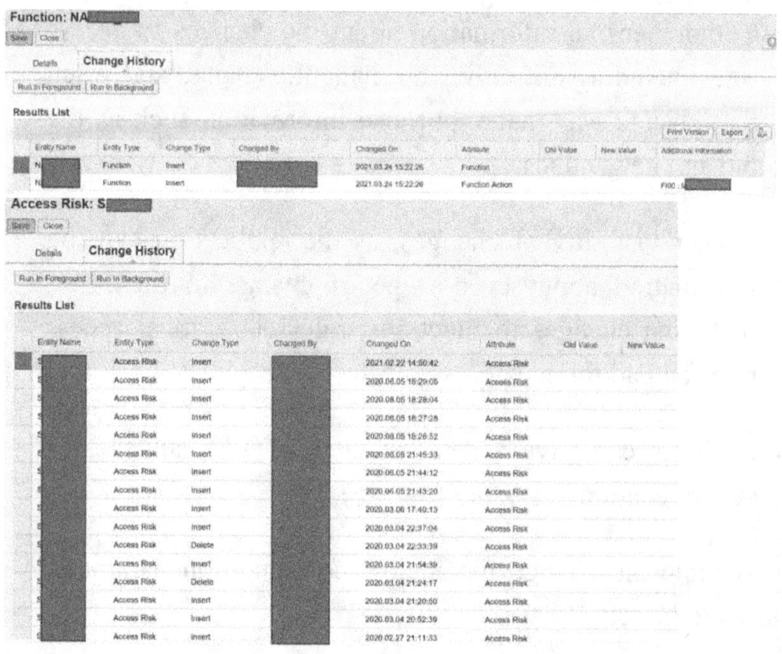

EAM– EMERGENCY ACCESS MANAGEMENT

1. Overview

2. Firefighter Application Types

3. Creating users and assigning roles

4. Verifying time zones

5. Creating reasons codes

6. Maintaining AC owners

7. Assigning owners to firefighter IDs

8. Assigning firefighter IDs and controllers to firefighters

9. Firefighting Session

10. FF Log Collection

11. Report Analysis

12. Role Based FFID

13. Decentralized Firefighting

1. <u>OVERVIEW</u>

- EAM allows user to take responsibility for tasks outside of their normal job function.

- Allows temporary access for users when assigned with solving a problem, giving them provisionally broad, but regulated access

- This temporary access is monitored and recorded in the application

- EAM provides the ability to manage and utilize firefighting activities centrally from the Access Control application

- The log file can be distributed to controllers and owner via workflow for additional approval.

- Emergency Access Management provides a centralized console through which firefighters can logon to different systems for firefighting

2. <u>FIREFIGHTER APPLICATION TYPES</u>

- ID Based Firefighter: The firefighter ID created in the remote system will be assigned to the user in the GRC system, either manually or via an access request. The firefighter accesses their assigned firefighter ID in the GRC server using the SAP GUI and transaction GRAC_SPM. The firefighter ID for all remote systems assigned to the firefighter will be accessed from this transaction.

- Role Based Firefighter: The firefighter roles created in the remote system will be assigned to the user in the GRC server. The firefighter directly logs into the remote system using their user ID and performs activities which are provided in the user's role and firefighter role assigned to the user.

- This is configured in IMG using parameter 4000 (Application Type) Only one application type can be configured at a given time.

3. <u>USER CREATION</u>

Create the below users in SU01 in GRC and Backend system as applicable. Remember to synchronize again the repository(program GRAC_REPOSITORY_OBJECT_SYNC)

1. Firefighter Id: Extra privileged user ID. All activities performed are tracked for audit. This Id is created in the target system (Backend System).

Role to be assigned : SAP_GRAC_SPM_FFID (This Role is maintained in the configuration parameter 4010 to identify the Firefighter Id). In addition, broader Role having the exceptional access to be assigned to this Id.

2. Firefighter User : Person who performs some additional activities by checking out a firefighter ID. This Id is created in GRC system.

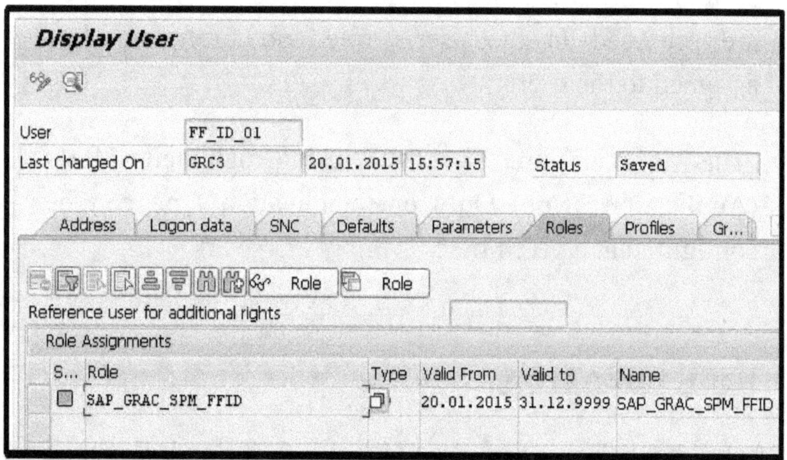

Role to be assigned : SAP_GRAC_SUPER_USER_ MGMT_ USER along with General GRC Roles (SAP_GRC_FN_ BASE and SAP_GRC_FN_ BUSINESS_ USER).

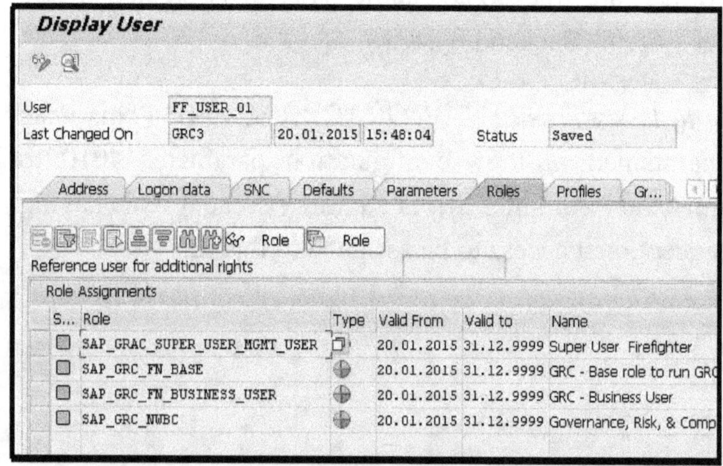

3. Firefighter ID owner : Person who owns the ID and has authority to assign firefighter IDs to others. This ID is created in GRC system.

Role to be assigned : SAP_GRAC_SUPER_USER_ MGMT_OWNER along with General GRC Roles.

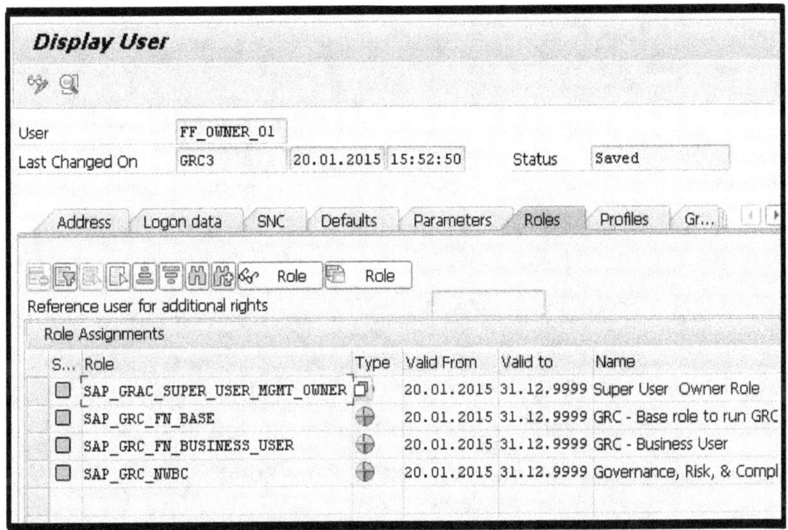

4. Firefighter ID Controller: Person who reviews the reason code/description and audit trail to ensure that access was used appropriately. The user can be notified when firefighter IDs are checked in/out and notified of all activities performed via email trigger. This Id is created in GRC system.

Role to be assigned : SAP_GRAC_SUPER_USER_ MGMT_CNTLR along with General GRC Roles.

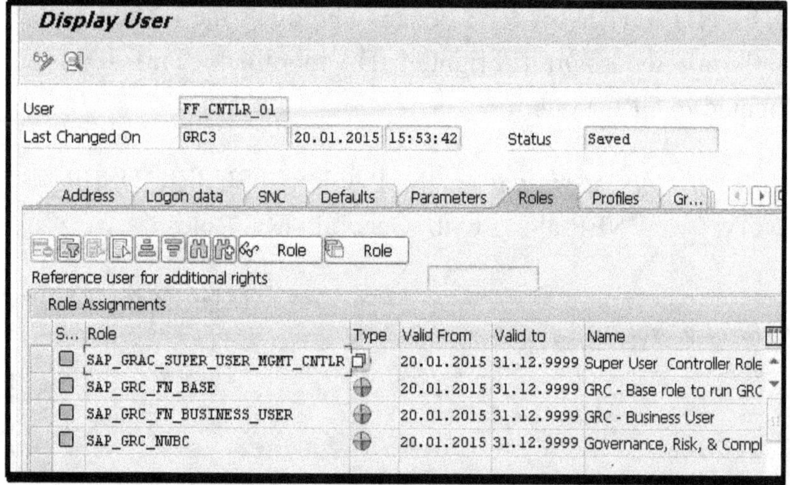

4. <u>VERIFYING TIME ZONES</u>

For logs to be properly captured the time zones in the connected ERP systems need to be configured to match the operating system and the AC server time zone.

Call SPRO -->SAP Reference IMG --> SAP NetWeaver --> General Settings --> Time Zones --> Maintain System Settings

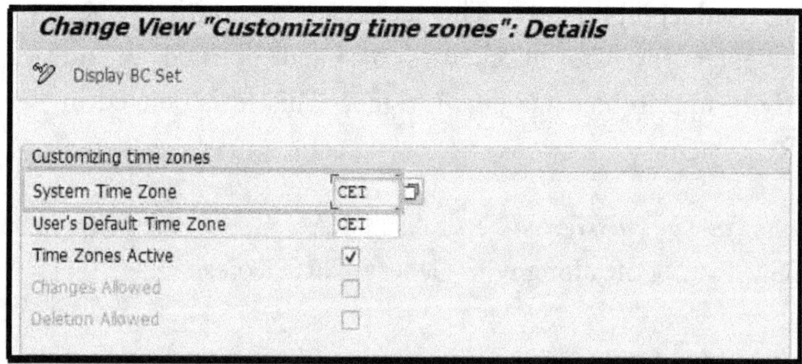

5. <u>REASON CODES</u>

When FF user login to FFID, system asks for a Reason Code to be selected. This Reason code is used to identify the reason due to which Firefighter is used.

To maintain Reason codes, go to NWBC, then Set up Work center, Click on Reason Codes under Super User Maintenance.

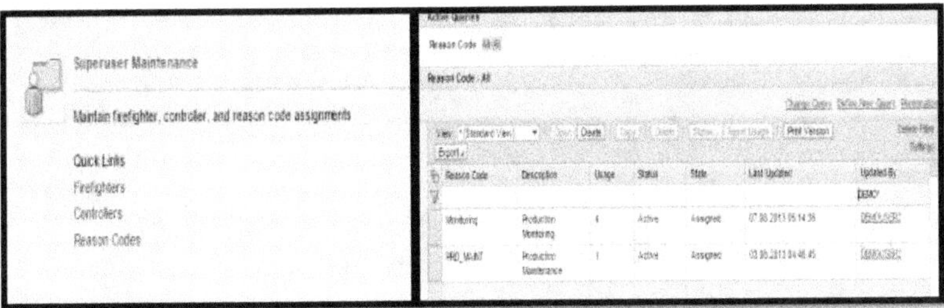

Click on create to enter a new Reason code. Mention the Reason code, description and set the status of Reason code to Active or Inactive. Add the systems to which this Reason code would be applicable. Click on Save.

To view or edit a reason code, click Open. Click Delete to delete the Reason Code.

In the list of Reason Codes, Usage column shows total no of times the Reason code has been used for Firefighter checkout. System wise usage count is displayed once a reason code is opened.

To reset the usage count, click on the Reset Usage button after selecting the Reason code.

Using the Status button, change the active reason code to inactive and vice-versa.

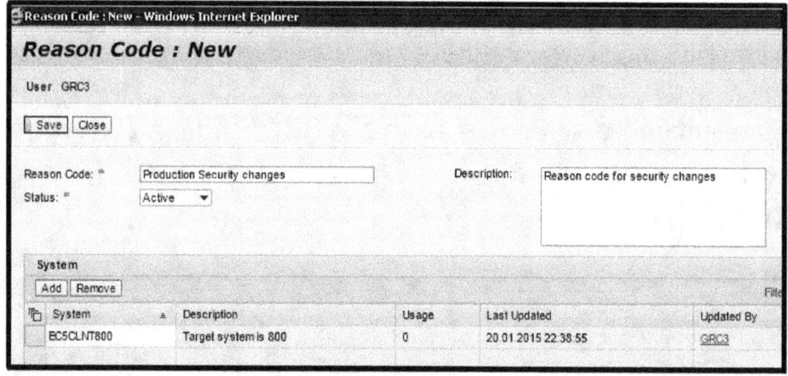

6. <u>ACCESS CONTROL OWNERS</u>

Open NWBC, go to Setup Work Center, then Click on Access Control Owners under Access Owners. In this activity, we will maintain the Firefighter Owner and Controller Ids created earlier in SU01 as Access Control Owner. Click on Create Button to maintain FF Owner and Controller. Enter the Id in Owner field and select Owner Type and click on Save.

There are 4 types of owners that can be maintained for emergency access

<u>ID BASED APPLICATION</u>

Firefighter ID Owner

Firefighter ID Controller

<u>ROLE BASED APPLICATION</u>

Firefighter Role Owner

Firefighter Role Controller

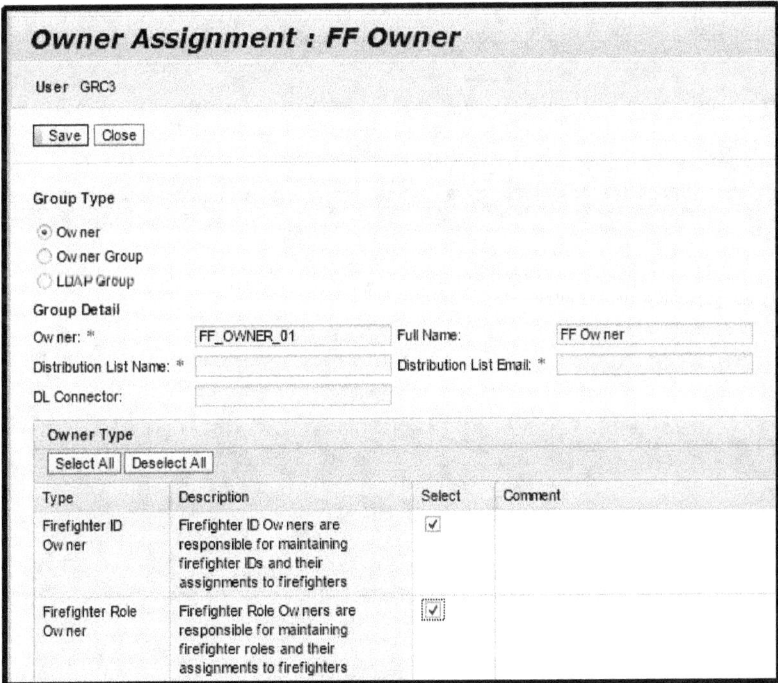

Type	Description	Select	Comment
Firefighter ID Owner	Firefighter ID Owners are responsible for maintaining firefighter IDs and their assignments to firefighters	✓	
Firefighter Role Owner	Firefighter Role Owners are responsible for maintaining firefighter roles and their assignments to firefighters	✓	

Group Type

- (•) Owner
- ( ) Owner Group
- ( ) LDAP Group

Group Detail

Owner: *	FF_CNTLR_01	Full Name:	FF Controller
Distribution List Name: *		Distribution List Email: *	
DL Connector:			

Owner Type

[Select All] [Deselect All]

Type	Description	Select
Firefighter ID Owner	Firefighter ID Owners are responsible for maintaining firefighter IDs and their assignments to firefighters	☐
Firefighter Role Owner	Firefighter Role Owners are responsible for maintaining firefighter roles and their assignments to firefighters	☐
Risk Owner	Risk Owners are assigned to risks and are commonly responsible for approving changes to risk definitions and violations of the risk. Risk Owners may also receive conflicting and critical action alerts.	☐
Role Owner	Role owners are responsible for approving either role content or user-role assignment or both	☐
Mitigation Monitors	Mitigation Monitors are assigned to controls to monitor activity and may receive control monitor alerts.	☐
Mitigation Approvers	Mitigation Approvers are assigned to controls and are responsible for approving changes to the control definition and assignments when workflow is enabled.	☐
Firefighter ID Controller	Firefighter ID Controllers are responsible for reviewing the log report generated during firefighter ID usage	☑
Firefighter Role Controller	Firefighter Role Controllers are responsible for reviewing the log report generated during firefighter role usage	☑

Central Owner POWL – Windows Internet Explorer

Active Queries

Cental Owner All (66)

Cental Owner - All

▸ Show Quick Criteria Maintenance

Change Query Define New Query Personal

View: [Standard View] ▼ [Open] [Create] [Copy] [Delete] [Print Version] [Export ▴]

Filter Setting

Owner	Owner Type	Comments	Updated On	Updated By
FF Controller	Firefighter Role Controller		20.01.2015 22:21:09	GRC3
FF Owner	Firefighter Role Owner		20.01.2015 22:19:55	GRC3
FF Controller	Firefighter ID Controller		20.01.2015 22:06:27	GRC3
FF Owner	Firefighter ID Owner		20.01.2015 22:05:26	GRC3

7. ASSIGN OWNERS TO FFID

Open NWBC, go to Setup Work Center, then Click on Owners under Super User Assignments. In this activity, we will assign FF Owner to Firefighter Id.

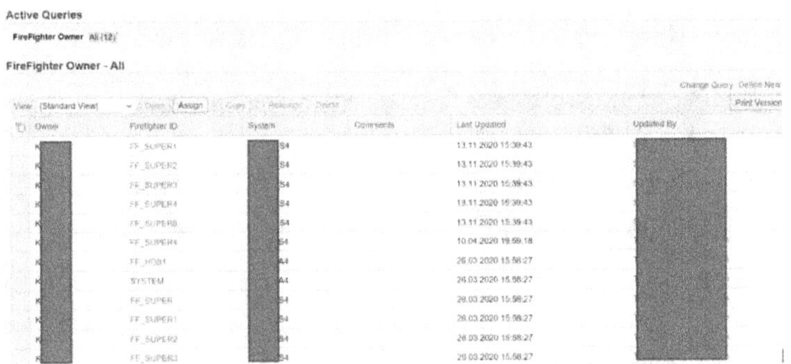

Click on Assign Button to maintain Owner for Firefighter. Select the Owner Id and Firefighter Ids for the owner. Click on Save.

Click on Open to view or edit the Owner to FFID assignment. Click on Delete to remove the Owner Assignment.

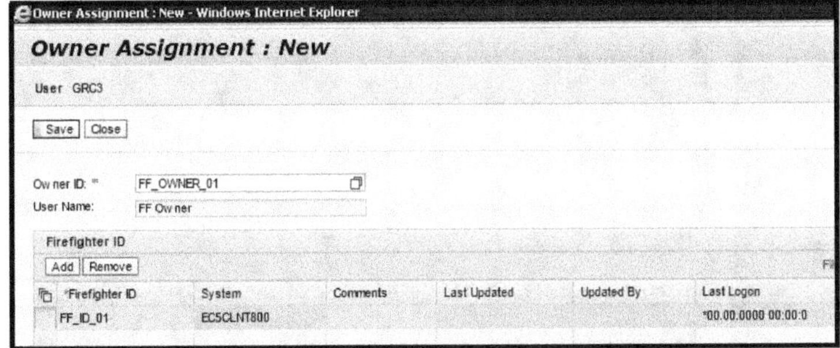

It is mandatory for a Firefighter ID/Firefighter Role to be assigned to the owner. Only then is further assignment possible, for example, Firefighter Controllers.

8. ASSIGN CONTROLLER AND FF USER TO FFID

Open NWBC, go to Setup Work Center, then Click on Firefighter IDs under Super User Assignments. The firefighter ID is assigned to a firefighter who can perform the activities in the backend system. Multiple firefighters can be assigned to a single firefighter ID. Controllers are also assigned to the firefighter ID for tracking and auditing the firefighter.

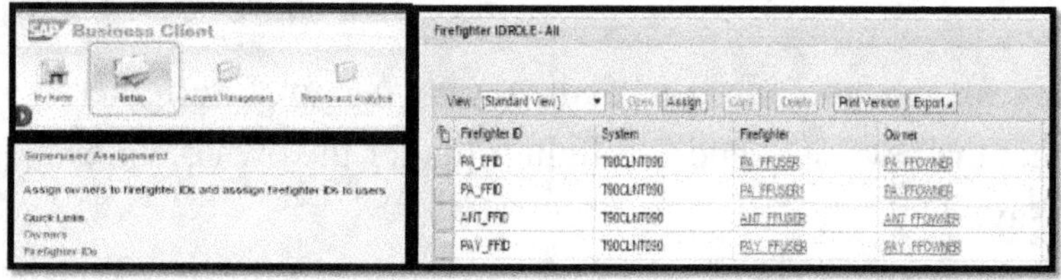

Click on Assign Button to maintain FF User & Controller to FF Ids. Select the Firefighter Id and Firefighter User along with Valid to and Valid from Date. Also, in controller tab,

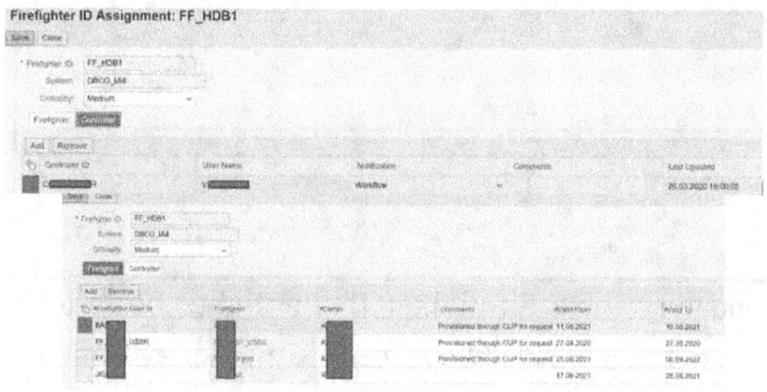

Assign the controller to the FF Id and select the notification type for controller if it should receive an email or workflow items for Log Review. Click on Save.

As an alternative method, instead of FF User and controller assignment to FFID, FF ID can be assigned to user and to controller. Use the below path to access the functionality.

FFID to user: Go to NWBC, setup work center and click on Firefighters under Super User Maintenance.

FFID to controller: Go to NWBC, setup work center, click on Controllers under Super User Maintenance.

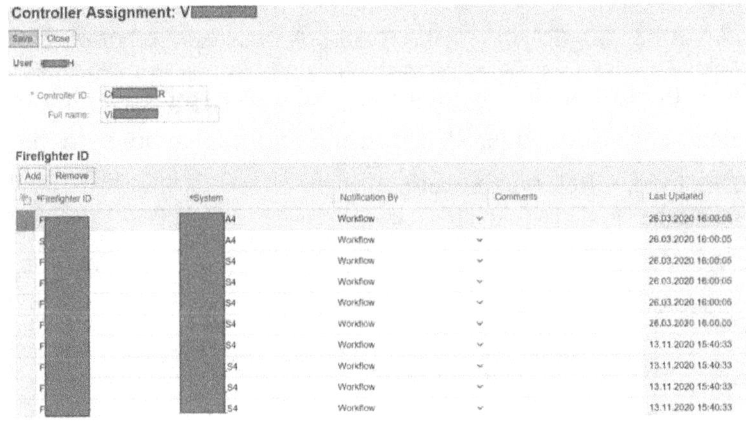

9. <u>FIREFIGHTER SESSION</u> (CENTRALIZED FIREFIGHTING)

Access Control 10.0 provides a centralized logon pad for accessing the firefighter IDs in all connected backend systems. The centralized logon pad allows:

• Displaying all firefighter ID assigned to the user

- Logging in to all connected backend systems

- Sending messages to other firefighters who are using a specific firefighter ID

- Unlocking a firefighter session not closed properly

Login to the GRC system using the firefighter user and launch transaction GRAC_SPM.

It will display all firefighter IDs which are assigned to the current firefighter in various systems.

Click on Logon to log in to any of the assigned system. Select a reason code, description, and the actions to be performed. Click on Execute.

The Firefighter can now do firefighting activities on the connected backend system. When finished you need to

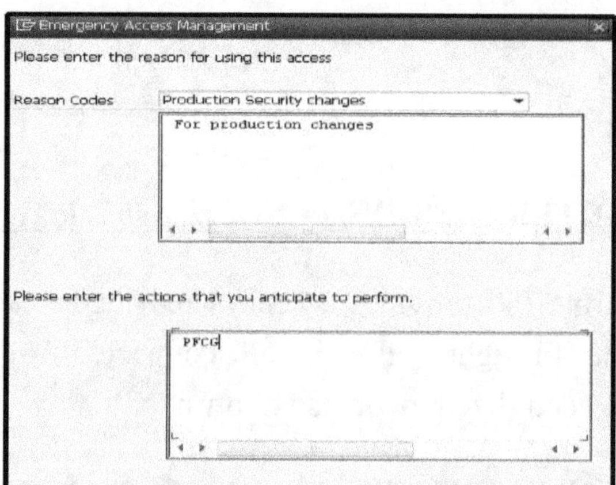

close the session.

- While a firefighter session is open the status of the firefighter ID will turn to red

- A firefighter can click Additional Activity any time to enter more information.

- If a firefighter ID is in use by another firefighter, then notification can be sent to the other firefighter by clicking Message

- Unlock can be used to unlock the firefighter ID in the event it is locked.

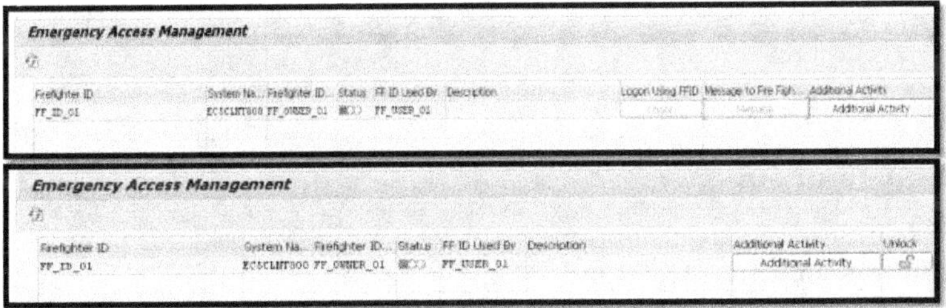

10. <u>FF LOG COLLECTION</u>

- The details of the transaction executed by the firefighter lies in the remote system in in the CDHDR, CDPOS, STAD, SM19, SM49, and debug & replace information.

- The data from the remote system can be fetched using the Log Collector which can be executed as a foreground or background job.

Foreground Job:

The foreground Job for Log Collection can be executed from the Update firefighter log button which can be found in the Consolidated Log Report.

Open NWBC, go to Report and Analytics Work Center, then Click on Consolidated Log report under Emergency Access User Management Reports.

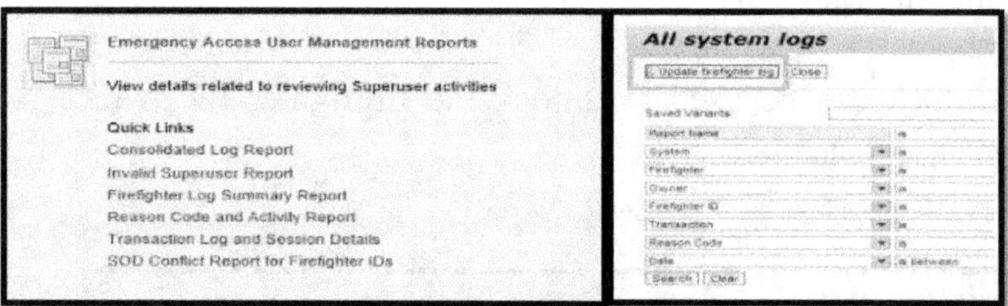

Background Job:

It can be scheduled from below IMG Path:

Call SPRO -->SAP Reference IMG --> Governance, Risk and Compliance --> Access Control --> Synchronization Jobs --> Firefighter Log Synch (T-code: GRAC_SPM_LOG_SYNC) Provide the connector name and select Execute or Execute in Background from Program.

Firefighter Workflow Synch:

Once the FF User completes the firefighter activities, Log Report notification is sent from the GRC Box to Controller.

FF Workflow Synch initiates FF log report review workflow based up on your workflow settings which sends the FF log report to FF controller for review.

If the Parameter 4007 is set to 'Yes' then the job 'GRAC_SPM_LOG_SYNC_UPDATE' will send the Log Report notification as well else if the parameter 4007 is set to 'NO' another job is required for log report notification to controller which is 'GRAC_SPM_WORKFLOW_SYNC'.

Call SPRO -->SAP Reference IMG --> Governance, Risk and Compliance --> Access Control --> Synchronization

Jobs --> Firefighter Workflow Synch (T-code: GRAC_SPM_WF_SYNC)

11. REPORT ANALYSIS

The Firefighter Log reports can be accessed using the NWBC or the Portal and are located under Reports and

Analytics Work Center --> Super user Management Reports

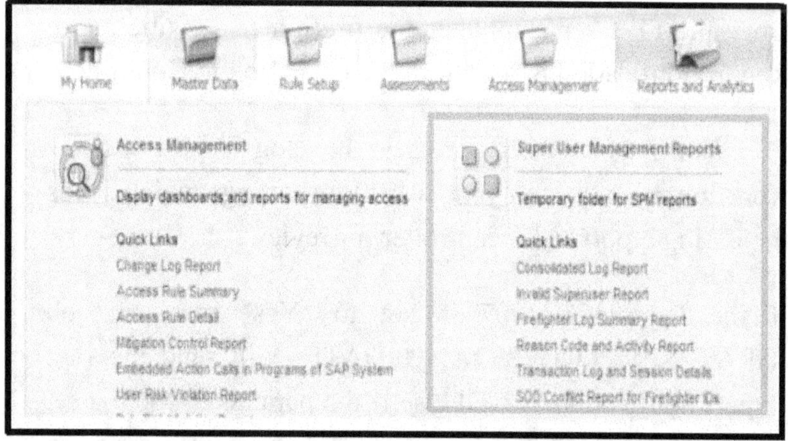

CONSOLIDATED LOG REPORT:

The consolidated log report is a new report which enables the user to segment the various logs collected or view them all in one combined report.

This report provides information based on the following logs from the remote system:

- **Transaction Log:** Captures transaction execution from transaction STAD

- **Change Log:** Captures change log from change document objects (tables CDPOS and CDHDR)

- **System Log:** Captures Debug & Replace information from transaction SM21.

- **Security Audit Log:** Captures Security Audit Log from

transaction SM20

- **OS Command Log:** Captures changes to OS commands

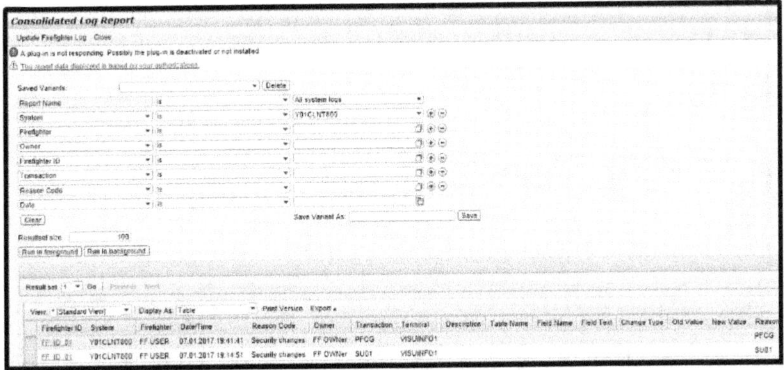

from transaction SM49.

The Change Log can be retrieved from the consolidated. Log Report by selecting the Report type

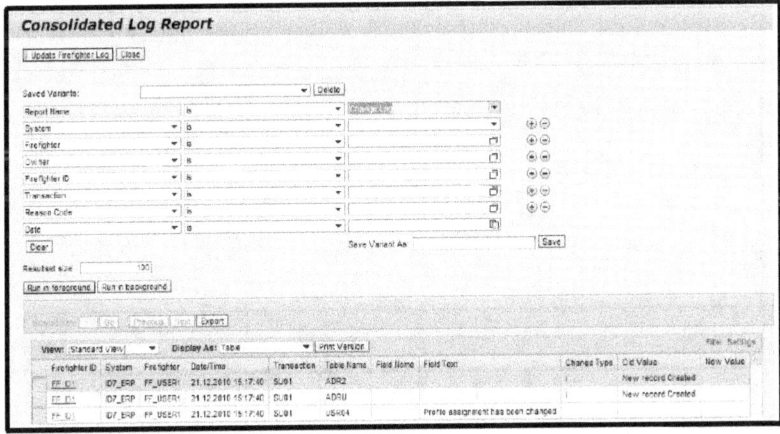

as Change Log.

The System Log can also be found in the consolidated Log. Report by choosing the Report type as System Log

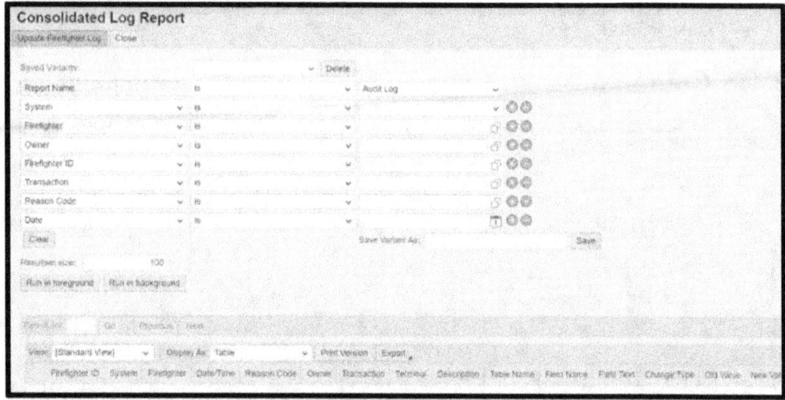

The Audit Log is also contained in the consolidated Log Report as Report type as Audit Log. This audit function will show the details of the user(s) subject to auditing. The user(s) to be audited are configured/selected in transaction SM19

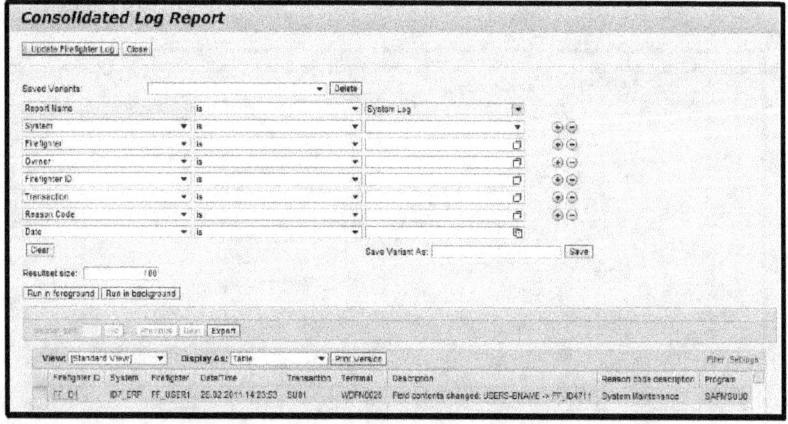

An OS Command Log can be retrieved from the consolidated. Log Report by selecting the Report type as OS Command. This log tracks the changes which the user makes in SM49 for OS Command

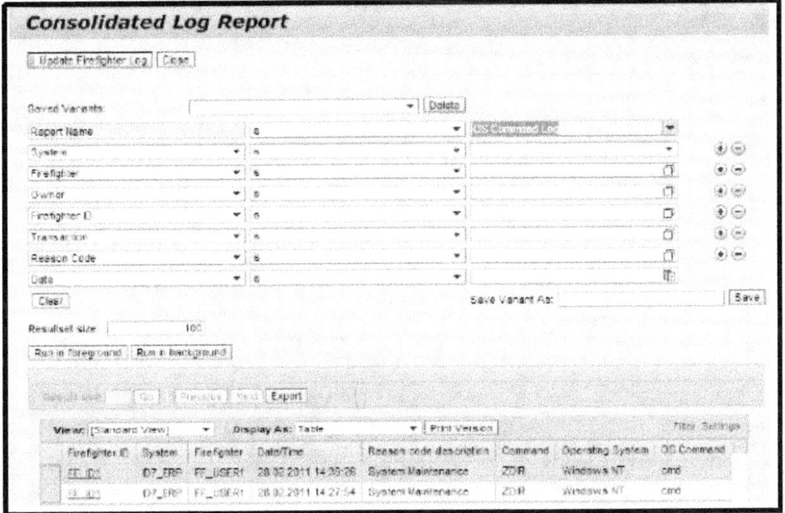

<u>INVALID SUPER USER REPORT:</u>

The Invalid Super User Log is launched by the Invalid Superuser Report from the Super User Management Reports area. This Log is used to analyze the users who are expired, locked, or deleted

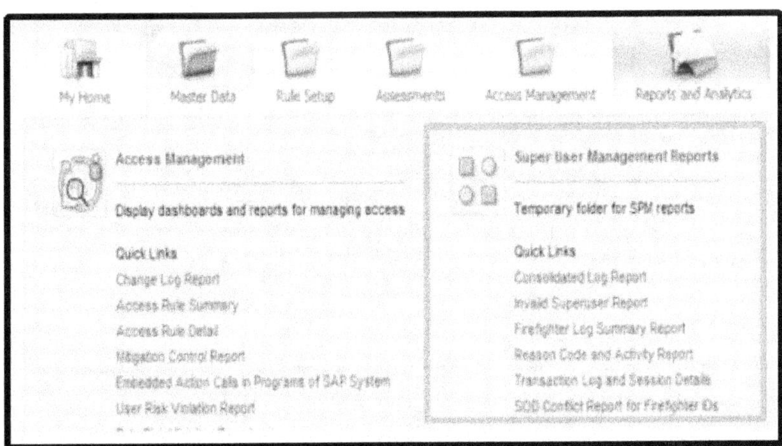

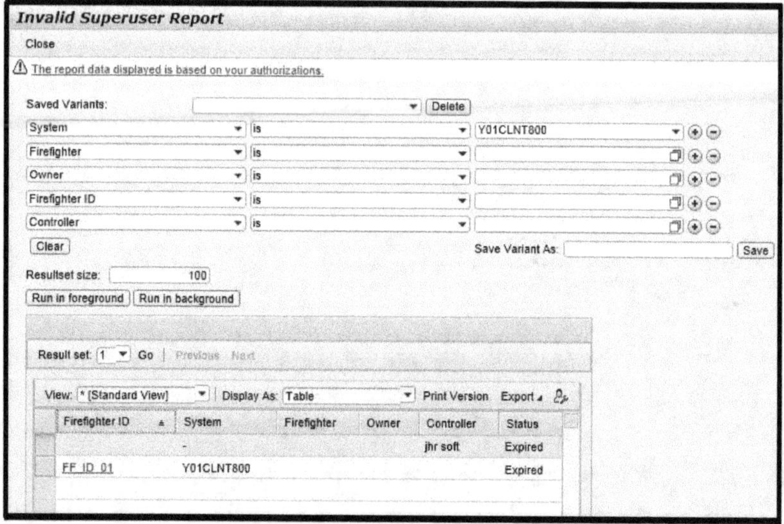

FIREFIGHTER LOG SUMMARY REPORT:

The Details of FFID Logged in sessions are captured in this Log Report.

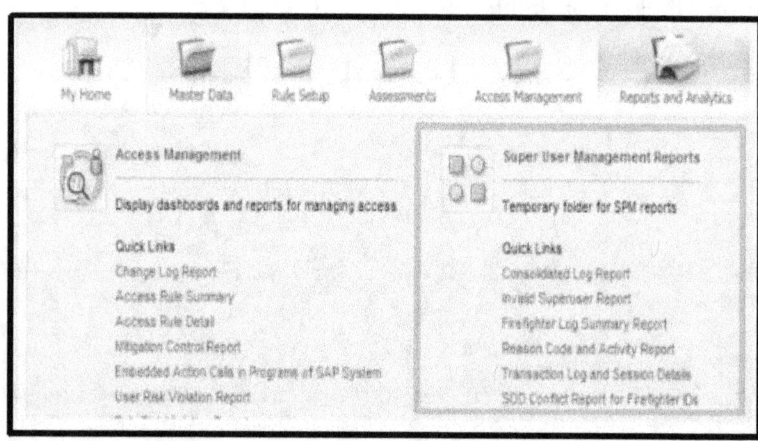

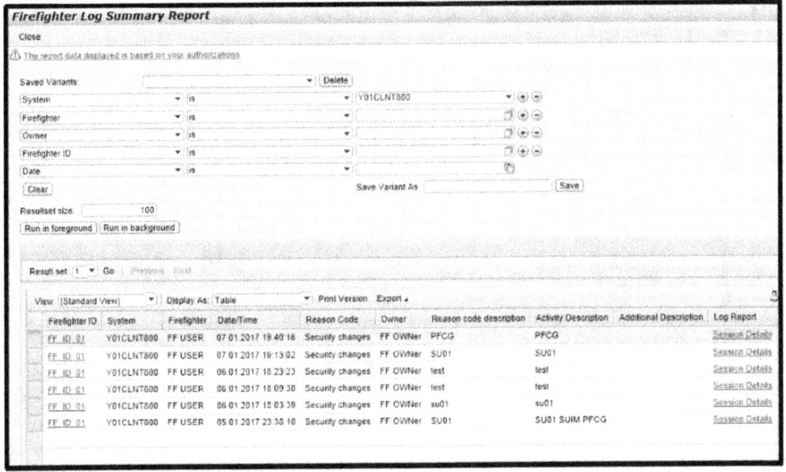

<u>REASON CODE AND ACTIVITY REPORT:</u>

Reason code and activity Report can be retrieved from the link in the portal for Reason Code and Activity. This Report Gives the Details of the Reason Code and Activity used when FFID Logs in to the Report System.

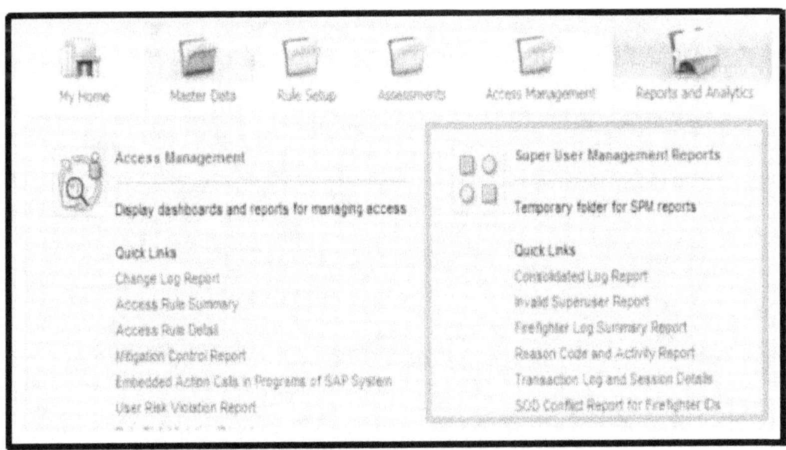

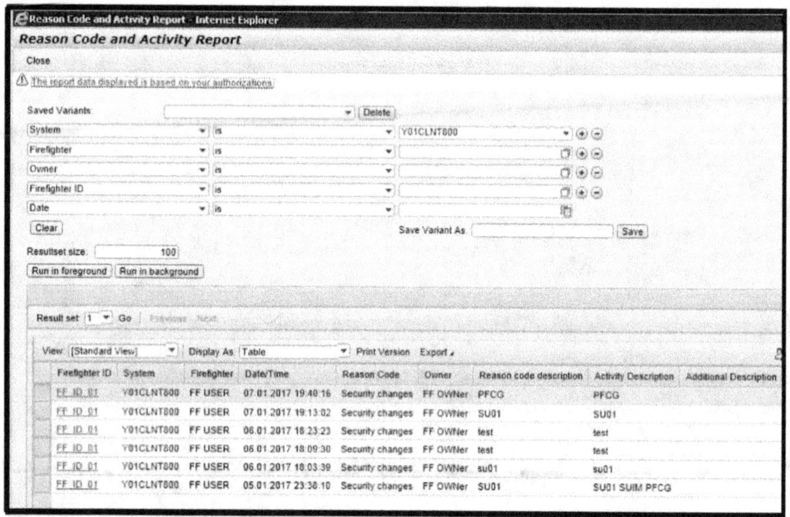

TRANSACTION LOGS AND SESSION DETAILS:

This report captures transaction data from the selected system connector for Firefighter IDs and Firefighters. It displays the number and type of transactions accessed for each session.

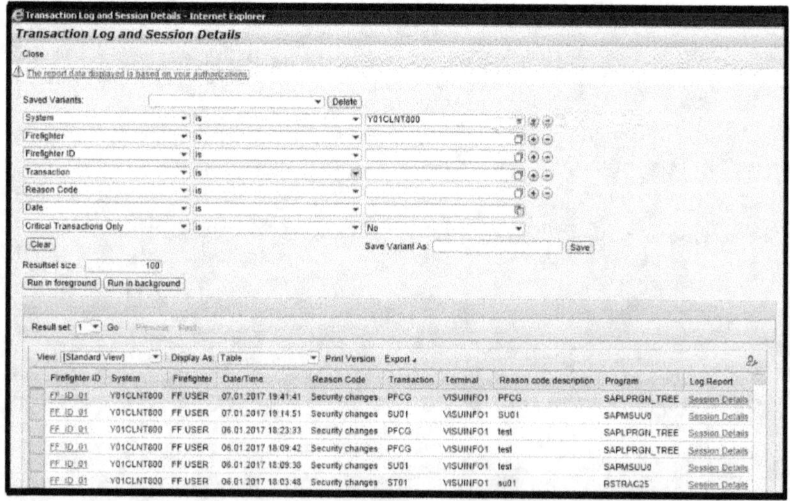

SOD CONFLICT REPORT FOR

FIREFIGHTER IDS :

This Report provide details regarding the SOD Conflict for the Firefighter Ids. If we need to get details of only the conflicts arising from the executed transactions, enable the Executed Transactions Only checkbox.

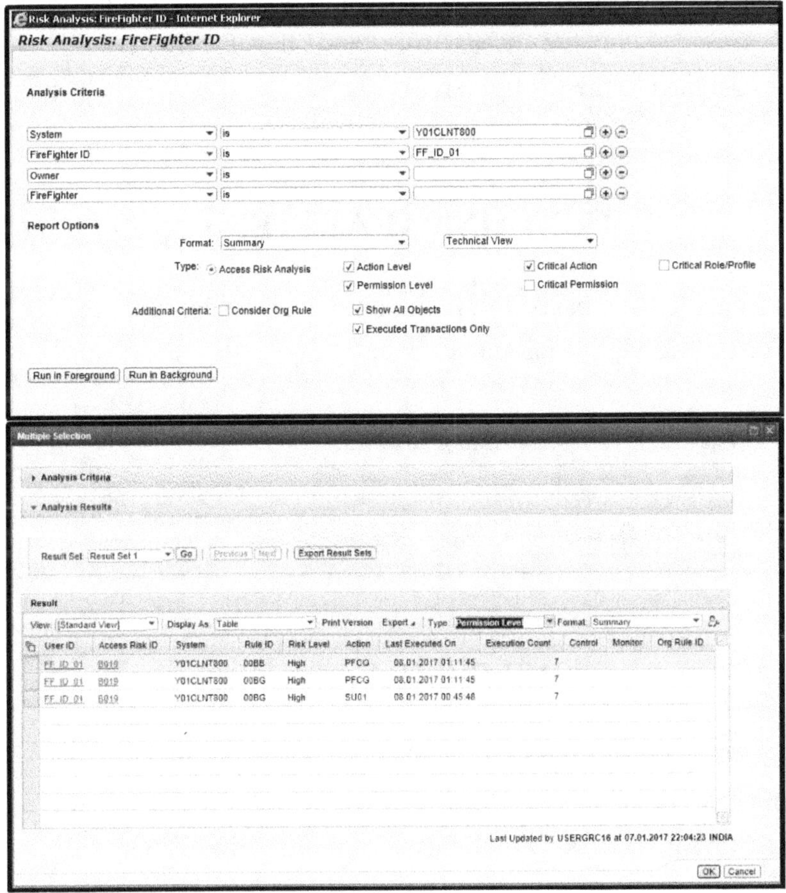

12. <u>ROLE BASED FIREFIGHTER</u>

- In Role Based Firefighter, the Dashboard is not used for logon as used with the traditional Firefighter ID.

- The Firefighter roles created in the remote system will be assigned to the user in the GRC server.

- The firefighter directly logs in into the remote system using their user ids and performs activities which are provided in the user's role and the firefighter role assigned to the firefighter.

MAINTAIN PARAMETER :

To enable Role based FF, maintain the parameter 4000 to 2. For ID Based, this parameter is 1.

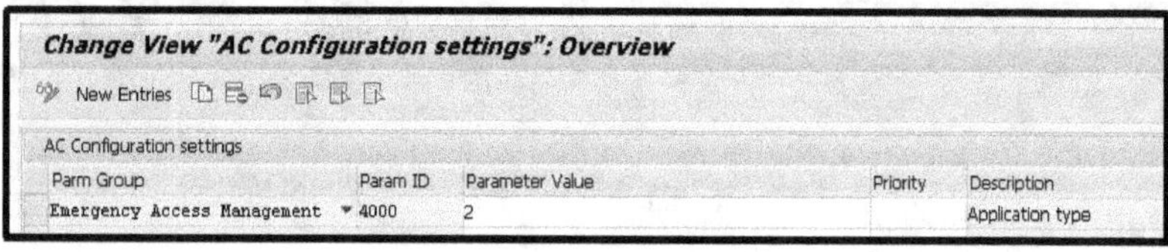

Parm Group		Param ID	Parameter Value	Priority	Description
Emergency Access Management	▾	4000	2		Application type

ROLE CREATION:

Create a role in transaction PFCG on the system to which the firefighter requires access. This Role will contain the additional access which user requires for Emergency activities.

ROLE IMPORT:

Import the role to GRC by going to NWBC Portal, Choose Access Management Work Center and click on Role Import under Role Mass Maintenance.

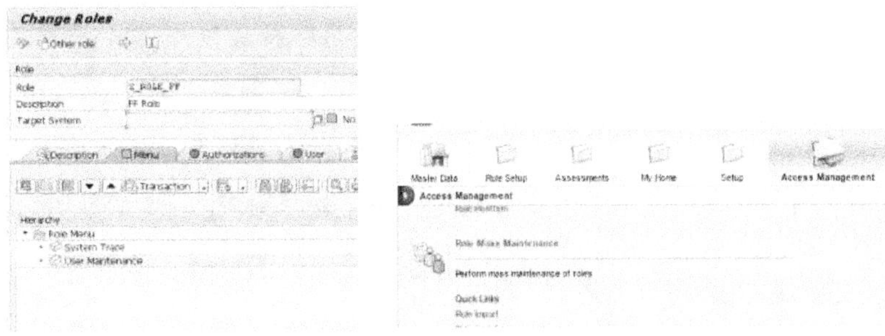

- Enter values for the following fields: Application Type, Landscape, Source system, Role from.

- Choose Next.

- In next screen, specify the Product release and set the Role status to Production.

- Choose "Next".

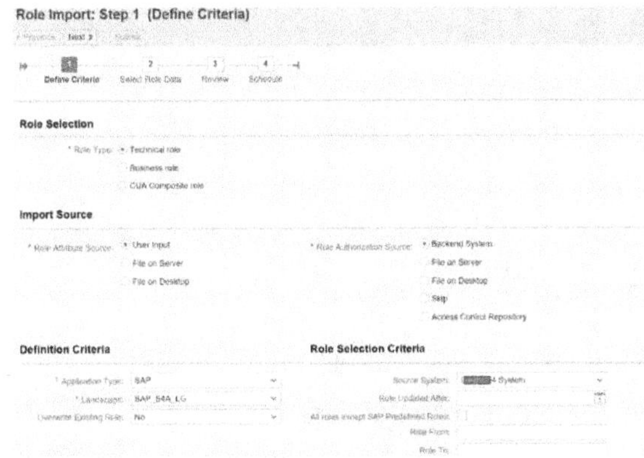

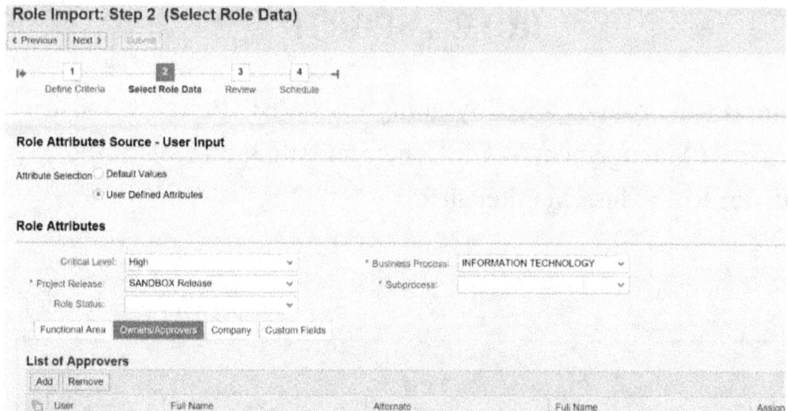

- Select Preview all Roles to view the selected Roles.

- Choose Next.

- Schedule the import in Foreground or Background.

Choose "Next". Role is imported

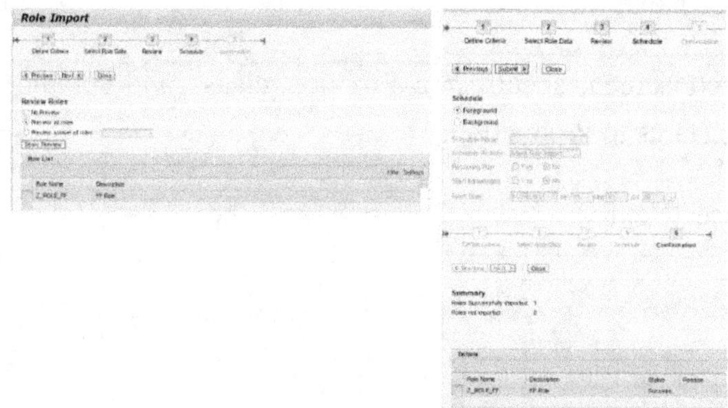

<u>Enable Role for Firefighting:</u>

Go to NWBC, Choose Access Management, Select Role Maintenance under the Role Management.

Select the role and click Open. Choose Define Role, go to Properties, select the Enable for Firefighting checkbox under User Provisioning, and save. Role is ready to be used as FF Role.

ASSIGN OWNER TO FF ROLE:

Create Owner and Controller in GRC system using SU01. Maintain the Ids under Access control Owners as FF

Role Owner and FF Role Controller respectively.

Add the Owner to the FF Role using NWBC portal, then Setup Work center, Owners link under Super User Assignment.

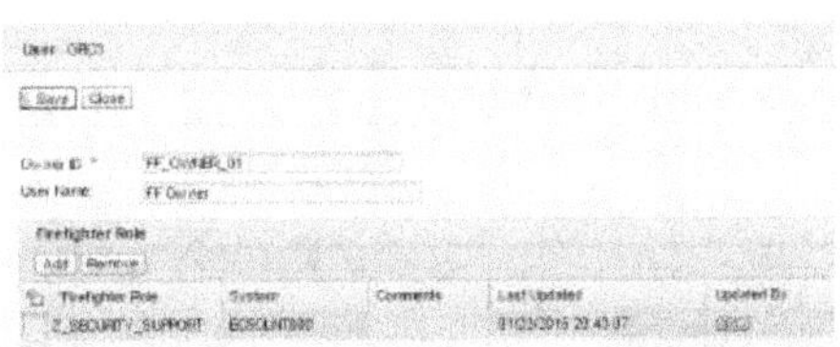

ADD CONTROLLER & FF USER TO FF ROLE:

Click on Firefighter IDs link under Super User Assignment in NWBC Setup Work center.

Assign controller to the Role and select the user along with Validity to which the FF Role would be assigned in plug-in system.

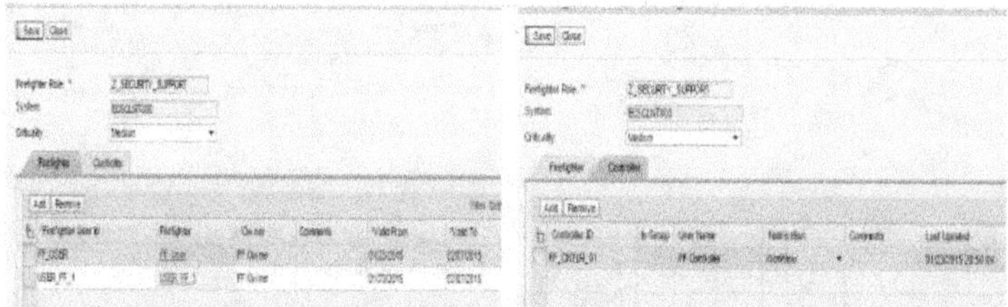

FIREFIGHTING SESSION :

• For role-based application reason codes need not be maintained, as firefighter user directly login into the client (plug-in) system.

• When the firefighter is assigned to firefighter role, the role is automatically assigned to the firefighter.

• Firefighter directly login into the client (plug-in) system using SAP GUI and perform operations

LOG UPDATE AND REPORTING:

From the Consolidated Log Report link in NWBC Reports and Analytics Work center, Click on Update Firefighter

Log.

Once Logs are updated, using the same report, you can get the list of T-codes executed as part of the Firefighter Role.

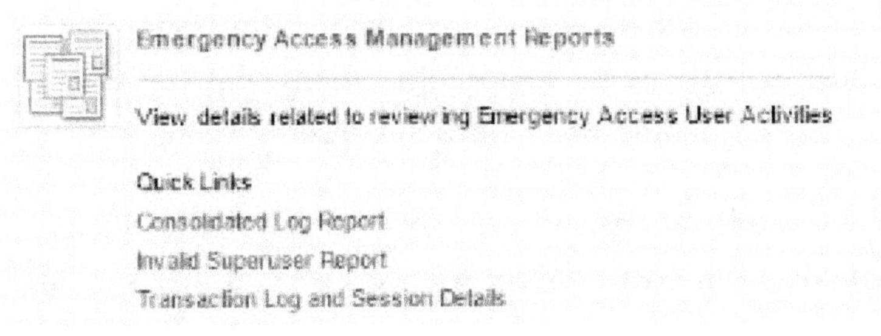

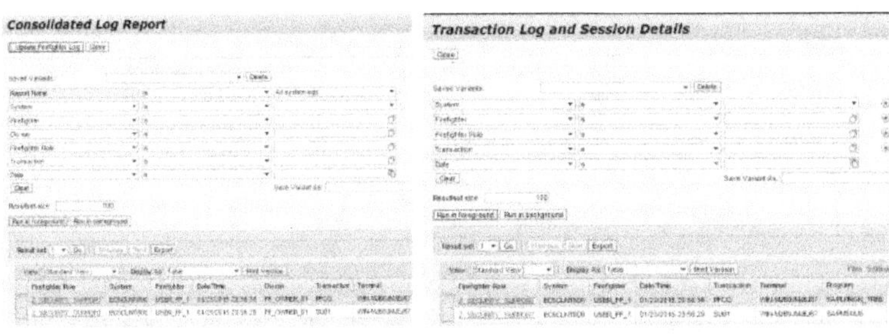

1. DECENTRALIZED FIREFIGHTING

- De-centralized firefighting feature in GRC 10.0 from GRC SP10. Depending on the client's needs, the option "log on centrally" (current version 10 behavior) or "log on locally" (5.3 behavior) can be configured in GRC 10, GRC 10.1 and GRC 12.X

- Also, system has the ability where both centralized and de-centralized approach can be configured but user can either login centrally or locally as there can be only one firefighter session at a time.

- Configuration parameter 4015 need to be maintained as "YES" in order to enable De-centralized firefighting

- FF Controller should also exist in the plug-in system with valid Email ID as FF login notifications will be sent to controller's Mail Id maintained in plug-in system.

- FF log notifications are sent to FF controller's mailed maintained in GRC system. Hence FF controller should exist in both GRC and Plug-in systems

Emergency Access Management	4015	YES	Enable Decentralized FireFighting

CONFIGURATION PARAMETERS –

PLUG-IN SYSTEM

It is required to maintain below configuration setting for De-centralized FF in both GRC and Plug-In System.

Call SPRO -->SAP Reference IMG --> Governance, Risk and Compliance (Plug-In) --> Access Control --> Maintain Plug-In configuration Settings

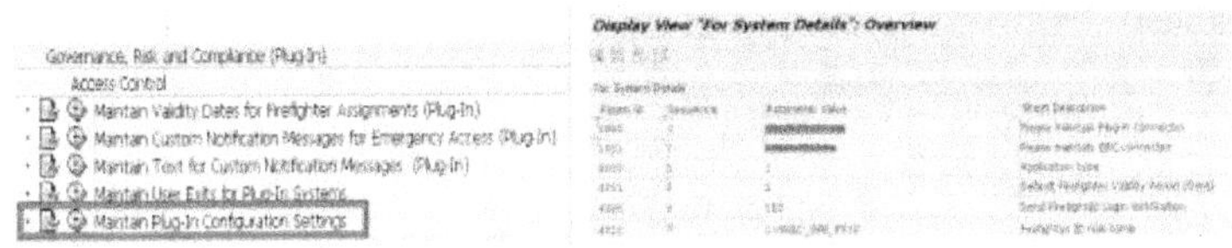

Parameter 1000 is for the connector name from GRC to Plug-in system. Parameter 1001 defines the connector from Plug-In to GRC system.

EAM MASTER DATA SYNCH :

This is the new job introduced as part of De-centralized firefighting. Synchronizes the EAM data from GRC box to Plug-in system. Once you have created all required users execute this job to synchronize the data from GRC to plug-in system.

Call SPRO -->SAP Reference IMG --> Governance, Risk and Compliance --> Access Control --> Synchronization Jobs --> EAM Master Data Synch

FFID LOGIN:

Once the FFID is assigned to user, the user directly logs in to Plug-In system and execute the T-code/n/GRCPI/GRIA_EAM from Plug-in system and login with firefighter Id's assigned to them. So, users no need to exist in GRC system anymore.

Once the user completes the activity, FF logs can be retrieved in similar way as it is done for centralized firefighting.

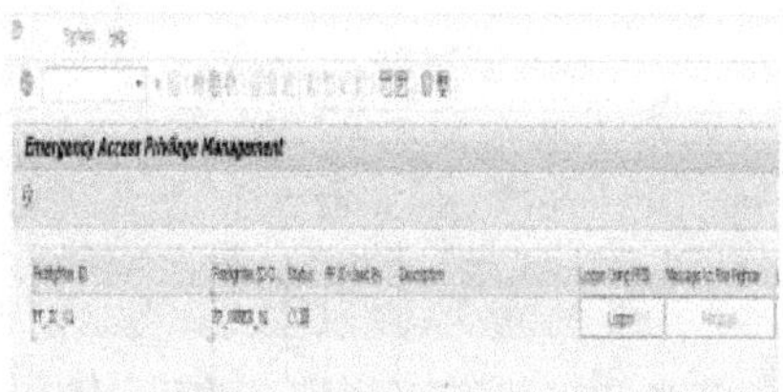

ADDITIONAL NOTES:

• All objects are transportable throughout the GRC 12.0 landscape, apart from mitigating controls.

<u>ARM– ACCESS REQUEST MANAGEMENT</u>

1. Perform Automatic & Task Specific Workflow Settings

2. Define Request Type

3. Maintain Priority Configuration

4. Define Employee Types

5. Maintain Number Range Intervals

6. Define Number Ranges

7. Maintain End User Personalization

8. Maintain Provisioning Settings

9. Maintain User Defaults

10. Maintain Review Rejection Reason

11. Creating users and assigning roles

1. PERFORM AUTOMATIC WORKFLOW CUSTO-MIZING AND TASK SPECIFIC CUSTOMIZING

Call SPRO --> SAP Reference IMG --> Governance, Risk and Compliance --> General Settings --> Workflow -->

Perform Automatic Workflow Customizing

• Execute Perform Automatic Workflow Customizing.

• Make sure that all tasks are green after the generation as show in the screenshot

• You may need to run program RHSOBJCH to fix HR control tables

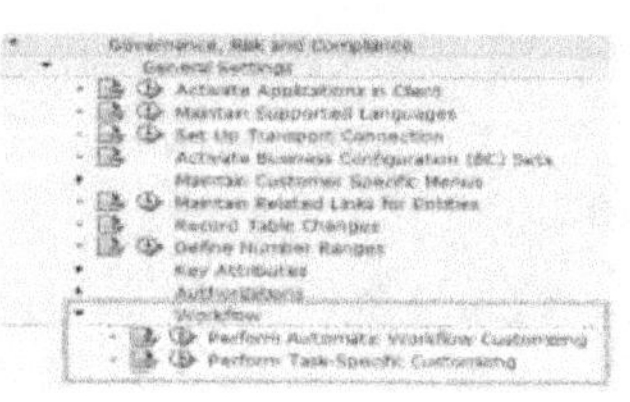

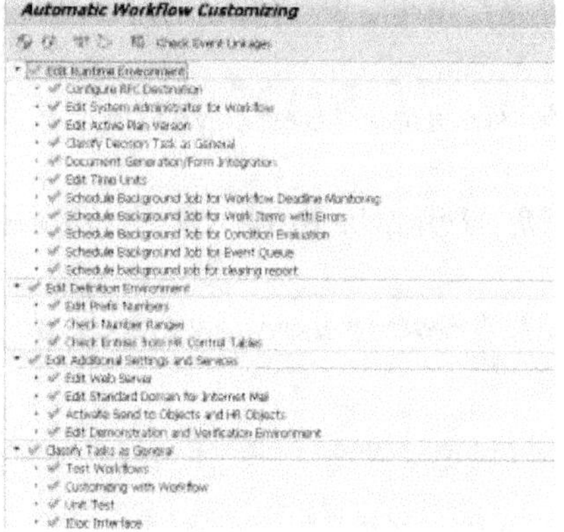

MAINTAIN PREFIX NUMBERS :

- Standard objects (workflow tasks, standard tasks, and so on) are identified with an eight-digit number.

- The last five digits of this number are assigned automatically by the system. The prefix number is used for the first three digits of this number.

- To guarantee unique identification, define a unique prefix number for each system and client.

- To perform this step, click on Edit Prefix Number under the Edit Definition Environment. This is available on the screen of Automatic Customization.

The prefix number applies for the following objects:

- Standard tasks

- Task groups

- Rules

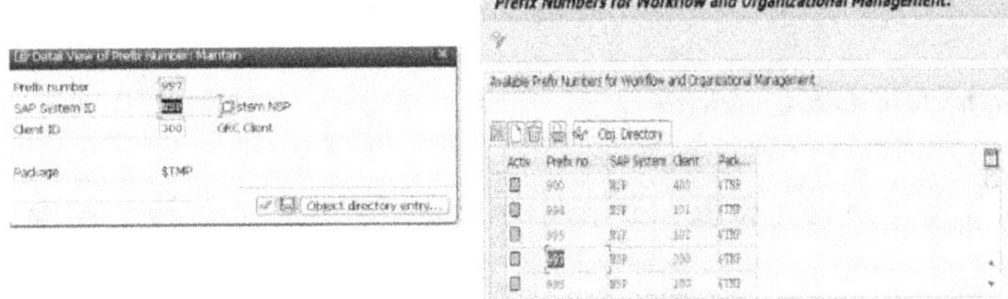

PERFORM TASK-SPECIFIC CUSTOMIZING :

Call SPRO -->SAP Reference IMG --> Governance, Risk and Compliance --> General Settings --> Workflow -->

Perform Task Specific Customizing

- In this Customizing activity, we establish the settings required to adapt the SAP tasks and SAP workflows in accordance with our requirements. This activity sets up the tasks and workflows that we need for the implementation phase. This activity to activate the triggering events for tasks and workflows.

- Possible agents must be specified for each task to define the organizational responsibility for processing.

- Workflows can only be started in a dialog by their possible agents. If a scenario requires that the relevant workflow be started in a dialog; this workflow must be assigned to its possible agents.

- A task or workflow can be started as a reaction to events created by the application functionality. For this, specific events are declared as triggering events for the task or workflow.

Expand the GRC node.

Click the Assign Agents link at the right side of the GRC node.

If no folders are visible below the

"GRC" folder please run report

"RS_APPL_REFRESH" in SE38.

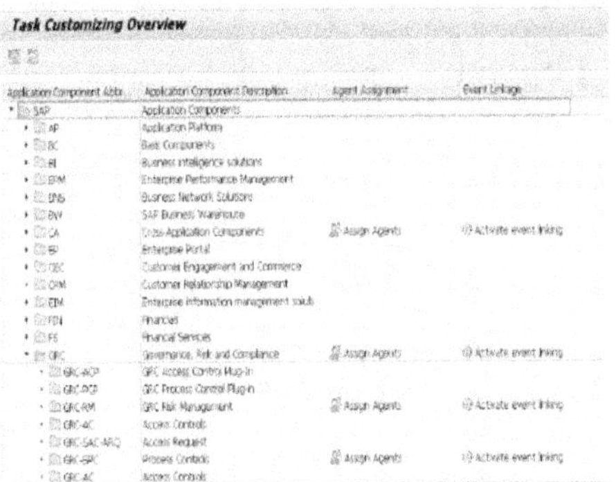

Assign Task as General Task via Task Attribute.

Make sure all tasks that are not using Background task have been assigned as General Task.

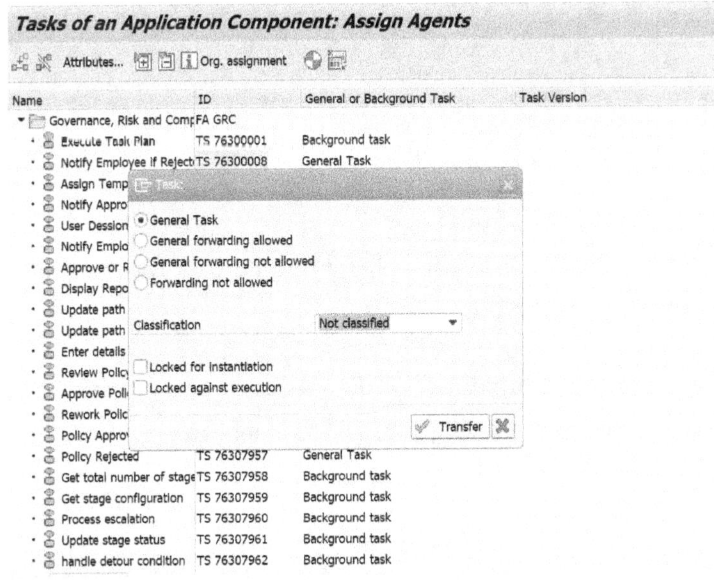

Click the Activate event linking link at the right side of the GRC node.

You need to perform below steps for all WS Tasks.

• Click the Properties icon

• Set the Linkage Status to No errors

• Make sure Event linkage activated is checked.

• Set Error feedback to Do not change linkage

• Be sure to activate all WS

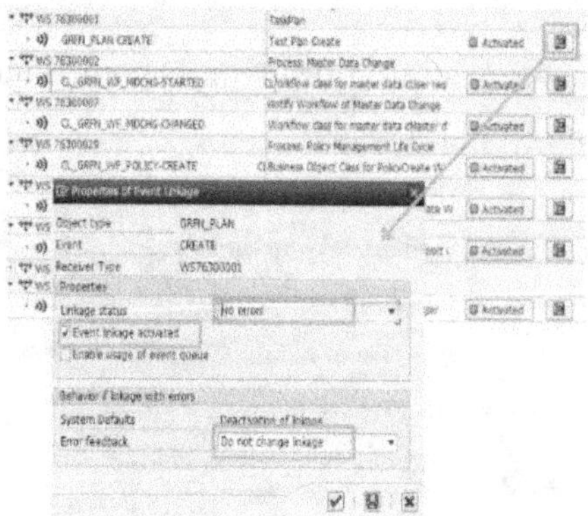

Repeat the all steps for GRC AC Folder. (e.g. for Access Control "GRC-AC")

Task-specific customizing for GRC-AC is not available in case you have the GRC plugins installed in your GRC system.

In case you have the GRC plugins installed also in the central GRC instance the task-specific customizing for

Access Control is not visible in IMG as shown below

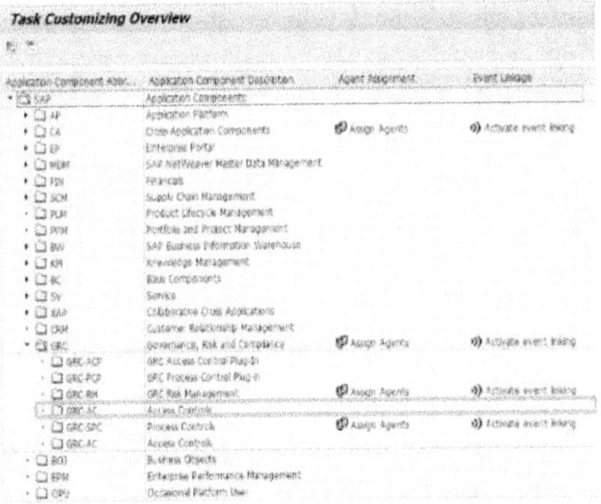

Event Linkage – Task Specific Customizing with plug-ins

Go to transaction SWE2 and maintain the following linkages by double clicking on each line in Change mode.

Set these parameters per event linkage item. Linkage Activated, do not change linkage and No errors in Receiver Status

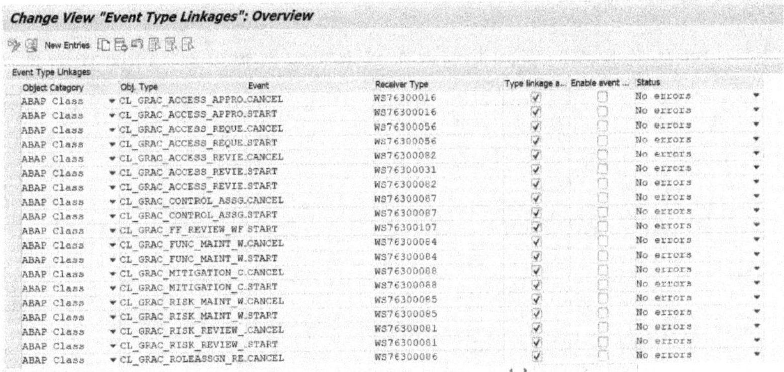

Object Category	Obj. Type	Event	Receiver Type	Type linkage a...	Enable event ...	Status
ABAP Class	CL_GRAC_ACCESS_APPRO.CANCEL		WS76300016	✓		No errors
ABAP Class	CL_GRAC_ACCESS_APPRO.START		WS76300016	✓		No errors
ABAP Class	CL_GRAC_ACCESS_REQUE.CANCEL		WS76300056	✓		No errors
ABAP Class	CL_GRAC_ACCESS_REQUE.START		WS76300056	✓		No errors
ABAP Class	CL_GRAC_ACCESS_REVIE.CANCEL		WS76300082	✓		No errors
ABAP Class	CL_GRAC_ACCESS_REVIE.START		WS76300031	✓		No errors
ABAP Class	CL_GRAC_ACCESS_REVIE.START		WS76300082	✓		No errors
ABAP Class	CL_GRAC_CONTROL_ASSG.CANCEL		WS76300087	✓		No errors
ABAP Class	CL_GRAC_CONTROL_ASSG.START		WS76300087	✓		No errors
ABAP Class	CL_GRAC_FF_REVIEW_WF START		WS76300107	✓		No errors
ABAP Class	CL_GRAC_FUNC_MAINT_W.CANCEL		WS76300084	✓		No errors
ABAP Class	CL_GRAC_FUNC_MAINT_W.START		WS76300084	✓		No errors
ABAP Class	CL_GRAC_MITIGATION_C.CANCEL		WS76300088	✓		No errors
ABAP Class	CL_GRAC_MITIGATION_C.START		WS76300088	✓		No errors
ABAP Class	CL_GRAC_RISK_MAINT_W.CANCEL		WS76300085	✓		No errors
ABAP Class	CL_GRAC_RISK_MAINT_W.START		WS76300085	✓		No errors
ABAP Class	CL_GRAC_RISK_REVIEW_.CANCEL		WS76300081	✓		No errors
ABAP Class	CL_GRAC_RISK_REVIEW_.START		WS76300081	✓		No errors
ABAP Class	CL_GRAC_ROLEASSGN_RE.CANCEL		WS76300086	✓		No errors

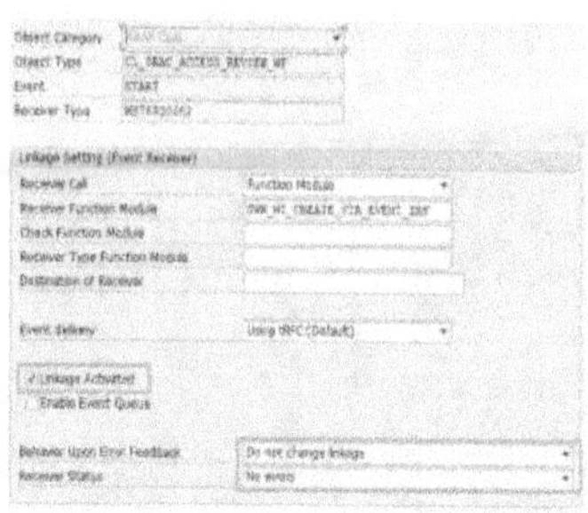

Assign Agents – Task Specific Customizing with plug-ins

Go to transaction PFTC and select the type and task as shown below. Click on Display.

Whole process needs to be repeated for each item.

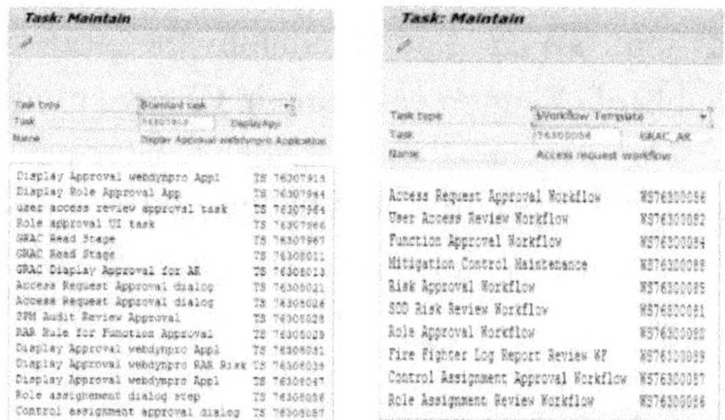

Then go to Additional Data - Agent assignment - Maintain. If the "Transfer container elements" window shows answer always No.

Now select "Attributes" and change the task to General Task

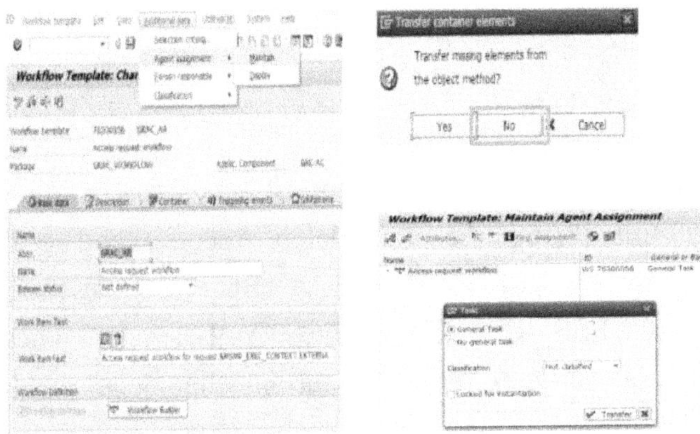

Once All Tasks have been changed, Activate the workflows tasks using transaction SWDD.

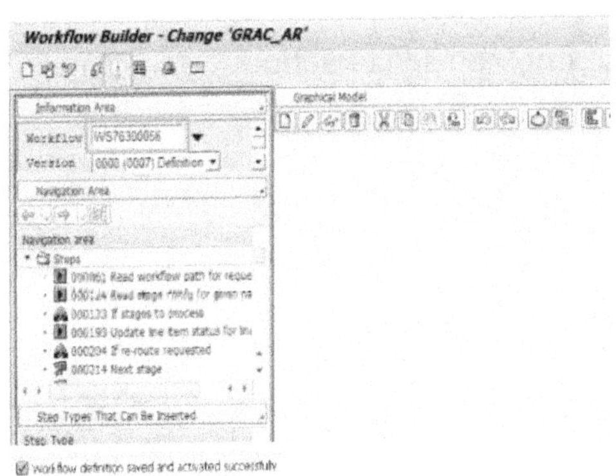

2. <u>DEFINE REQUEST TYPES</u>

In this Customizing activity, we can maintain the request types, and then assign actions to the request types.

Call SPRO --> SAP Reference IMG --> Governance, Risk and Compliance --> Access Control --> User

Provisioning -->

Define Request Type

SAP delivers several standard request types for example, New Account, Change Account, Delete Account, and so on. as part of BC Set activation (GRAC_ACCESS_REQUEST_REQ_TYPE). These standard request types represent actions that occur in the back end systems.

You can choose to change these request types, or you can create your own. Click on Active checkbox to activate/deactivate the request type.

To view or change the associated action with the request type, select it and click on select action.

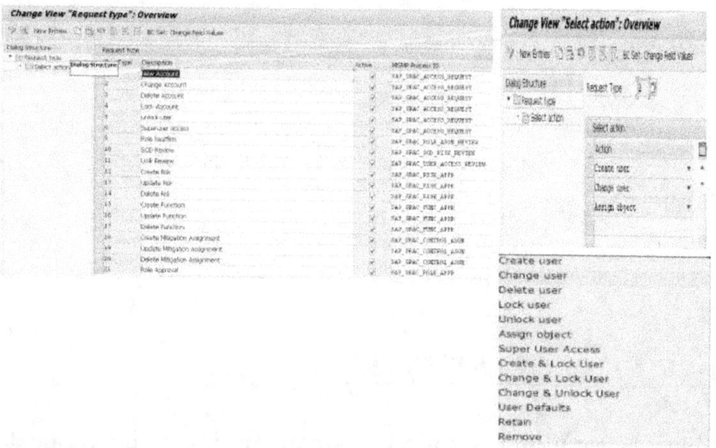

- **Create User** - Action to create a new user without user default settings

- **Change User** - Action to change user detail except for

user default settings

• **Delete User** - Action to delete existing user

• **Lock User** - Action to lock existing user

• **Unlock User** - Action to unlock locked user

• **Assign Object** - Action to assign and remove roles

• **Superuser Access** - Action to assign and remove emergency access IDs and roles

• **User Defaults** - Action to apply user defaults to the user, during provisioning.

3. <u>MAINTAIN PRIORITY CONFIGURATION</u>

In this Customizing activity, you can create a priority for a request to determine how quickly a request is approved. The priorities we define appear on the Priority tab page of the Create Request screen.

Call SPRO -->SAP Reference IMG --> Governance, Risk and Compliance --> Access Control --> User Provisioning ->

Maintain Priority Configuration

SAP standard priority value are loaded after the activation of BC set: GRAC_ACCESS_REQUEST_PRIORITY

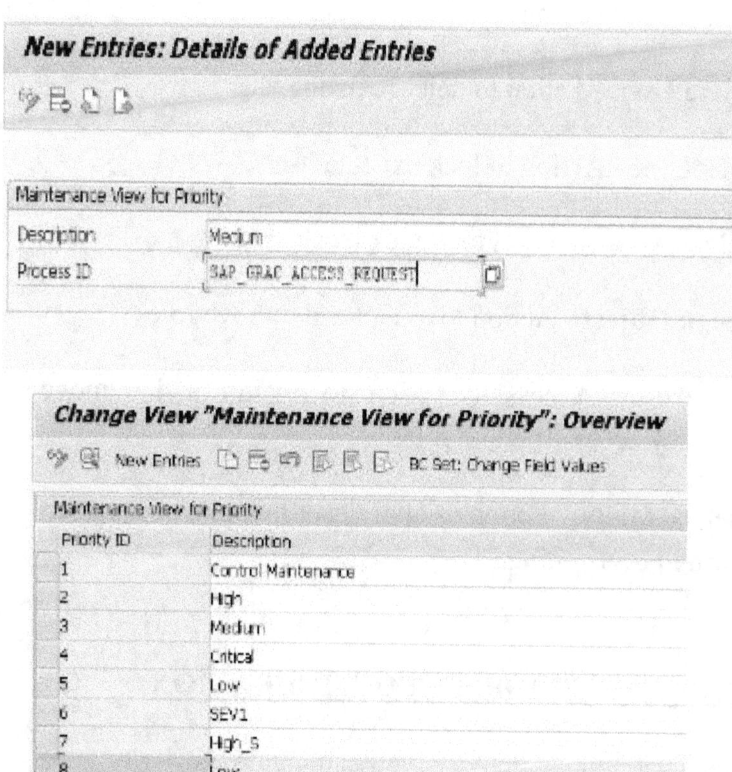

To create a new Priority, enter Description and select the Process Id for which it is applicable.

4. <u>DEFINE EMPLOYEE TYPE</u>

In this Customizing activity, we can maintain the list of available employment types such as full time, part time, and so on. The employment types appear in a dropdown list on the Access Request screen

Call SPRO -->SAP Reference IMG --> Governance, Risk

and Compliance --> Access Control --> User Provisioning -
->

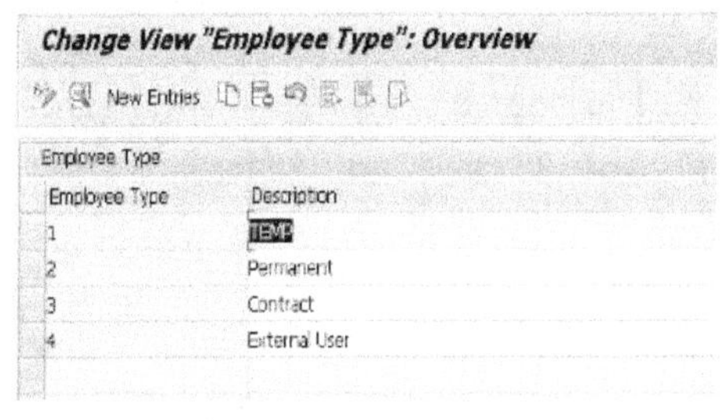

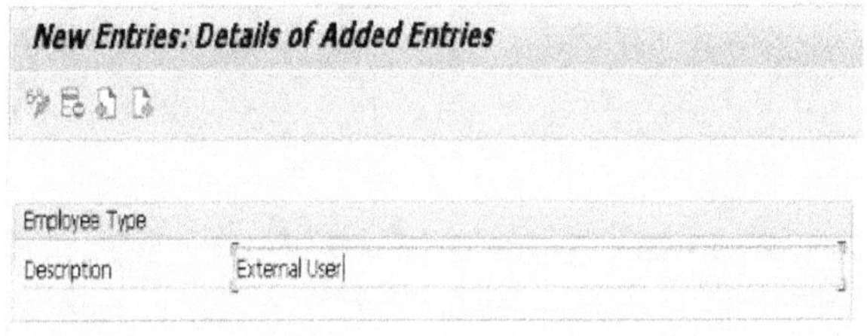

Define Employee Type

To create a new Employee Type, click on New Entries.

5. <u>M AINTAIN NUMBER RANGE INTERVAL</u>

Maintaining number ranges is one of the required activities because without maintaining number ranges, you can't create any type of request.

Call SPRO -->SAP Reference IMG --> Governance, Risk and Compliance --> Access Control --> User Provisioning -->

Maintain Number Range Intervals for Provisioning Requests.

Transaction SNRO can also be used to maintain the number range intervals for the object GRACREQNO, which is meant for user access requests.

Use the object GRACREQNO and click on Interval Editing (In GRC 12.X It will appear as Number Ranges). Click on change interval and provide the Number Range.

Click on change NR status to reset the current number in the range.

Click on + symbol to add a New entry and provide the From and to values. Make sure the EXT checkbox is unchecked.

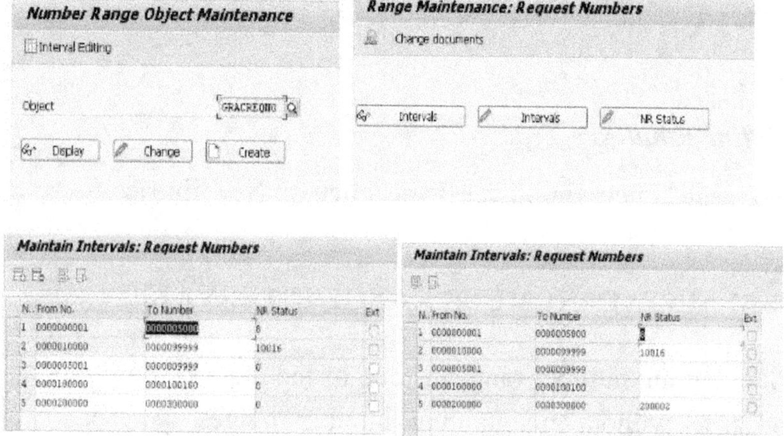

6. <u>DEFINE NUMBER RANGES</u>

In this Customizing activity, we can active the current number range that the application uses to process User Provisioning requests.

Requests for User Provisioning are identified through a system of distinct numbers. We can define a range of unique request numbers.

Call SPRO -->SAP Reference IMG --> Governance, Risk and Compliance --> Access Control --> User Provisioning - ->

Define Number Range for Provisioning Requests

Click on New entries to add a new interval in the list. This interval are already created in SNRO t-code in previous step.

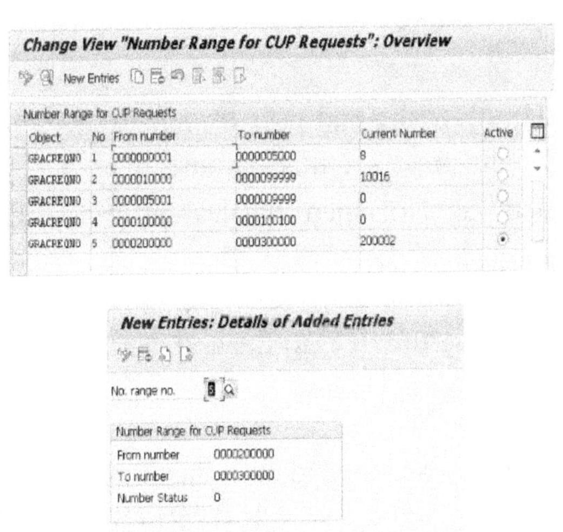

7. **<u>MAINTAIN END USER PERSONALIZATION</u>**

In this Customizing activity, we can set the parameters that define the behavior of the fields and the pushbuttons on the

Request Access screen.

Call SPRO -->SAP Reference IMG --> Governance, Risk and Compliance --> Access Control --> User Provisioning -->

Maintain End User Personalization

The following parameters and options are available:

• **Default Values** - These values are automatically populated in the fields.

• **Mandatory** - If you want the end user to enter a value in the selected field (for submitting a request), then you must set this parameter as Yes.

• **Editable** - To allow the end user to edit the value in the selected field, you must set this parameter as Yes. If the parameter is set as No, then the value in the field is displayed as read-only

• **Visible** - To display the field to the end user, you must set this parameter as Yes.

SAP standard values are loaded into customizing table by activation of BC Set: GRAC_ACCESS_REQUEST_EUP

To edit the fields properties, select the EUP Id and click on Maintain EUP fields. This will open the screen to maintain different properties for various fields.

Perform the changes and click save.

Similarly, a new EUP can be created by clicking on New Entries. Give the EUP Id and Name and click Save.

Select the new EUP Id and click on maintain EUP fields to provide the parameter values.

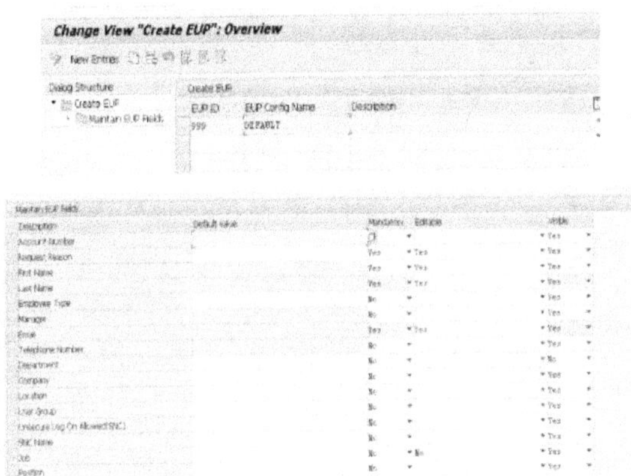

8. <u>MAINTAIN PROVISIONING SETTINGS</u>

In this configuration step, you maintain global and system-specific provisioning settings. These settings impact the provisioning process flow at the end of user request approval

Call SPRO -->SAP Reference IMG --> Governance, Risk and Compliance --> Access Control --> User Provisioning -->

Maintain Provisioning Settings

You can specify as to whether auto provisioning must be done globally or by system. All global auto provisioning

features are superseded by the system settings. You need to

Maintain at least the Global Provisioning settings.

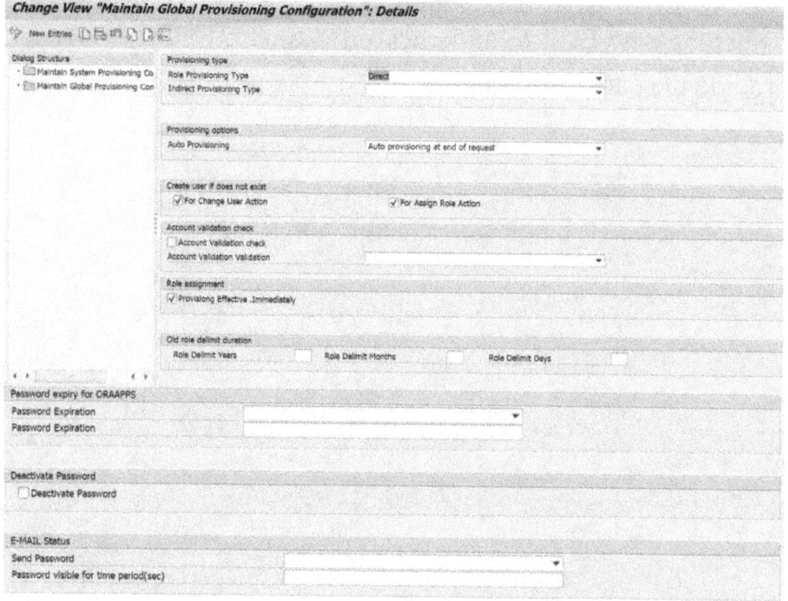

1. Select the Role Provisioning Type as described below:

• **Direct** : The application carries out provisioning directly on the user master record.

• **Indirect** : The application uses the SAP HR system to carry out provisioning. You must also select one of the following HR object types, which the application needs to transmit to the HR system: Position, OrgType, or Job.

• **Combined** : The application first uses indirect provisioning. If it is unsuccessful, then the application uses direct provisioning.

You must choose the HR object type that the application

uses for indirect provisioning.

2. Choose Auto Provisioning options:

• **Auto Provision at End of Request** : Select this option to begin provisioning when all the workflow paths in the submitted request are approved.

• **Auto Provision at End of Each Path** : Select this option to provision the access requested for each path as the path is approved. This method works only when the request splits into parallel workflows.

• **No Provisioning** : Select this option to turn off auto provisioning.

• **Manual Provisioning** : Select this option if provisioning must be done by an approver at an approval stage. This can be done at the last stage using stage configuration.

• **Manual Provisioning with Auto Password Generation** : This case is the same as Manual Provisioning; however, the approver cannot set the user password.

3. Choose Create User Options :

Use this feature if you want the provisioning process to automatically create a user in case no record is found for the user. You can select one of the following options:

• **For Change User Option** : Apply this feature only for

requests of the action Change User.

- **For Assign Role Option** : Enable this feature only for requests of the action Assign Role.

4. Maintain Account Validation Check : You can choose whether the application displays a warning message or an error. The application performs the following two checks:

• Whether or not the target connector is working properly

• Whether or not the user exists in the target system; for example, if the user exists in the target system, the application does not create a request for user creation.

5. Maintain the Role Assignment : From the Provisioning Effective Immediately dropdown list, select one of the following options:

• **Yes:** The provisioning takes place immediately.

• **No:** The provisioning takes place later.

6. Maintain the Old Role Delimit Duration :

Enter the length of time in Years, Months, and Days for transitioning from an old position to a new position. Use this setting with SAPHR indirect provisioning only.

8. Maintain the Password Expiration for ORAAPPS :
Select the basis on which the password expires: number of days, number of accesses, or none. For Days and Accesses, you must also enter the number.

9. Deactivate Password :

Select the checkbox to enable this feature if you are using Single Sign-On (SSO) and do not want to allow dialog logons. If you set this option in the Global Provisioning Configuration, it applies to all systems.

If you set this option in the System Provisioning Configuration, it applies only to the specified system.

Once you enable this feature, the application disables passwords for all new access requests. For all users with passwords activated prior to this, you must disable the passwords via transaction SU01.

Note : If you have chosen to deactivate passwords here, but you have enabled PSS for the connector, when the user tries to use PSS, the application displays a message indicating the connector is not valid for password activation.

10. Maintain E-mail Status.

Choose whether the application must send the user's password in an e-mail. If you choose Yes, then you must also specify the number of seconds for which the password is valid.

If you choose No, then the application includes a link in the e-mail notification. The link opens an HTML page with the details of the password.

You can maintain system specific provisioning settings as well by selecting the Maintain System Provisioning settings.

These settings will override the global settings for that system.

Click on New entries and then select the connector and the various provisioning settings like Auto provisioning, Role Provisioning type, Password deactivation etc. Once done, click on Save.

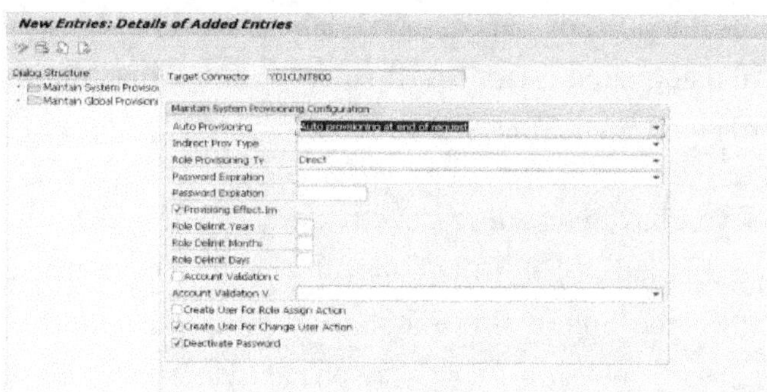

9. <u>MAINTAIN USER DEFAULTS</u>

In this Customizing activity, you can assign user defaults in the SAP back end system for new users.

You can set defaults for the following: Start menu, Time

zone, Decimal number, Date format, Output device, User group, set user groups, set parameter IDs, Set the connectors

Call SPRO -->SAP Reference IMG --> Governance, Risk and Compliance --> Access Control --> User Provisioning -->

Maintain User Defaults

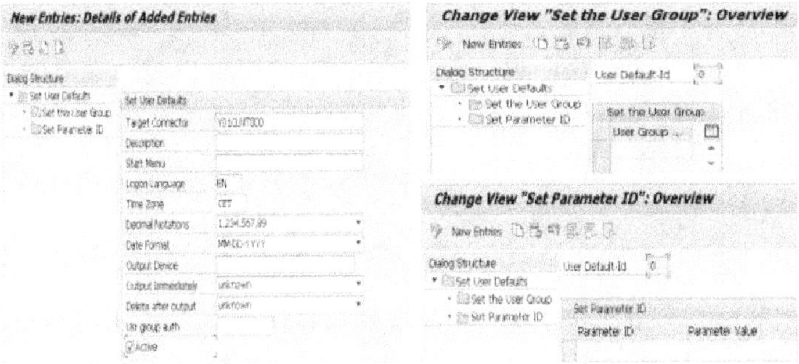

10. <u>MAINTAIN REVIEW REJECTION REASONS</u>

In this Customizing activity, you maintain the reasons due to which the respective user provisioning request is rejected. The reasons appear in a dropdown list on the Request Review screen.

Call SPRO -->SAP Reference IMG --> Governance, Risk and Compliance --> Access Control --> User Provisioning -->

Maintain Review Rejection Reasons

Click on New entries to add new Rejection reason. Select the type (Role, User or Risk), select the active checkbox and mention the Description of the reason.

Choose the Active radio button against a row to enable that Number Range for request creation.

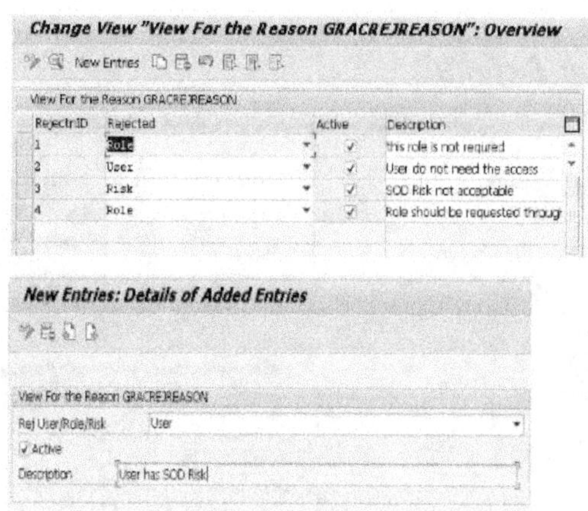

11. <u>CREATE USERS FOR ACCESS MANAGEMENT</u>

• Create Point of Contact Manager, Role Owner & Security admin in SU01 (GRC) and assigned necessary roles.

• Assign them to access control owners via NWBC.

• Make sure to maintain valid email address to get the request in inbox.

Assign below Roles to the 3 sets of users.

1. **Manager** : General Roles and SAP_GRAC_ ACCESS_APPROVER.

2. **Role Owner :** General Roles, SAP_GRAC_ ACCESS_APPROVER, SAP_GRAC_ROLE_MGMT_ROLE_OWNER and SAP_GRAC_RISK_ANALYSIS

3. **Security Admin :** General Roles, SAP_GRAC_ ACCESS_APPROVER

4. **General Roles :** SAP_GRC_FN_BASE, SAP_GRC_ FN_BUSINESS_USER and SAP_GRC_NWBC

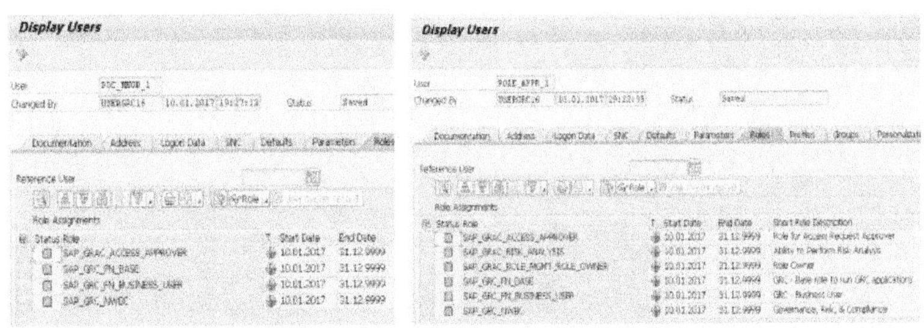

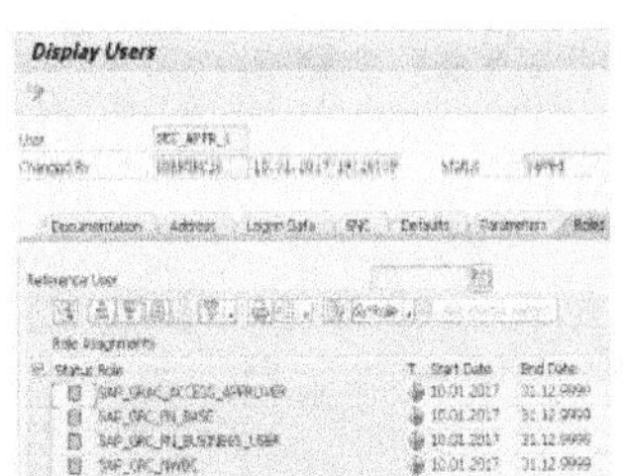

ASSIGN APPROVERS TO ACCESS

CONTROL OWNER :

Go to NWBC – Setup – Access Owners – Click on Access
Control Owners.

Click on Create to assign the Owners.

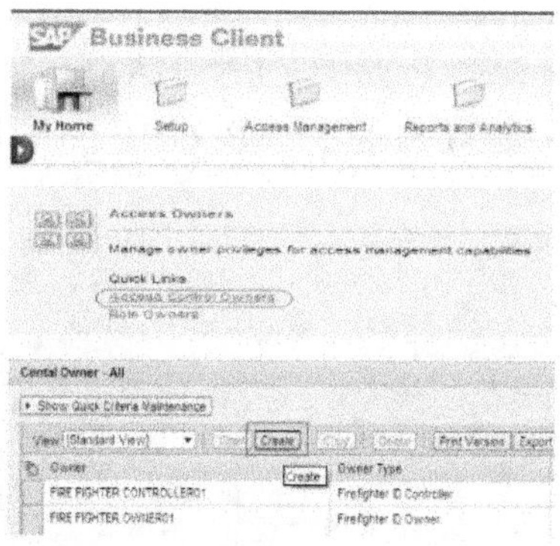

POC MANAGER:

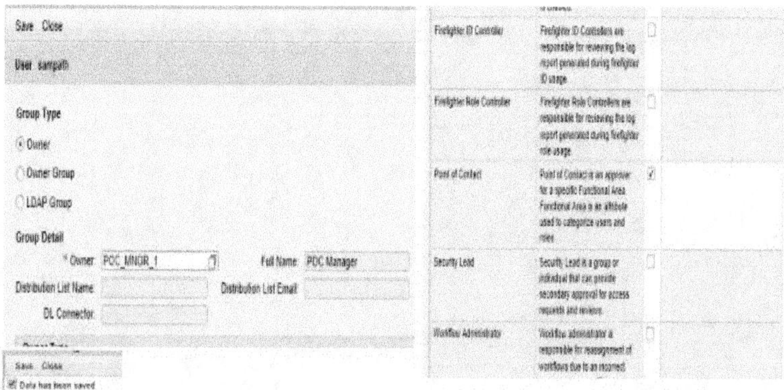

SECURITY ADMIN:

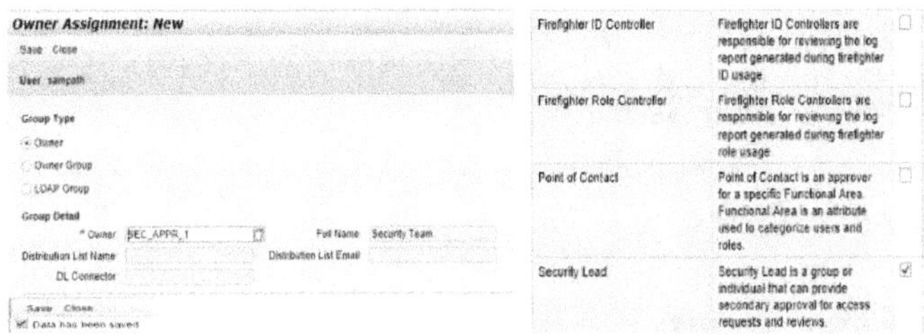

ROLE OWNER:

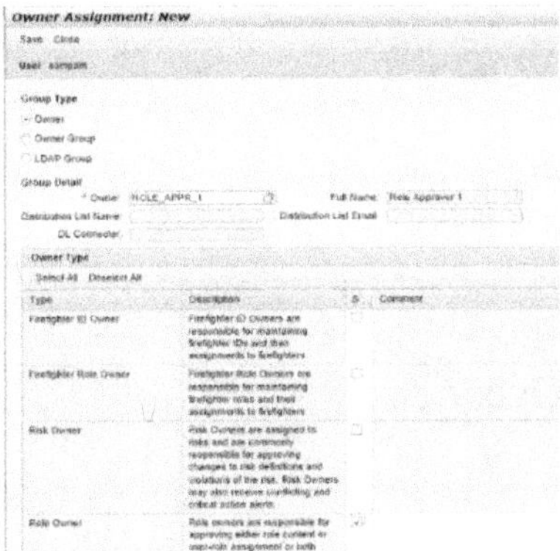

MSMP WORKFLOW

1. Process Global Settings

2. Maintain Rules

3. Maintain Agents

4. Variables and Templates

5. Maintain Paths

6. Maintain Route Mapping

7. Generate Versions

MSMP Workflow Overview

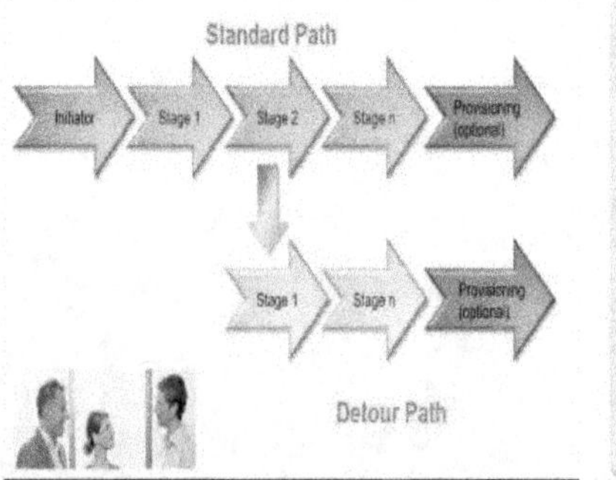

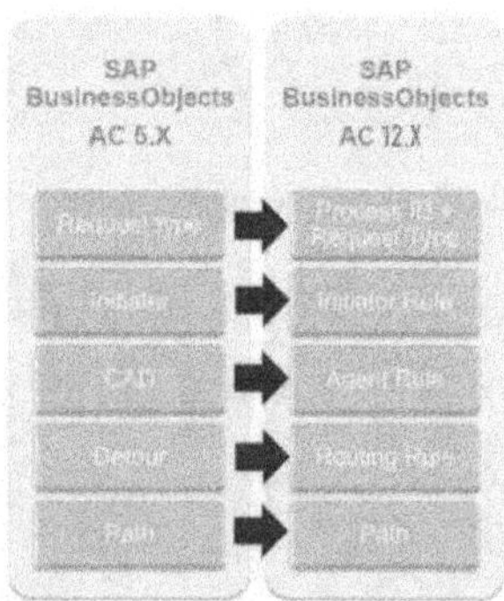

• MSMP is the new workflow engine used within SAP Access Controls 10.0 and is capable of directing requests down multiple approval routes simultaneously.

• It's used for the management of automated approval workflows in User Access Management but can also be triggered for the other SAP Access Control modules, including Access Risk Analysis master data updates or role building approval workflows.

Call SPRO -->SAP Reference IMG --> Governance, Risk and Compliance --> Access Control --> Workflow for Access control --> Maintain MSMP Workflow

T-code for MSMP Workflow: GRFNMW_CONFIGURE_ WD

These activities allow you to customize and maintain the Multi-Stage Multi-Path (MSMP) process workflows for Access Control 10. There are total 7 steps for MSMP configuration discussed in following topics.

Activate below BC Sets to populate the standard Workflow provided by SAP.

***GRC_MSMP_CONFIGURATION* :** For standard and sample configuration GRC_MSMP_SAMPLE_CONF: For sample paths

GRC_MSMP_STD_CONF : For standard configuration

1. <u>PROCESS GLOBAL SETTINGS PRE-DELIVERED PROCESS IDS :</u>

Access Request Approval Workflow

Access Request Approval Workflow for HR OM Objects

Control Assignment Approval Workflow Mitigation Control Maintenance Workflow Fire Fighter Log Report Review Workflow Function Approval Workflow

Risk Approval Workflow Role Approval Workflow SOD Risk Review Workflow

User Access Review Workflow

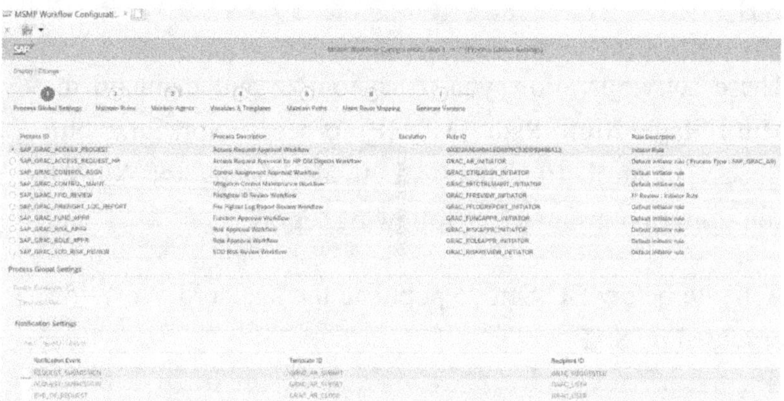

In this step, global settings for each process Ids are maintained such as escape conditions and notifications settings.

Select a Workflow process (Access Request Approval Workflow in this example) and click on Display/Change. Below are MSMP Workflow Initial Screen fields which can be maintained based on the requirements.

Under process global settings there are two variables for you to set.

1. **Enable Escalation** : If this checkbox is checked, it enables global escalation on any workflow that was pending for approval and the deadline monitoring for the fixed date. After this date, all work items escalate for this process.

2. **Escalation Date** : This is the date on which all work items for this process are escalated. This field is required if escalation is enabled

Under Notification Settings, the variables you should set are:

1. **Notification Event** : There are two events like notification upon request submission and upon completion of request need to be configured in order to send the notification to the respective users at the trigger of these events.

2.**Template ID** : The template is maintained for the message that has to be sent either at submission of request or at the end of request processing notifying the requestor or user of the outcome as message what is the request number that had been created with details or approval information after the end of the workflow process.

3. Recipient ID : This is the recipient of the end of request notification message. (configured as an agent), which can be a user or requestor.

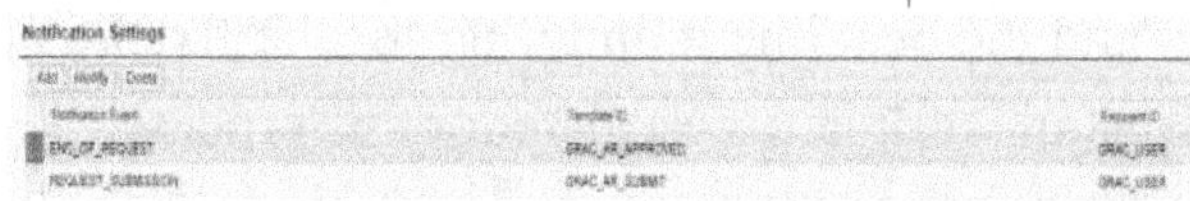

Under Escape Conditions, the variables you should set are:

1. **Escape Conditions :** This table has two entries, one each for two escape conditions: Approver Not Found and Auto Provisioning Failure.

2. **Set Escape Routing :** This checkbox needs to be set to activate the respective escape paths. Activation is optional.

3. **Escape Path :** Path the request follows if no agents are found for any stage or failure during auto- provisioning. This is set in step 5 and is required when Escape Routing is enabled.

4. **Escape Stage :** This escape stage number dictates at which approval stage this escape routing should be triggered in case of if any escape condition arises.

5. To maintain the escape path, it should be created in Step 5 to set the stage for the above-mentioned escape path to which the request should follow.

The next step in the configuration of MSMP is to maintain rules and rule results. Select a process Id and click on Next to setup other six stages for that process Id.

2. <u>MAINTAIN RULES</u> :

Maintain Rules includes a list of all available rules to be used when configuring a workflow. If a new rule is created, it must be added to this list. This is also where the default initiator is configured.

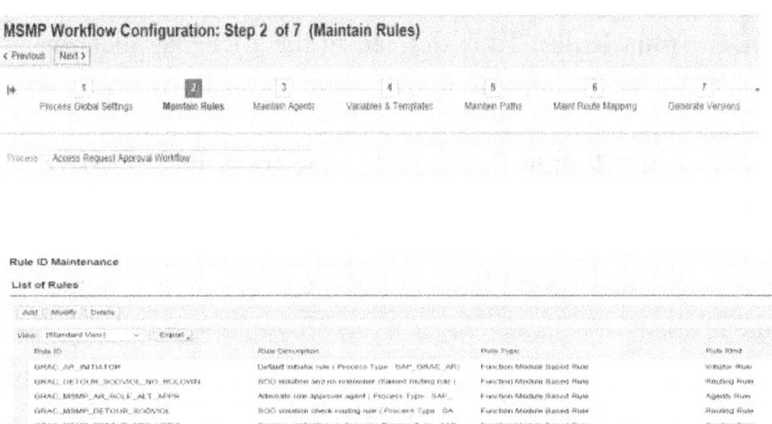

Under the Rule ID Maintenance table, a list of rules is provided by default, which can be modified, or new rules can be added as needed. The fields in the table are described:

• **Rule ID :** Unique name for the rule to identify different rule types and rule kinds that are used in the MSMP workflow process. This is a mandatory field.

• **Rule Description :** Meaningful description to the purpose of the rule.

• **Rule Type :** There are four rule types based on the underlying technology that helps to make decisions. In SAP Access Control, there are several ABAP class-based and function module-based rule types available. The BRF+ rule is a more simplified rule engine that helps the business user define the rules without much technical skill.

The following rule type options are available:

1. **BRF plus Rule :** Rule defined in the BRF+ application to get rule results depending on conditions inside the rule.

2. **Function Module Based Rule :** Function module coded to output rule results.

3. **ABAP Class Based Rule :** Class method coded to output rule results.

4. **BRF plus Flat Rule (Line-item by Line-time) :** BRF+ rule defined for only one line item. (This rule is called once for each line item in the request.)

• **Rule Kind :** Four different rule kinds are used during the execution of the MSMP workflow process to determine results for initiator, agents, routing and notification variables.

The rule kinds in the workflow process are described here:

1. **Initiator Rule :** This rule is used to direct the workflow path based on the rule result which is defined by the rule type. Only one initiator rule per process can be defined in the bottom window Global Rules area with the Process Initiator field.

2. **Routing Rule :** You can use this rule to route a request from one path to another based on the rule result. It determines a detour routing based upon an attribute of the request (for example, SoD Violations Exist, Training Verification, No Role Owner).

3. **Agent Rule :** You can create multiple rule IDs for the agents rule kind based on your definition of multiple agents such as role owner, risk owner, or any other custom agent. It determines the recipients of a stage.

4. **Notification Variables Rule :** This is also defined once per process in global settings. This rule helps to send notifications to various agents. It determines the variable values at runtime used in the notification e-mails.

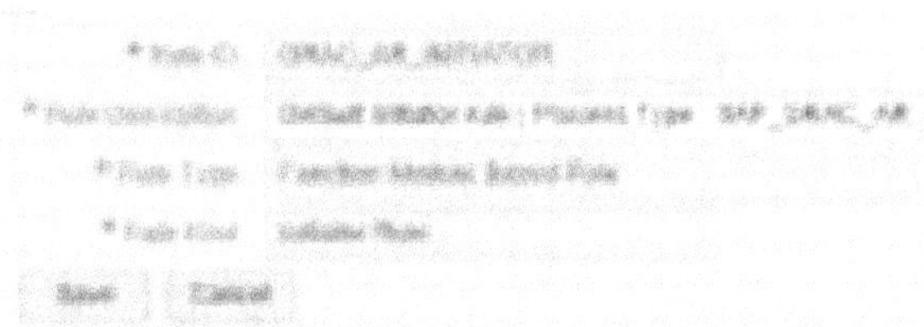

RULE RESULTS:

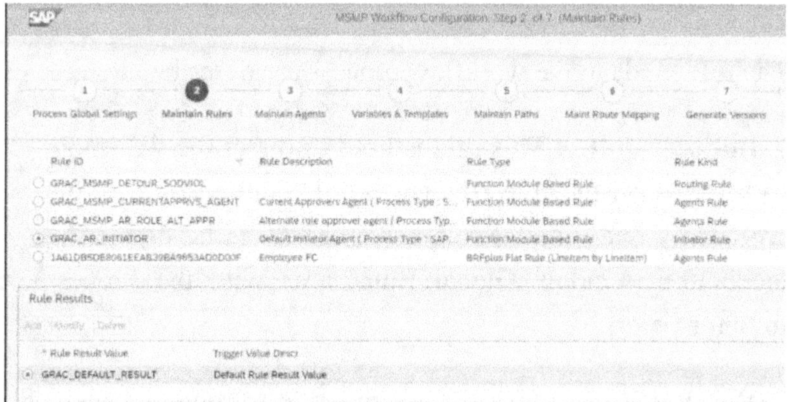

It is required to maintain a list of all possible results returned by an initiator/routing rule by using the Results button. The rule result value can be a single result or multiple results, which is used in workflow paths or stages to determine either agents or paths depending on the rule kind. These values will be mapped to a path on step 6.

• **Rule Result Value** : Initiator or routing rules have rule results which are results derived from rule types. The result value is configured as the path to be taken by the workflow.

• **Trigger Value Description** : Rule results require meaningful description, which you maintain here

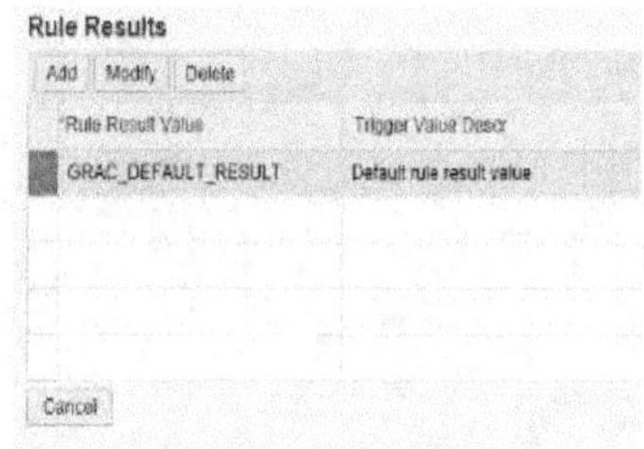

We need to configure Global Rules at the bottom part of the screen.

The fields that are important in the configuration of global rules are described in further detail here:

• **Process Initiator :** Associate the rule comprising possible initiators to a process. There can be only one active initiator per process. This initiator needs to cover all paths defined for the process that are to participate in the process.

• **Notification Rule :** Rule to determine notification variables used in notification templates.

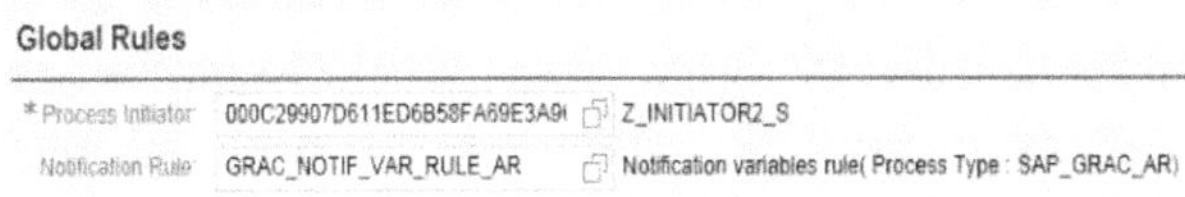

The next step in the configuration of MSMP is to Maintain Agents.

3. <u>MAINTAIN AGENTS</u>

A list of all available agents for a workflow is maintained in this step. Agents have a type and a purpose assigned.

In this step, we define various access request approvers such as immediate managers, role owners who own the business, security team or notification agents (e.g., requestors and users involved in the workflow process) and how individual users are mapped to these agents to determine the correct stage approver.

To add new agents or modify their determination procedure,

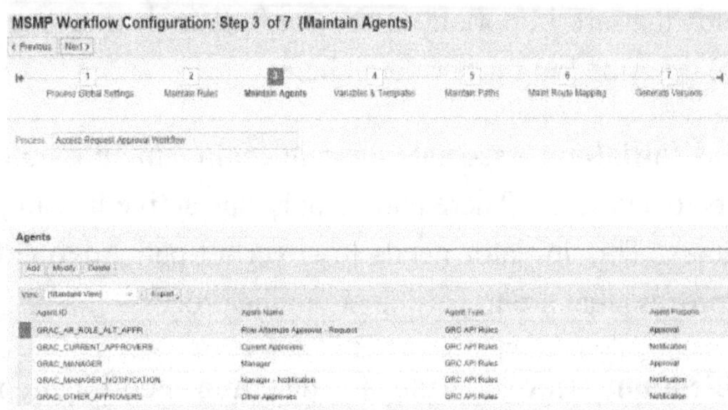

select respective buttons either to Add or Modify in the Agents screen.

For each Agent you need to maintain below fields:

1. **Agent ID :** Define the logical approver ID, which is a required field.

2. **Agent Name :** Give a description of the logical approver ID.

3. **Agent Purpose :** Agents are defined in the MSMP workflow for either approval purposes or to notify about the activities.

• **Approval :** This agent will get work item from workflow for approval purpose.

- **Notification :** This Agent is used for notification purpose to convey the information about the workflow.

  This needs to be selected from the drop-down list of Agent Purpose.

4. **Agent Type :** Define dynamic approvers that can be assigned to any workflow stage. Agents are logical approvers determined or supported by the following mapping:

- **Directly Mapped Users :** This configuration is used for defining static user groups used within.

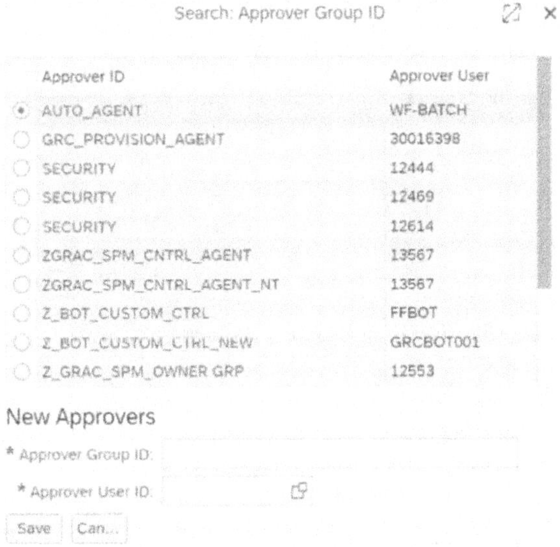

- Workflow processes for example, to define a security group consisting of one or more SAP users. This group can be assigned to any approval stage for a workflow process.

Click on the search option in Approver Group Id which will open a new screen. You can maintain Group to User mapping.

• **PFCG Roles** : PFCG roles assigned to a user as agent and workflow determines the agent based on the role assignment.

• **PFCG User Groups** : PFCG groups assigned to a user for example, this can be specific process owners that are defined in a user group.

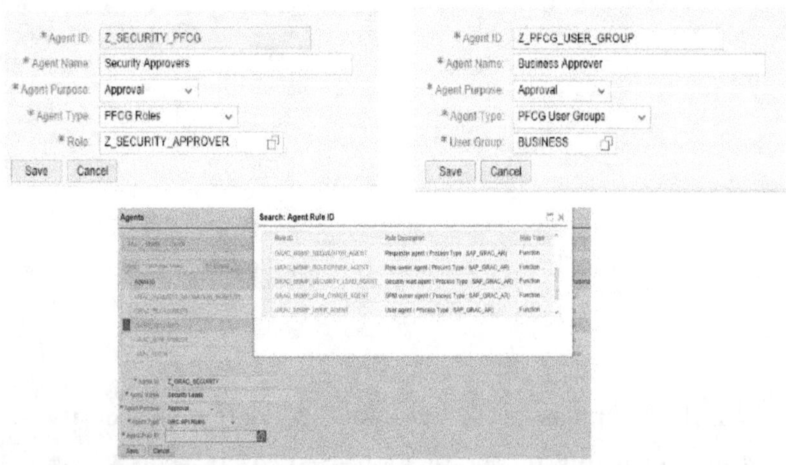

GRC API Rules : This is used to fetch rule-based approvers such as manager, role owners, risk owners, and so on via associated function modules. This agent type will determine the recipients based on a rule maintained in step 2.

4. <u>MAINTAIN VARIABLES AND TEMPLATES</u>

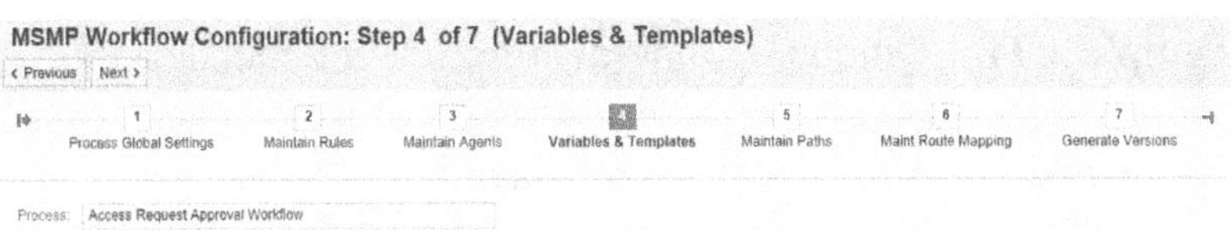

Notification variables and templates must be configured to be used as part of a specific MSMP workflow. These templates are used to send email messages to the approvers/notification receivers that contain some fixed texts and variables, such as user ID, user name, request type, role or provisioning details, system name, to give the message to the receiver of this workflow content for decision making on approval or rejection.

The customization can be done to these templates and variables from the ABAP stack using Transaction SE61 which we will cover in separate topic.

Notification Templates

Add   Delete

Template ID	Message Class	Message number	Docu. Object	Owner
GRAC_AR_APPROVED	0MSMP_AR_APPROVED	000	GRAC_MSMP_AR_APPROVED	SAP
GRAC_AR_APP_BY_EMAIL	0MSMP_AR_APP_REJ	000	GRAC_MSMP_AR_NEWWORKITM_APP	SAP
GRAC_AR_CLOSE	0AC_AR_CLOSE	000	GRAC_AR_CLOSE	SAP
GRAC_AR_ESCALATION	0MSMP_AR_ESCALATION	000	GRAC_MSMP_AR_ESCALATION	SAP
GRAC_AR_FORWARD	0MSMP_AR_FORWARD	000	GRAC_MSMP_AR_FORWARD	SAP
GRAC_AR_NEW_WORK_ITEM	0MSMP_AR_NEWWORKITM	000	GRAC_MSMP_AR_NEWWORKITM	SAP
GRAC_AR_REJECTED	0MSMP_AR_REJECTED	000	GRAC_MSMP_AR_REJECTED	SAP
GRAC_AR_SUBMIT	0AC_AR_SUBMIT	000	ZSUB	Customer
GRAC_EMAILRMDR_CUP	0MSMP_EMAILRMDR_CUP	000	GRFNMW_EMAILRMDR_CUP	SAP

Notification Templates : Templates for each notification type are configured here along with the corresponding messages class/number for each template. In this area of the screen, you can either add a new template or delete one if you don't need it.

Template ID : Unique ID that identifies each template.

Message Class : ID where the message is stored.

Message number : Number assigned to the message.

Document Object : Object maintained through SE61 which contains the text of the message.

• **Notification Variables :** Variables used in the notification message that will be replaced by valid values in the runtime by the MSMP engine.

• **Temp. Variable :** Unique name for each variable used in the template message.

• **Variable Description :** Meaningful description for the variables used in the message.

Notification Variables

Temp. Variable	Variable Description
APPROVED_BY	Request Approver
FIRST_NAME	Requester First Name
LAST_NAME	Requester Last Name
LINK_APPROVE_REJECT	Link to Approve/Reject by Email
LINK_GET_APPROVERS	Link to get Approvers
LINK_GET_REQ_STATUS	Link to get Request Status
PATH	Path ID
PROVISIONING	Request Provisioning Details

5. <u>MAINTAIN PATHS</u>

Here the actual workflows are configured. Multiple paths relevant to a specific Process ID are configured by assigning a sequence of stages.

Each stage is configured in this screen as well as notifications setting specific to stage.

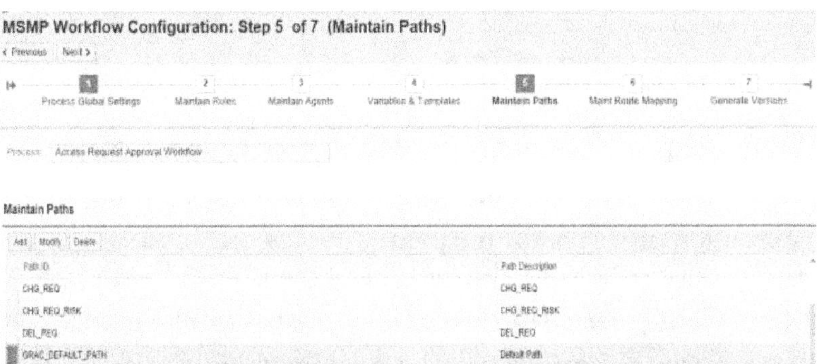

To create a new path, you can click on Add from Maintain Paths. Similarly, existing path can be modified or deleted. Mention the Path Id which define the Path Name. Enter the description of the path in Path Description field. Next step is to Maintain Stages. Select a path to view the stages assigned to it.

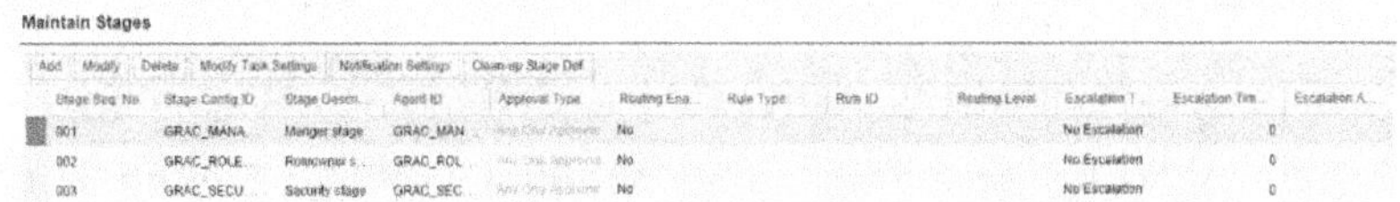

In the Maintain Stages area of the screen, you'll maintain approval stages and stage-relevant task and notification settings, which can be associated to the workflow path. You can configure the application-specific actions/tasks for a process in Modify Task Settings and maintain notifications by selecting the Notifications Settings button.

To create a new stage, select the Add button and maintain the Attributes as mentioned Below:

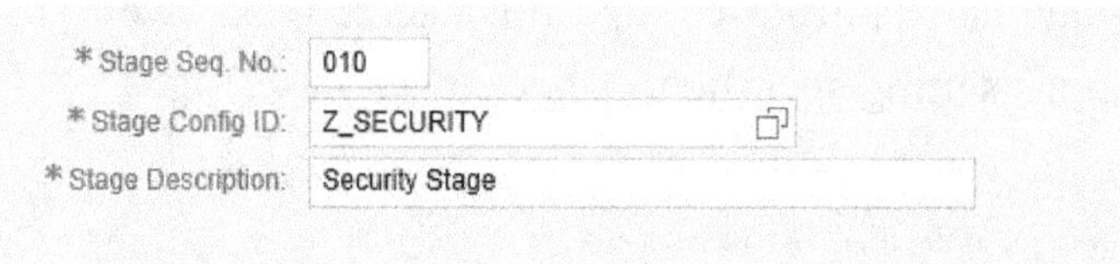

- **Stage Seq No :** Number to define the sequence of the stage in the path. This number will determine the order of execution of stages for the path.

- **Stage Config ID :** This is a unique ID that can be used to identify the stage and it can be used in multiple paths, for example, for manager, role approver, and so on. You can use an existing Config Id or mention a new name to create one.

- **Stage Description :** Maintain meaningful text to describe the stage.

Click on Show details to maintain more values. If the Stage Config Id is existing one, below fields will be auto-populated with the global Stage Settings. You can maintain different values which will overwrite the settings for this particular path.

- **Agent ID :** The dropdown menu shows all the agents that are maintained in the Maintain Agents step. Logical

Approver ID can be chosen from this dropdown menu.

- **Approval Type :** Maintain the value that this stage level needs; either all approvers or any one of the approvers is enough to move the workflow to the next stage.

- **Routing Enabled :** Select this optional checkbox if routing needs to be enabled for this stage. If this checkbox is chosen, the following additional two fields will be shown on the screen.

1. **Rule ID :** Maintain based on what routing rule is needed at this stage.

2. **Routing Level :** Indicate in routing whether to route the entire stage or only the failed line items as a result of routing. This is mandatory if routing is enabled.

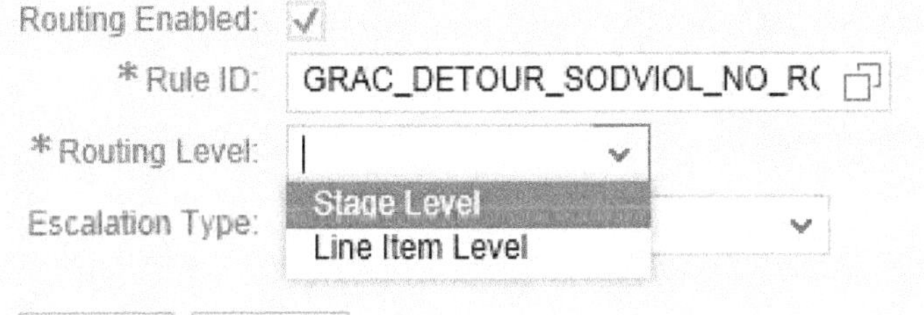

• ESCALATION TYPE:

1. **Use Defaults :** When you select Use default, then the default settings defined for the process are used for escalation:

2. **Escalate to Specified Agent :** If this value is selected,

then an additional field is shown in the same screen to escalate to provide agent that is maintained in Agent ID field.

3. Skip to Next stage : This selection escalates the request to the next stage.

4. No escalation : This is an optional setting to use if you don't want to escalate.

• **Escalation Time Mins :** Escalation should start after a specified time in minutes. This field is required if Escalation Type is set with Escalate to Specified Agent or Skip to next stage.

• **0Escalation Agent :** Agent ID is used to determine approvers for escalation. This field is required if Escalation Type is set to Escalate to Specified Agent is chosen.

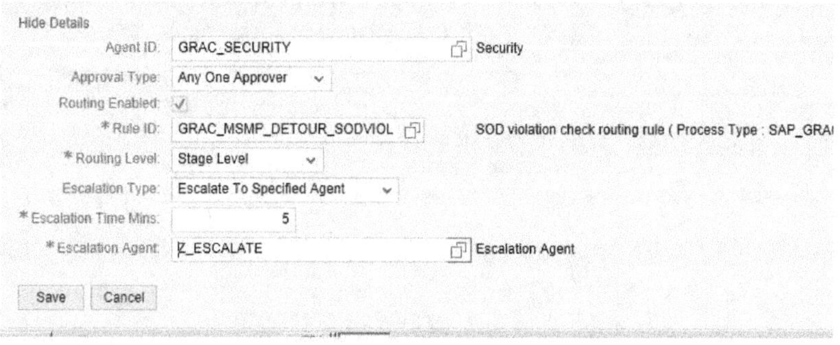

MAINTAIN GLOBAL STAGE SETTINGS AND STAGE TASK SETTINGS

Select a stage and click the Modify Task Settings button to open the Stage Definition screen.

In Stage Details, you can maintain the global Stage Values such as Agent, Approval Type, Escalation type etc. Whenever the same Stage Config Id is used in any path, these values would be auto-populated in local stage settings. Local settings can be changed to overwrite these values.

Stage Details

Stage Config ID:	Z_NEW_STAGE_MGR
* Agent ID:	GRAC_AR_ROLE_ALT_APPR
* Approval Type:	All Approvers
Routing Enabled:	
Escalation Type:	No Escalation

In this stage definition, you need to maintain the values for application-specific configuration for actions that can be performed in a given stage and activities that are needed to be performed by the stage approvers.

These values will remain same across all paths in which the Stage Config Id is used.

• **Path Reval New Role :** Checks whether path revaluation

is to be performed if a new role is added. The following possible values are available from the dropdown list:

1. Only New Roles in Evaluation Path (evaluate)

2. All Roles in Evaluation Path (reevaluate)

3. No Path Revaluation for New role

• **Risk Analysis Mandatory** : Ensures that risk analysis is performed for a stage.

• **Comments Mandatory** : Makes adding comments mandatory while approving or rejecting.

• **EUP ID** : End User Personalization (EUP) template that should be shown at this stage level.

• **Rejection Level** : This value allows the stage level approver to reject either one of the defined level such as Role, Request, System and Role.

1. **Request** : Approvers have the authority to reject all roles in a request. For example, security approvers can reject any role relevant to a request.

2. **Role** : Approvers can only reject those roles that belong to them.

3. **System and Role** : Approvers have the authority to reject systems and roles.

• **Approval Level** : This setting allows the stage approver to approve either one of the defined level such as role, request, system and role.

• **Runtime Config Change OK :** If there are any configuration changes in the stage settings, should it be considered for any work items that are already in process path effected with these new changes.

• **Add assignment :** Allows approvers to add assignments for roles or systems to the request.

• **Request Rejected** Enables the stage approver to reject a request.

• **Reroute :** Allows approvers to reroute the request to a previous stage as an alternative to rejecting the request.

• **Confirm Approval :** Once approved, this enforces approval confirmation by pop-up window.

• **Confirm Rejection :** Enforces rejection confirmation by pop-up window.

• **Reject by Email :** Enables the approver to reject the request via emails by clicking the link received in the approver's inbox.

• **Approve by Email :** Enable the approver to approve via email.

• **Forward Allowed :** Allows the approver to forward the request to another approver.

• **Approve Despite Risk :** Enables request approval though risk exists in the request without mitigation or remediation action.

- **Display Review Screen** : Enables the display of the request review screen.

- **Reaffirm Approve** : Enables approvers to confirm their identities before approving requests by means of logon with a user ID and password.

- **Reaffirm Reject** : Enables approvers to confirm their identities before rejecting.

- **Change Request Det** : Enables changing of the request parameter.

- **Allow Manual Prov** : Allows approvers to provision directly from the stage approval screen.

- **Override Assign Type** : Enables the override of the default setting of direct, indirect, or combined provisioning. For this function, manual provisioning should be checked.

MULTISTAGE MULTI PATH WORKFLOW

- In this way, we can maintain the configuration for stage-related maintenance activities for one specific workflow path.

- If your workflow path contains more than one stage, then follow the same processes to complete other stages in the workflow path.

- Every stage is a decision-making point for the request in the process.

- If there are multiple workflow paths for the same process, select all the paths involved in this process one by one, and define the entire stage level configuration to complete this step configuration.

NOTIFICATION SETTINGS

From the Notification Settings screen, you need to configure the notification templates mapping to the notification event and recipient. You can create a new entry or delete one from the screen.

- **Notification event :** Notification triggering events such as APPROVED, REJECTED, and so on.

- **Template ID :** Notification template to be used for getting the message. If you select a new work item as the event, this template might be the approval or rejection notice.

- **Recipient ID :** Any agent who may be an approver of this stage or receiver of this stage activity result, such as a requestor or user.

- **Disable email :** If this checkbox is enabled only work item from workflow will be sent to the agent but not email.

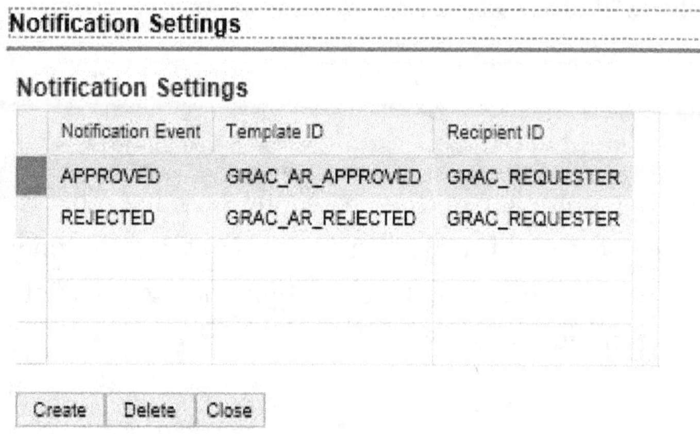

Notification Event	Template ID	Recipient ID
APPROVED	GRAC_AR_APPROVED	GRAC_REQUESTER
REJECTED	GRAC_AR_REJECTED	GRAC_REQUESTER

6. <u>MAINTAIN ROUTE MAPPING</u>

In this step you define the mapping between rule results and paths to route the requests.

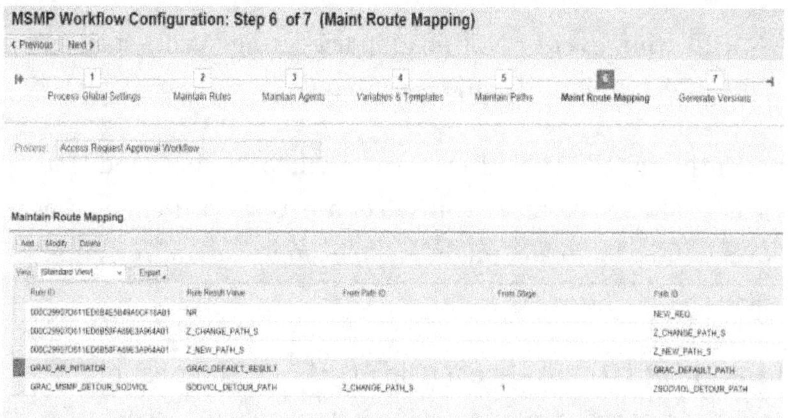

- **Rule ID :** Rule ID of the path.

- **Rule Result Value :** Result returned by the rule.

- **Path ID :** Path ID to be started in case this trigger value is returned by the rule.

If the Rule is for Routing rather than Initiator, there are two additional fields to be maintained.

- **From Path Id :** Path from which the new path will be triggered if there are SOD violations.

- **From Stage :** Stage of the current path from which new path will be triggered if there are SOD violations.

7. <u>GENERATE VERSIONS</u>

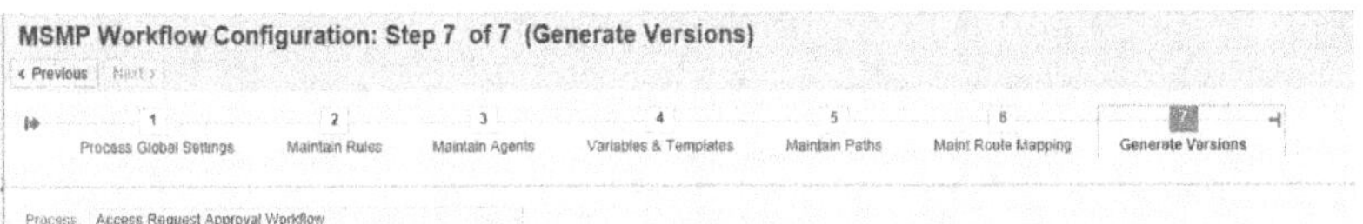

- Other than agent, approver, and process global settings, all other workflow configuration settings are versioned by SAP Access Control to track the changes as well as transport them to other systems, which is like a technical object in the ABAP system.

- If you select the Save/Simulate button, this action will simulate generation to confirm that there are no errors in the MSMP workflow process so far.

- If there are errors that need to be addressed, the error message will give some lead to resolve the issue.

- Once completed with this action, activate this process to make it ready to use in the specified workflow process.

• During the save and simulation phase, a popup screen will ask whether to save against new or old transport requests or without transport.

• Save this to transport all the settings to another environment of the SAP Access Control system.

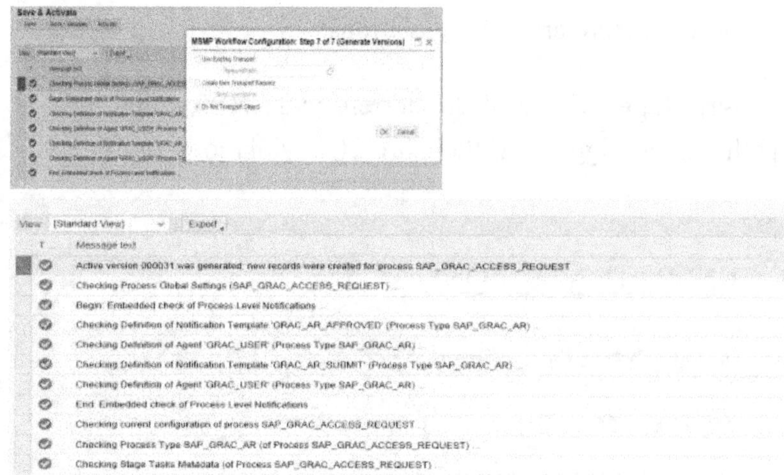

Access Request Creation

Call NWBC -->   Go to Access Management Work center -> Under Access Request Creation work item click on Access Request

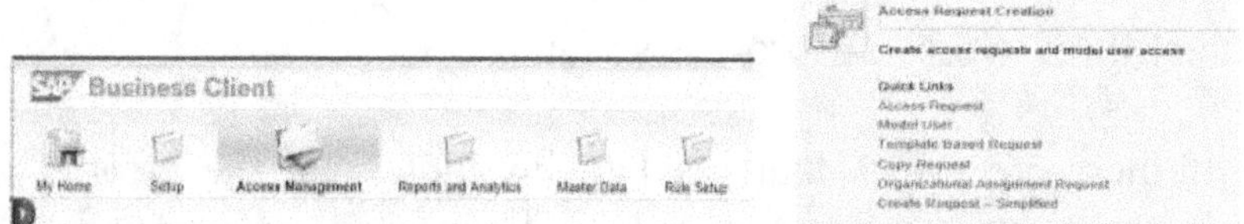

1. **Description :** Enter Description for the Request Reason.

2. **Request Type :** Select the type of request like New

Account, change user, lock User etc. In this example, we will select New Account to create a New user.

3. **Request For :** Select if the request is for Self, Other User or Multiple Users. In case of multiple users, a new tab will be opened to provide user details. If Another user is selected, provide the User Id in the User field.

4. **Business Process :** Select the Business Process to which user belongs.

5. **Priority :** Select the Request Priority if it is low, high, critical or any other defined value.

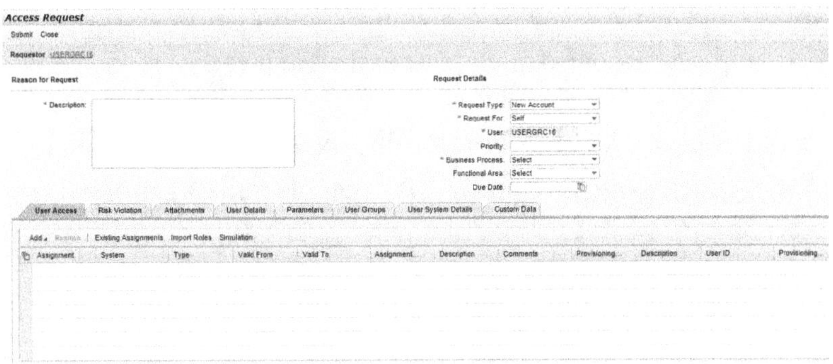

USER ACCESS TAB :

From the User Access Tab, Add Systems and Role details.

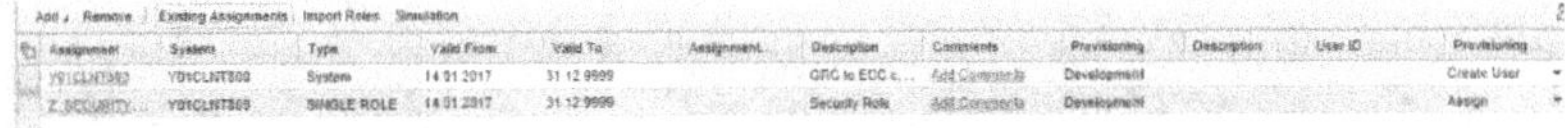

Change the Valid from and Valid To details and Add comments if any. From the Provisioning dropdown you can select the action to be performed. Like for System, Create User or Change User. For Role, it will be either Assign, Remove or Retain.

From the Existing Assignments option, you can view the Roles assigned to the user.

From the Import Roles, you can mass import no of Roles from backend so that they can be selected in the request.

From the simulation button, you can view the Risks arising from the new assignments.

From the Risk Violation tab, you can run the Risk Analysis for the selected assignments while creating the Request. This step is optional while creating the Request.

From the User Details tab, enter the details of user like First Name, Last Name, Email, Manager Details, Employee Type etc. From this screen, you can mention the defaults to be maintained for the user.

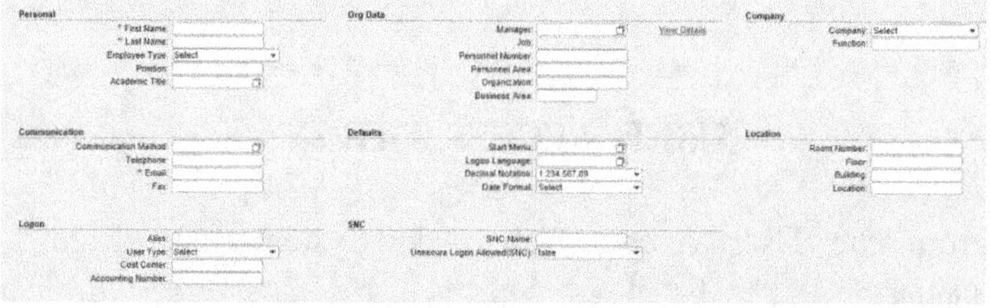

From the User Groups tab, enter the User Groups which will be maintained in Groups tab in SU01. This will not be maintained in the User Group field in Logon Tab in SU01.

From the parameter Tab, you can maintain the various parameters to be assigned to User in SU01 Parameters Tab. From the User System Details, you can maintain the User group to be maintained in SU01 Logon Data. Also password can be updated for the user else system generated password would be sent to the user. Password is deactivated if corresponding settings in Provisioning setting in SPRO is set to Deactivate Password. Click on Submit to create the Request.

For the current path for Access Request, the request will go to Security Approvers. Login with Security Approver Id and click on Work Inbox to view the approval Request.

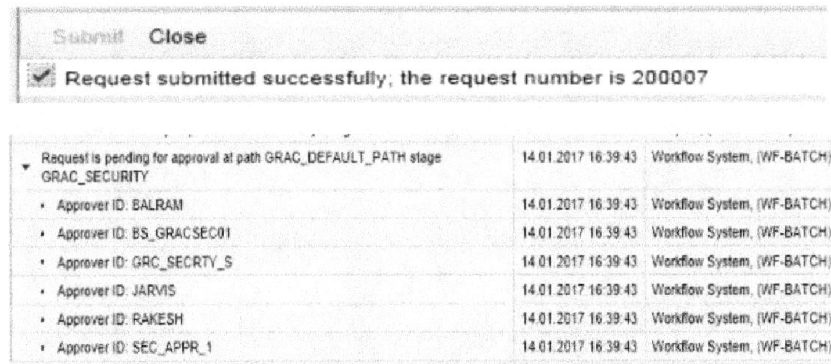

If the Approver do not act on the request within the

specified escalation time for the stage, Request will flow to escalation agent for that stage approval.

Select Approve or Reject for each line item and click on Submit to approve the Request.

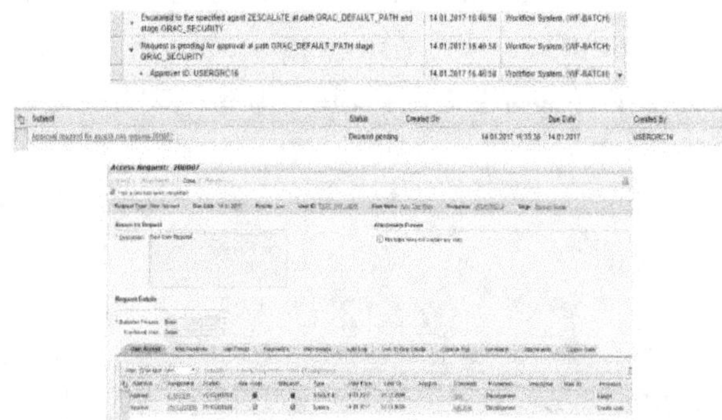

If Comments are mandatory, then enter the Approval comments also.

Once the Request is approved at all stages, User provisioning will be performed in Backend system.

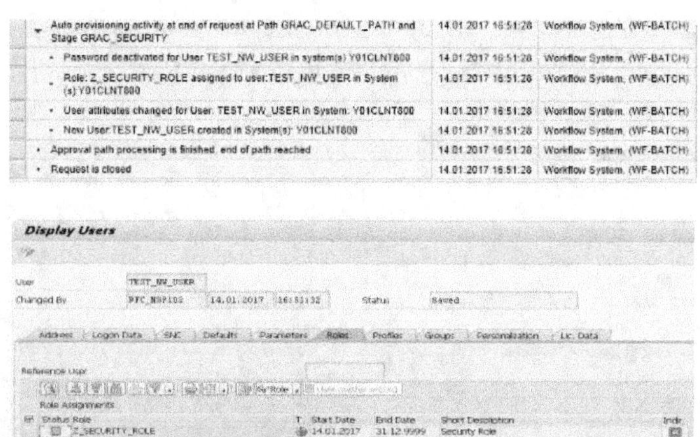

Verify the new user from SU01 in backend system.

BUSINESS RULE FRAMEWORK

1. Overview

2. Define Workflow Related MSMP Rules

3. Define Business Rules Framework

4. Simulate Rule Result

5. Map Rule to MSMP Workflow

6. Access Request for Change User

7. Access Request for Lock / Unlock User

8. Access Request for Delete User

9. Access Request for Firefighter

1. OVERVIEW

• If we use the default initiator Rule in MSMP workflow for Access Request, there will be same workflow path for all type of requests such as Lock User, Create User, Change User etc.

• This is because default initiator Rule has only one Rule result which can be mapped to a single path.

• To provide the flexibility to create different paths for

different type of access Request or deciding path based on other Request attributes, custom Rules can be created with multiple Rule Results which can then be mapped to different workflow paths.

• Business Rules Framework provides this flexibility, not only for initiator Rules but for Agent Rules, Routing Rules and Notification Rules.

• The BRFplus Workbench is a User Interface (UI) that enables users to define, test and maintain rules for various business scenarios without the need of ABAP code.

2. <u>WORKFLOW RELATED MSMP RULES</u>

Using this activity, we can create rules for initiators, agents, and for routing. This will only create an empty rule that will be maintained later through BRF workbench.

Call SPRO -->SAP Reference IMG --> Governance, Risk and Compliance --> Access Control --> Workflow for Access Control --> Define Workflow Related MSMP Rules

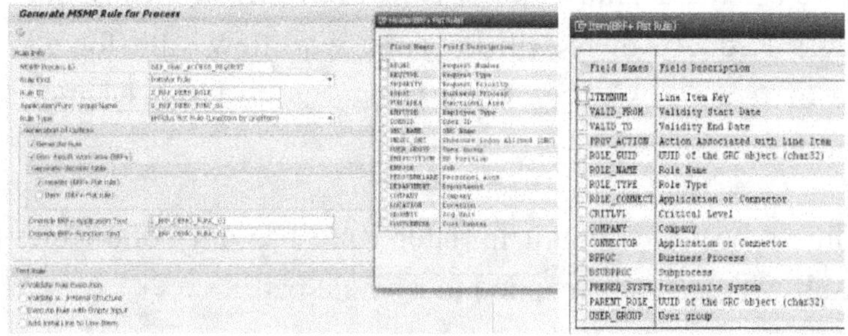

1. Process Id : Maintain the relevant MSMP process ID that needs a BRF+ rule.

2. Rule Kind : It is used to get results from one of the types such as agent, initiator, routing, or notification variables. This needs to be maintained accordingly in the MSMP workflow depending on the requirement.

3. Rule Type : There are four different Rule Types available: BRFplus based, Function Module based, ABAP Class based, and BRFplus Flat Rule. This rule type is used to define what kind of rule generation process is used. Here we will use BRFplus Flat Rule (LineItem by LineItem).

4. Enter any appropriate name for the Rule ID and Application/Function Group Name.

5. Check the default Generate Rule and Gen Result Work-area (BRF+) checkboxes, along with Validate Rule Execution.

6. To create Actual BRF+ rule, you need a decision table to make decisions based on request header characteristics such as request type and request priority. Choose the Header (BRF+ Flat rule) checkbox and select the fields based on which decision needs to be made.

7. Select the checkbox Item (BRF+ Flat Rule) to make decisions based on Request items like Role Name, Role critical level etc.

8. Click on execute to generate the Rule.

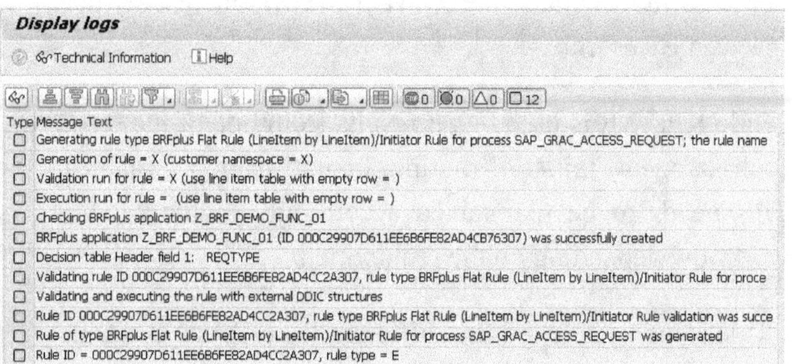

As a result of successful generation, screen will show log with details of the activity carried out along with an Application ID and Function that are created in the BRF+ with Z names entered and the GUID that is returned. This long alphanumeric GUID is referred to repeatedly in the message, which is the rule ID/function generated.

3. <u>DEFINE BUSINESS RULE FRAMEWORK</u>

• The next step in working with actual BRF+ is to create a rule to suit the needs.

• The rule we need to create is a decision table based on a request type and system combination. To achieve this, define a business rule using the BRF+ Workbench in combination with the decision tree

Call SPRO -->SAP Reference IMG --> Governance, Risk and Compliance --> Access Control --> Workflow for Access Control --> Define Business Rule Framework. (T-code BRF+)

This action opens a new Web Dynpro application in a browser window as the BRF+ Workbench, and the rule GUID that was created earlier would be visible.

Double-click on the function name to display the details of the function from the right side.

MAINTAIN CONDITIONS

Using this activity, you maintain the request fields that will be checked in a decision table.

The decision table is empty by default and is located under Expression - Decision Table where the necessary request fields can be added by inserting column.

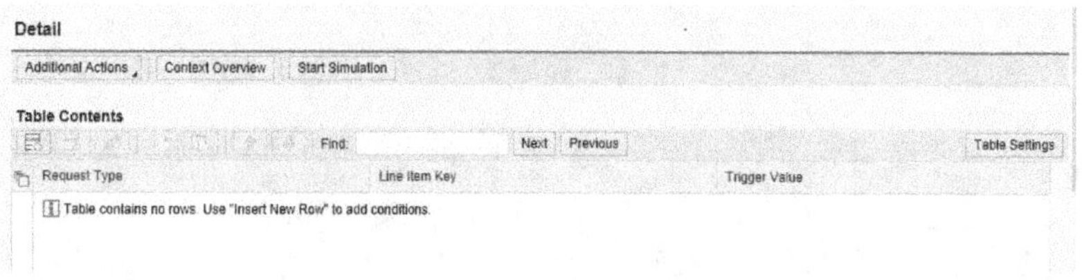

By using the Table Settings button, the condition columns can be maintained.

In the Conditions Columns, click Insert Column, then select Context Data Objects in order to add items that will be used as the Condition Factors in the Decision Table.

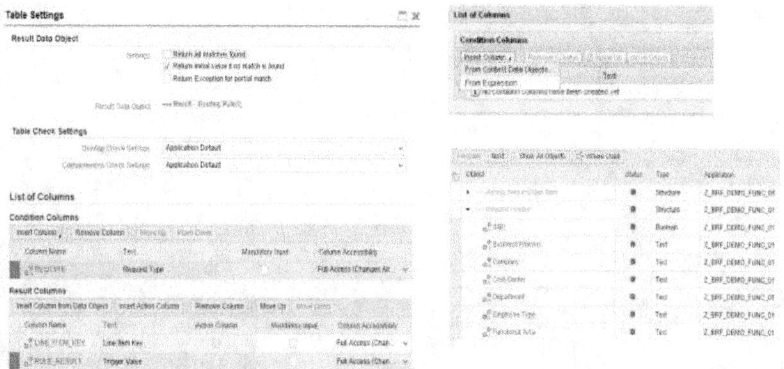

Navigate to the structure that contains the Condition Items and select the columns from Request header or Request Line item based on the requirements.

The Condition columns are now selected into the Decision Table settings. Click OK, on the bottom of the screen, to complete Table Settings.

• Once Table settings are done, Click on Insert New Row to configure new conditions statements and results. and create your decision table.

• Each line will match a specific condition based on the request attributes depending on the columns you selected.

• Each line will be mapped to a path in the MSMP workflow configuration, so make sure to give it a unique result value in the RULE_RESULT column, which is used in MSMP Workflow Configuration to get the result from here.

• Once a new Row is inserted, Click the icon in each field. Select Direct Value Input to enter value(s) 0 for the Condition:

Choose the Expression Type (is equal to, is not equal to) from the dropdown list. Enter the value that the Condition

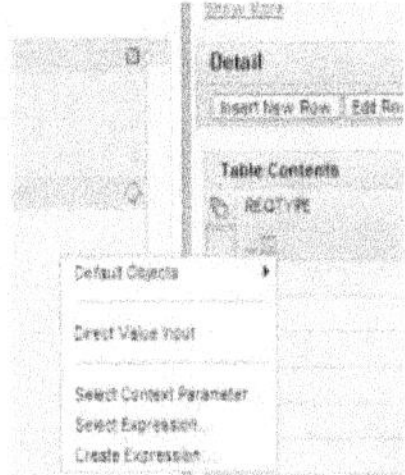
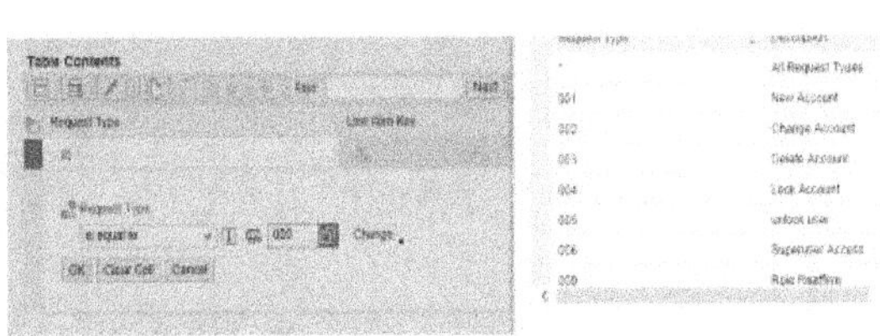

should match.

Finally, set the results column values.

• Initiator/Routing Rules : the result column is RULE_RESULT which will be used for mapping the path in the MSMP Workflow Configuration

• Agent Rules : the result column is USER_ID, which will return an agent (notification or approval).

• Once all conditions are maintained for different rule results, table will look like this:

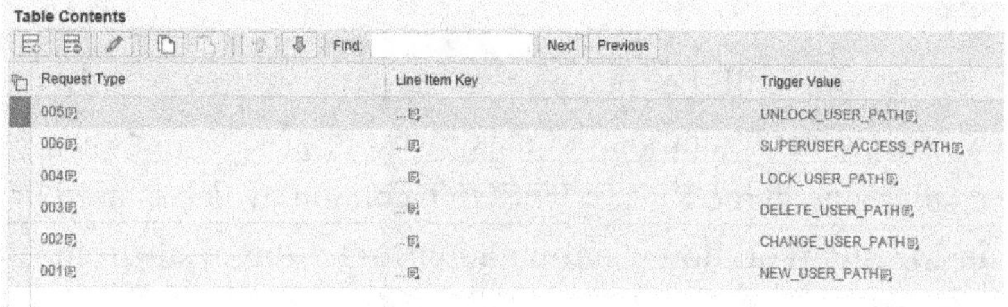

• Make Sure there is a green light next to the decision table and function names. You need to click on Save and then Activate to achieve this.

• Now the BRFplus rule can be used in MSMP Workflows.

• MSMP Workflow will use the Function Id instead of Rule.

4. <u>SIMULATE RULE RESULTS</u>

To ensure that BRF Rule is working fine, use simulation with values to check whether the expected results are appearing in the Rule Result table. To start using simulation for an existing BRF+ menu, select the decision table and

click on simulation from Tools. Click on continue and then select the input values and click on execute to get the result.

5. <u>MAP RULE TO MSMP WORKFLOW</u>

In this step, we need to maintain the MSMP workflow to trigger the correct workflow with a BRF+ rule as an initiator rule.

Call SPRO -->SAP Reference IMG --> Governance, Risk and Compliance --> Access Control --> Workflow for

Access control --> Maintain MSMP Workflow

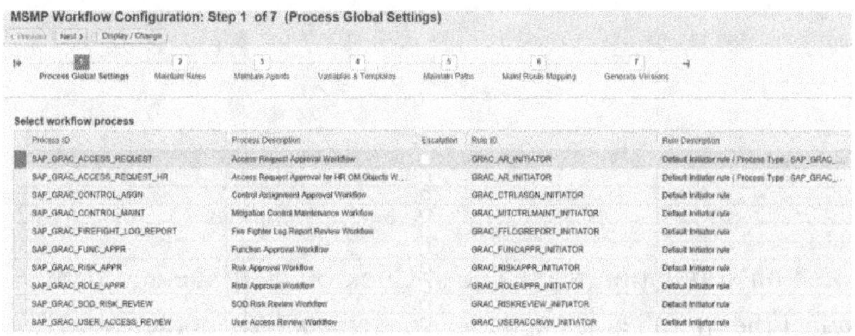

• Click on the Display/Change button to maintain the BRF+ initiator rule configuration.

• Select the correct Process ID, and choose the Maintain Rules step.

• Click the Add button from the List of Rules window, add the BRF+ Rule ID, and enter the Rule Description, Rule Type, and Rule Kind, which is Initiator Rule. Save the settings

• In the same window, click on the Results button to add all the result values that are created in the BRF+ result tab.

- Maintain the new Rule under Process Initiator in Global Rules.

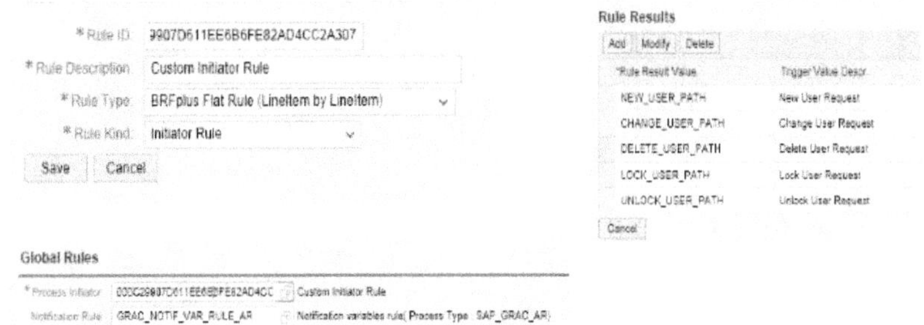

From the Maintain Path Step, create different workflow paths and stages for the Rule Results. Same path can be used for multiple Rule Results as well.

For the FF User workflow, use the SPM Owner as the Approval agent for the workflow stage.

For other workflow, set the stages as required.

After all the paths are maintained, go to the next step Maintain Route Mapping.

Map the Rule Result with the path in this step, and based on the result value passed by the BRF+ rule, the resulting path will be chosen to execute the workflow.

Once done, Activate and generate the Version for the

Workflow using Step 7.

6. <u>ACCESS REQUEST FOR CHANGE USER</u>

Create Access Request for Change User and verify the path the Request follows:

From the Search Requests link under Access Request Administration in Access Management Work center, search the Created request number. Select the Request and click on Audit Log.

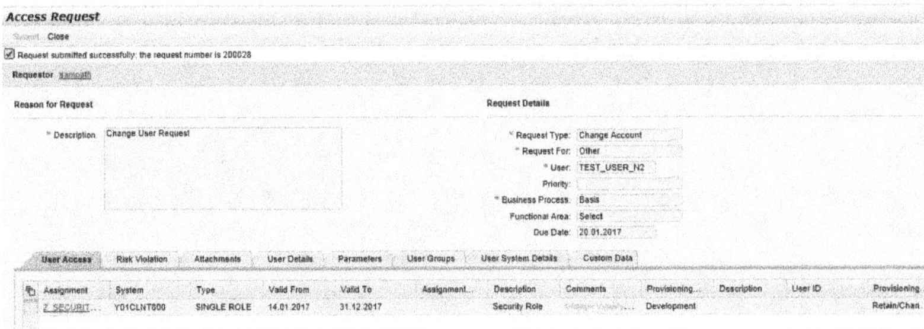

Verify if the request is flowing to correct path and the approver as maintained in MSMP workflow.

Once the Request is approved at all stages, Changes for the user would be performed in Plug-In System. Verify the changes using SU01.

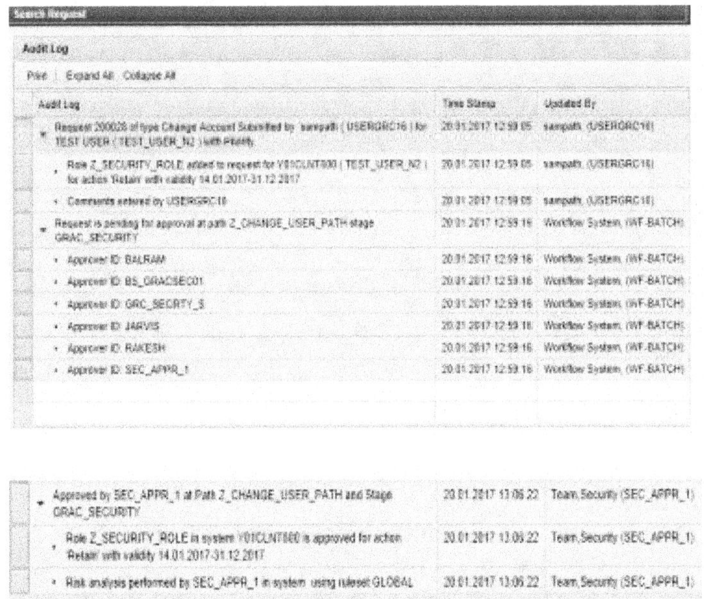

7. <u>ACCESS REQUEST FOR LOCK/UNLOCK USER</u>

Create an Access Request for Lock/Unlock User and verify the path the Request follows:

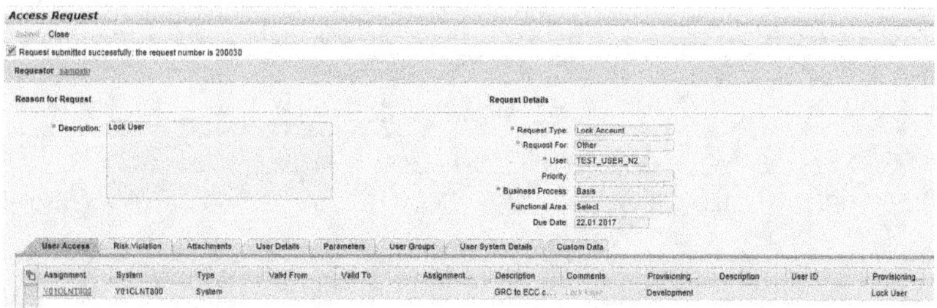

From the Search Requests link under Access Request Administration in Access Management Work center, search the Created request number. Select the Request and click on Audit Log.

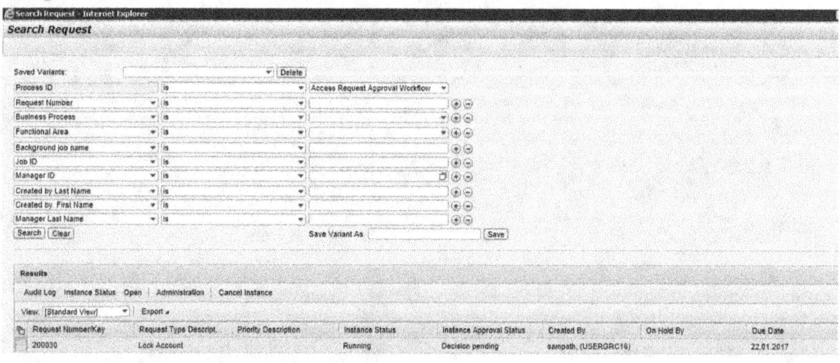

Verify if the request is flowing to correct path and the approver as maintained in MSMP workflow.

Once the Request is approved at all stages, User would be locked in plug-in system. Verify the changes using SU01.

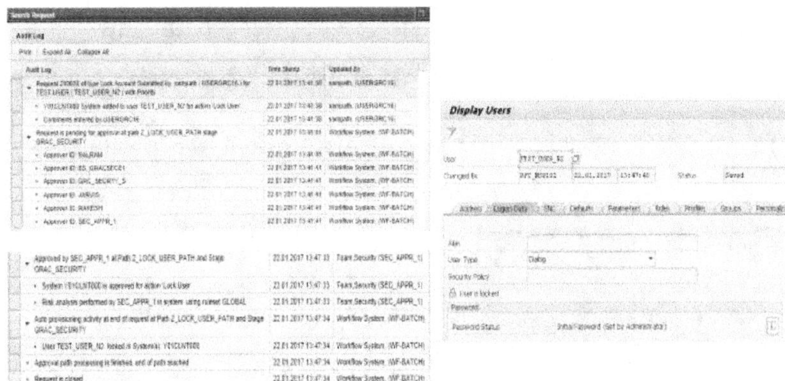

8. <u>ACCESS REQUEST FOR DELETE USER</u>

Create a Access Request for Delete User and verify the path
the Request follows:

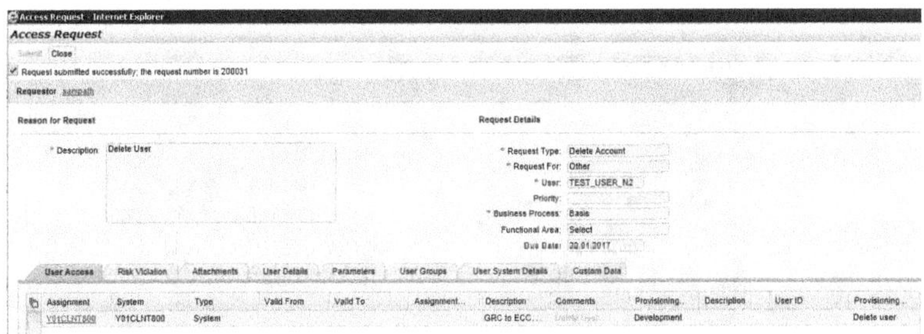

From the Search Requests link under Access Request
Administration in Access Management Work center, search
the Created request number. Select the Request and click on
Audit Log.

Verify if the request is flowing to correct path and the approver as maintained in MSMP workflow.

Once the Request is approved at all stages, User would be

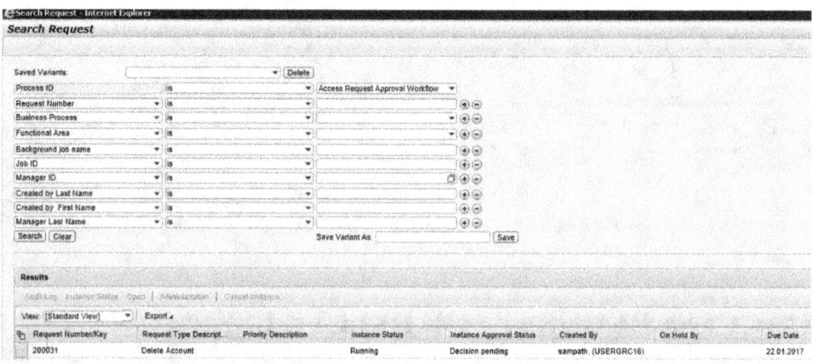

deleted in plug-in system.

Verify the changes using SU01.

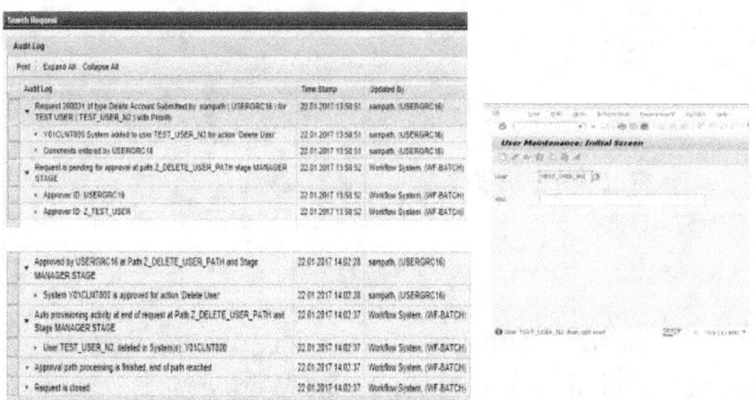

9. <u>REQUEST FOR SUPER USER ACCESS</u>

Create a Access Request for Super User Access and verify the path the Request follows:

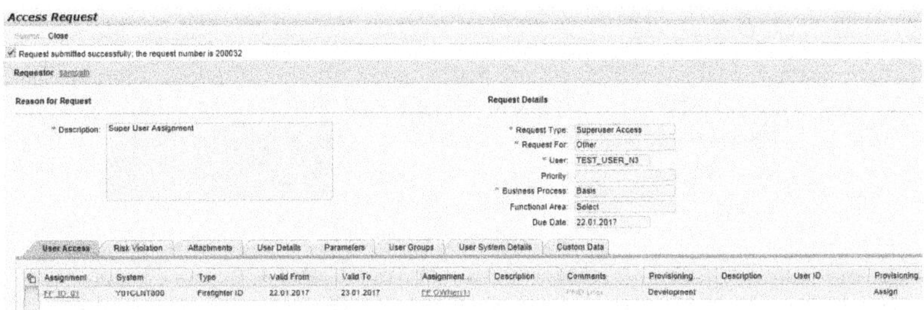

From the Search Requests link under Access Request Administration in Access Management Work center, search the Created request number. Select the Request and click on Audit Log.

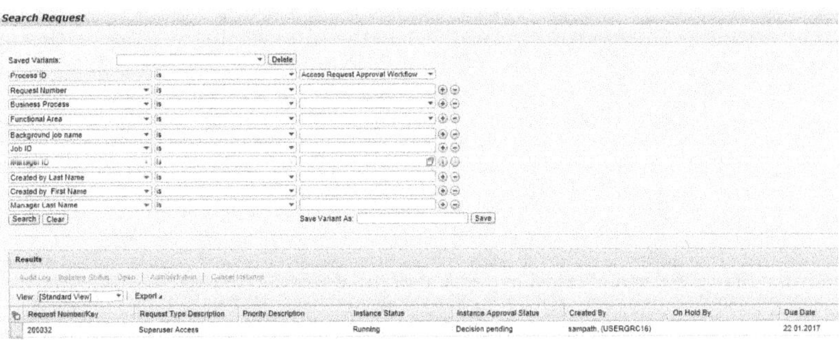

Request will flow to FF ID Owner for Approval. Once approved by Owner, FFID would be assigned to the selected user. Verify the assignment by selecting Firefighters link under Setup Work Center.

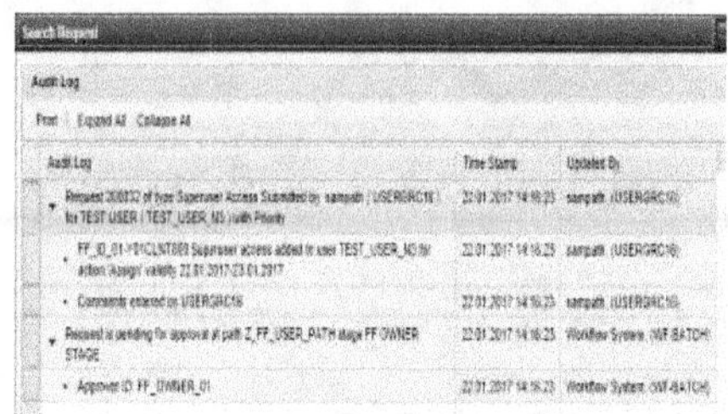

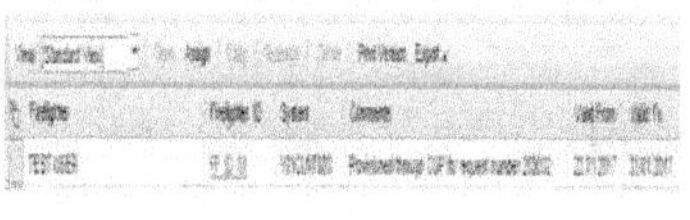

TEMPLATE MANAGEMENT

Template Management is useful to create different types of access request Forms based on employee type or any other parameters.

Using the steps described in Maintain EUP Settings, create a new EUP Id and provide the settings for different field types.

As an example, we will create a form for Contract Employees. To achieve this, create a new EUP Id and maintain settings for various fields.

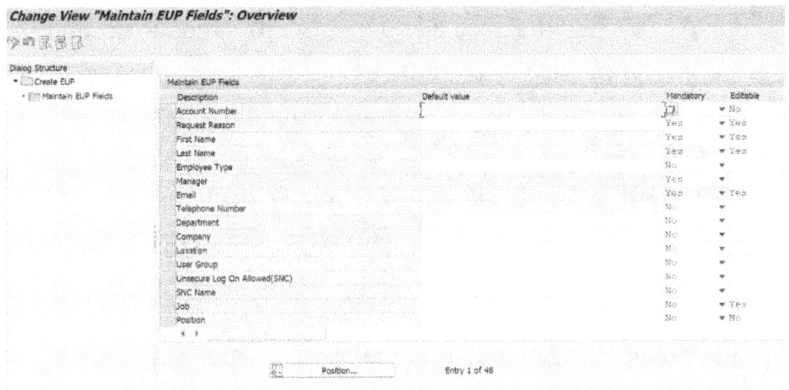

From NWBC, go to the Access Management tab. Navigate to Access Requests Administration and choose Template Management. Click on create.

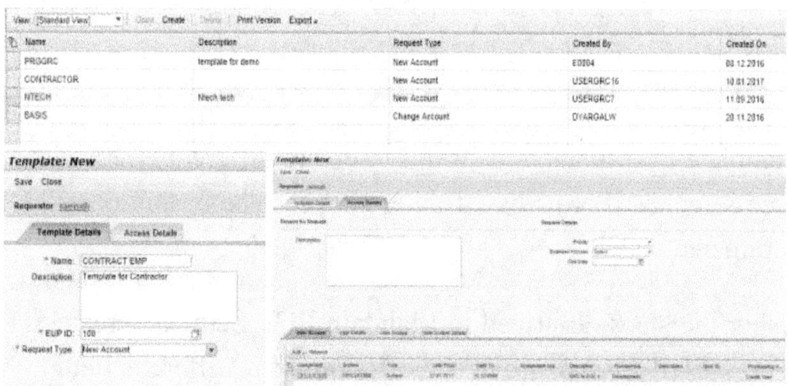

In the Template Details tab, enter Name, Description and the EUP ID and choose the Request Type for which template is created.

In the Access details tab, add any user details, Role and System assignments which must be pre-filled for the Access Request. Once the details are entered, save the changes.

To create a request in the new Template, from NWBC, go to the Access Management tab. Navigate to Access Request Creation, and then choose Template Based Request.

In this screen, choose the template name created previously, and then choose Next.

| CONTRACT EMP | Template for Contractor | New Account | USERGRC16 | 22.01.2017 |

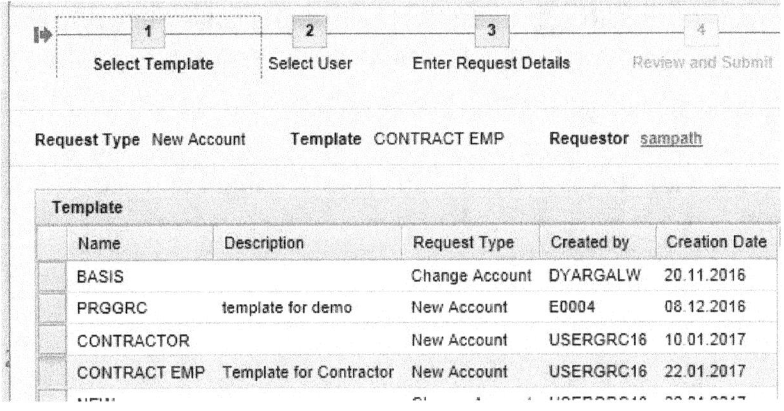

Enter user details in the next screen, and then choose Next.

Here the values maintained in EUP and template would be pre-filled and based on EUP settings, fields would be visible and editable.

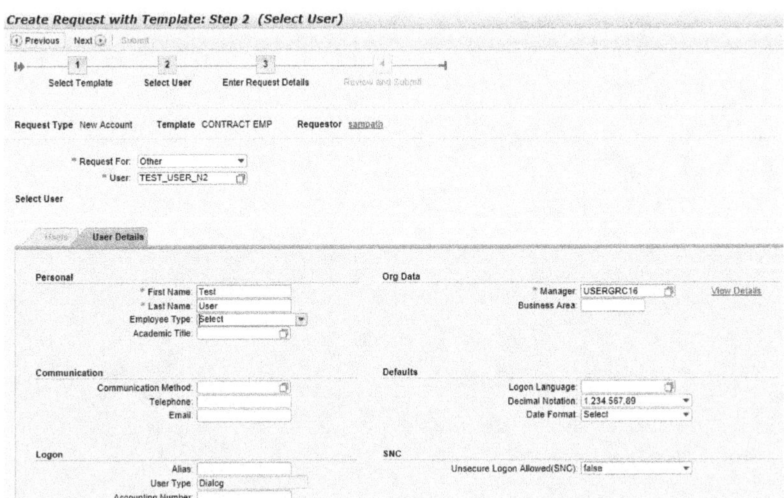

Enter Access Request details. (You will see any roles that were added in the template on this screen), and then choose Next.

Review the Request details and click on submit to create the Request.

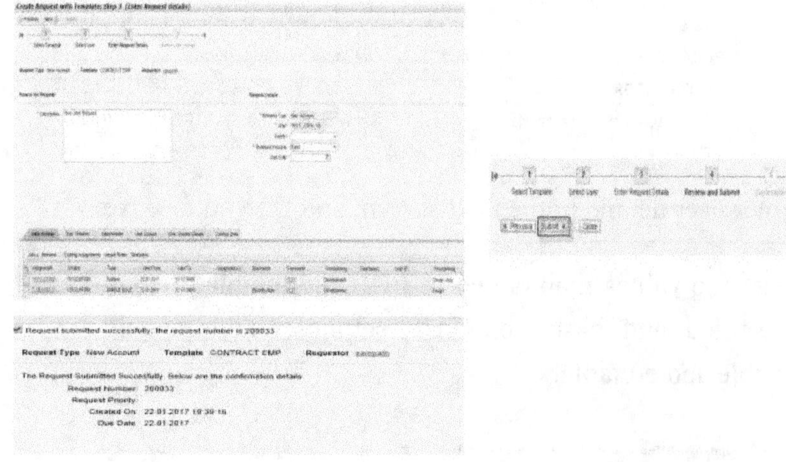

PROCESS ID CONFIGURATION

1. Control Assignment Approval Workflow

2. Mitigation Control Maintenance Workflow

3. Fire Fighter Log Report Review Workflow

4. Function Approval Workflow

5. Risk Approval Workflow

6. Role Approval Workflow (Discussed in BRM Module)

7. SOD Risk Review Workflow (Discussed in SOD Risk Review Topic)

8. User Access Review Workflow (Discussed in User Access Review Topic)

1. CONTROL ASSIGNMENT APPROVAL WORKFLOW

Using MSMP Workflow, we can Maintain the Workflow for the Mitigation Control Assignment.

Steps are mentioned as below:

Open the MSMP Workflow Configuration page using the T-code GRFNMW_ CONFIGURE_WD

Select the Process Id SAP_GRAC_CONTROL_ASGN and click on Display/Change button to edit the Workflow settings.

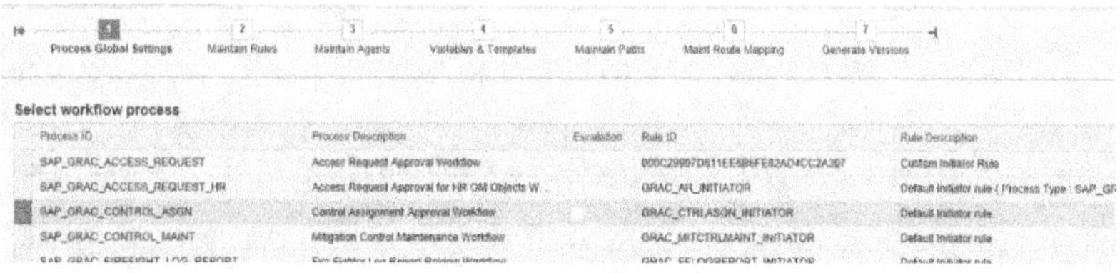

Maintain Process Global Settings, Notification Templates and Escape Conditions in the 1st step.

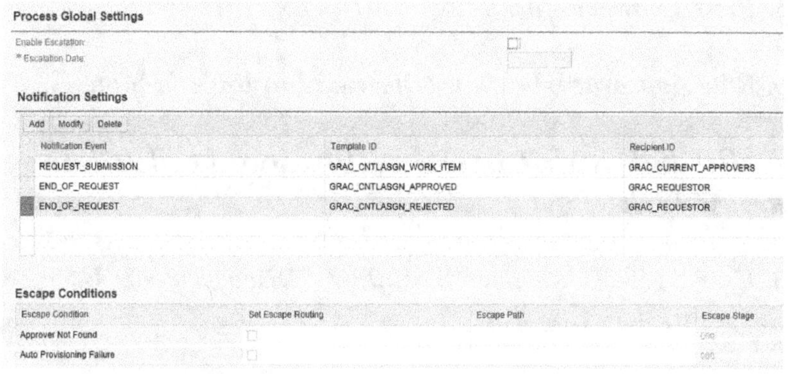

MAINTAIN RULES

In this step, you can maintain new Rules if created other than the standard Rules provided by SAP. Select the Process Initiator (Standard or Custom as required) and Notification Rule under Global Rules.

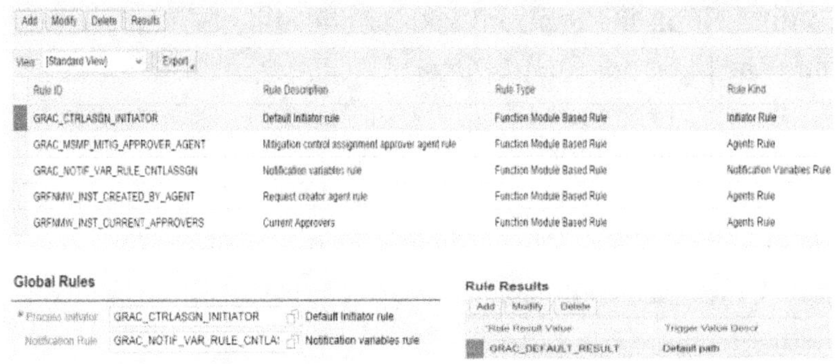

MAINTAIN AGENTS

In this step, you can maintain new Agents if required other than the standard Agents provided by SAP.

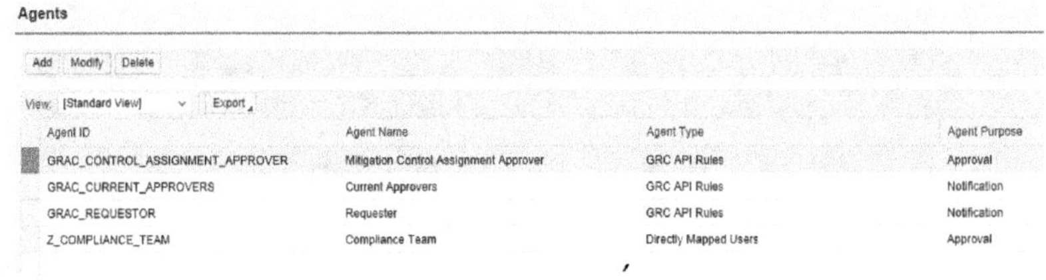

VARIABLE AND TEMPLATES

In this step, you can define the Notification templates for the current Process Id.

MAINTAIN PATH

In this step, approval path and the stages would be

configured. In the Standard Path provided by SAP, there is only one Stage for Control Owner.

We can create multiple stages in the path or create a new path. For this example, we have created two stages: One is the Control Owner Stage (Agent would be Control Owner) and Other is Compliance Stage (Agent is compliance Team)

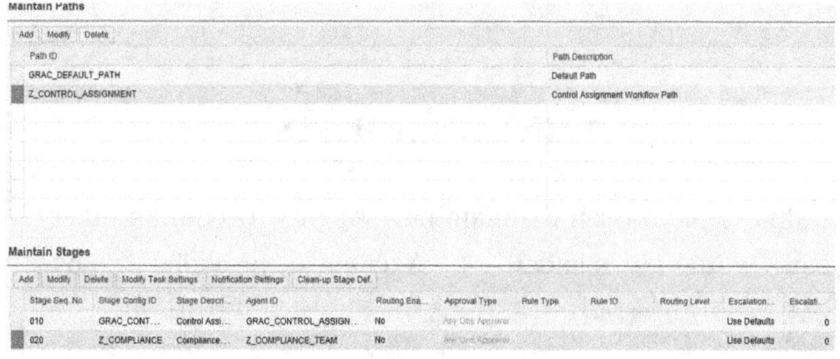

MAINTAIN ROUTE MAPPING

In this step, Map the Initiator or Routing Rules and Result Values to Workflow Path.

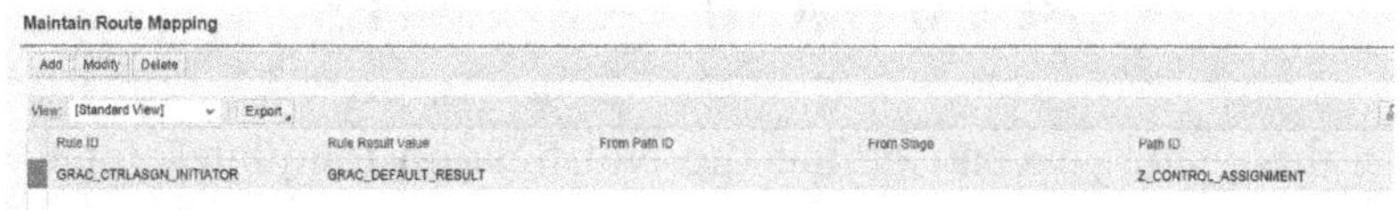

GENERATE VERSIONS

Save the changes and Activate the Version.

BRF RULE

If new Rule needs to be created based on different Line Items, you can create a BRF Rule similar to steps mentioned in Access Request Process Id.

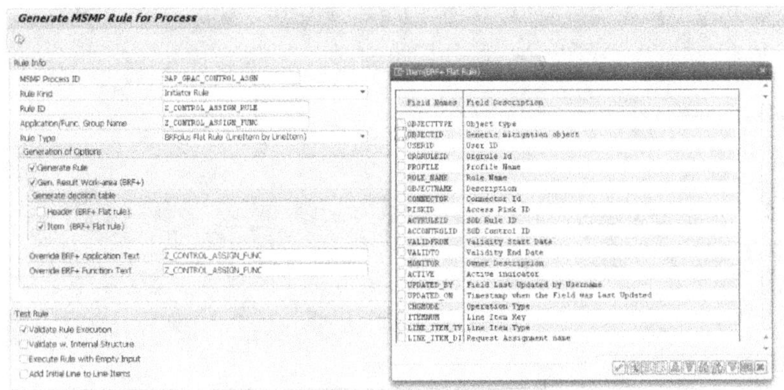

2. <u>MITIGATION CONTROL MAINTENANCE WORK FLOW</u>

Using MSMP Workflow, we can Maintain the Workflow for the Mitigation Control Maintenance.

Steps are mentioned as below:

Open the MSMP Workflow Configuration page using the T-code GRFNMW_ CONFIGURE_WD

Select the Process Id SAP_GRAC_CONTROL_MAINT and click on Display/Change button to edit the Workflow settings.

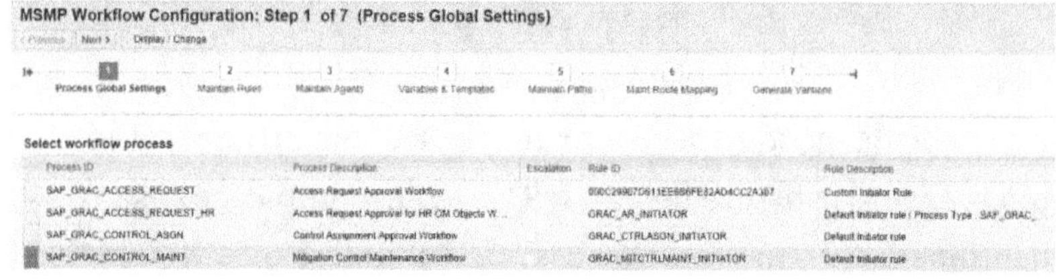

Maintain Process Global Settings, Notification Templates and Escape Conditions in the 1st step.

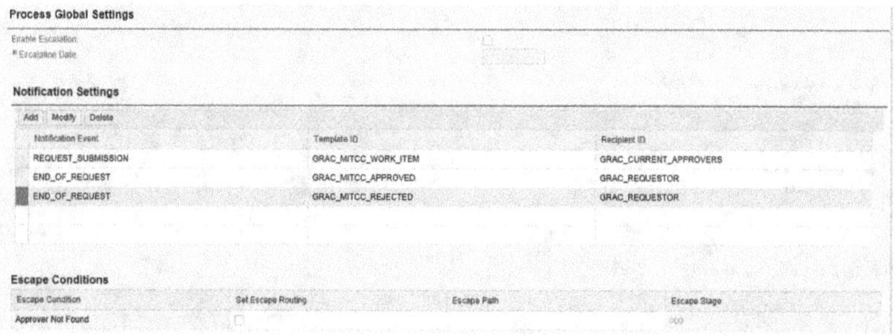

MAINTAIN RULES

In this step, you can maintain new Rules if created other than the standard Rules provided by SAP. Select the Process Initiator (Standard or Custom as required) and Notification Rule under Global Rules.

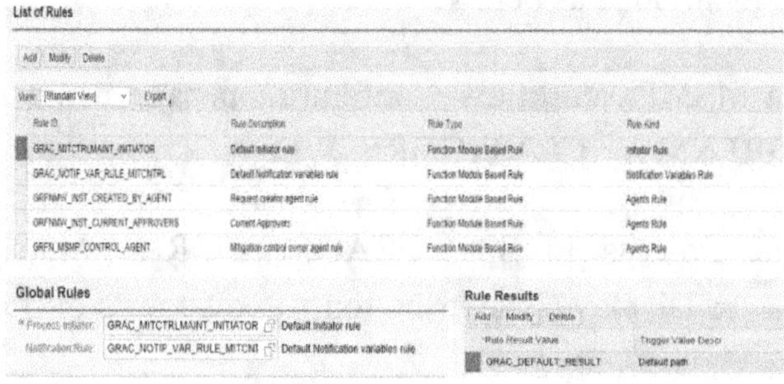

MAINTAIN AGENTS

In this step, you can maintain new Agents if required other than the standard Agents provided by SAP.

VARIABLE AND TEMPLATES

In this step, you can define the Notification templates for the current Process Id.

MAINTAIN PATH

In this step, approval path and the stages would be configured. In the Standard Path provided by SAP, there is only one Stage for Control Owner.

We can create multiple stages in the path or create a new path. For this example, we have created two stages: One is the Control Owner Stage (Agent would be Control Owner) and Other is Compliance Stage (Agent is compliance Team)

MAINTAIN ROUTE MAPPING

In this step, Map the Initiator or Routing Rules and Result Values to Workflow Path.

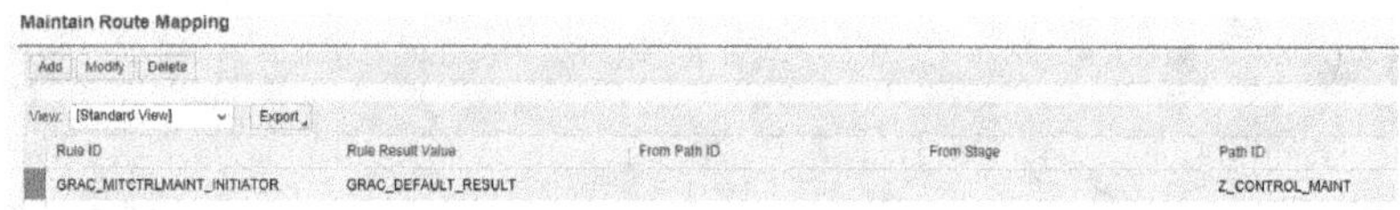

GENERATE VERSIONS

Save the changes and Activate the Version.

BRF RULE

If new Rule needs to be created based on different Line Items, you can create a BRF Rule similar to steps mentioned in Access Request Process Id.

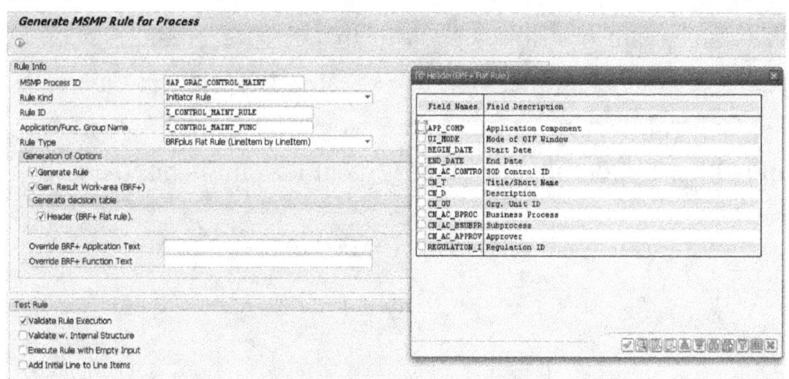

3. <u>FIREFIGHTER LOG REPORT REVIEW WORK - FLOW</u>

Using MSMP Workflow, we can Maintain the Workflow for the FF Log Report Review.

Steps are mentioned as below:

Open the MSMP Workflow Configuration page using the T-code GRFNMW_ CONFIGURE_WD

Select the Process Id SAP_GRAC_FIREFIGHT_LOG_ REPORT and click on Display/Change button to edit the Workflow settings.

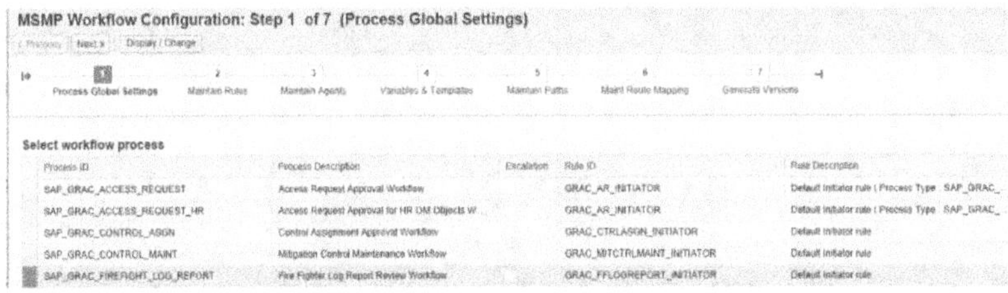

Maintain Process Global Settings, Notification Templates and Escape Conditions in the 1st step.

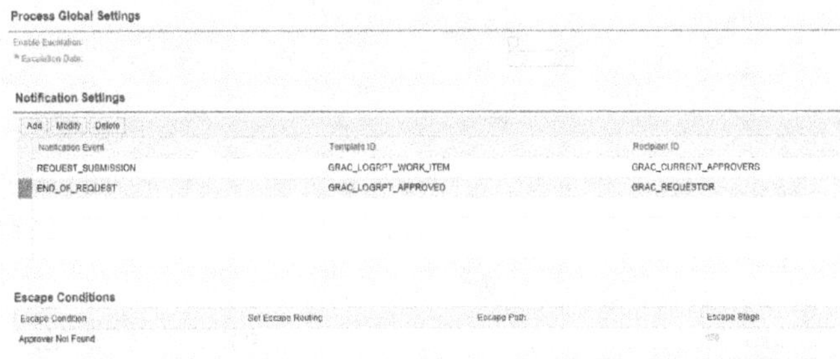

MAINTAIN RULES

In this step, you can maintain new Rules if created other than the standard Rules provided by SAP. Select the Process Initiator (Standard or Custom as required) and Notification Rule under Global Rules.

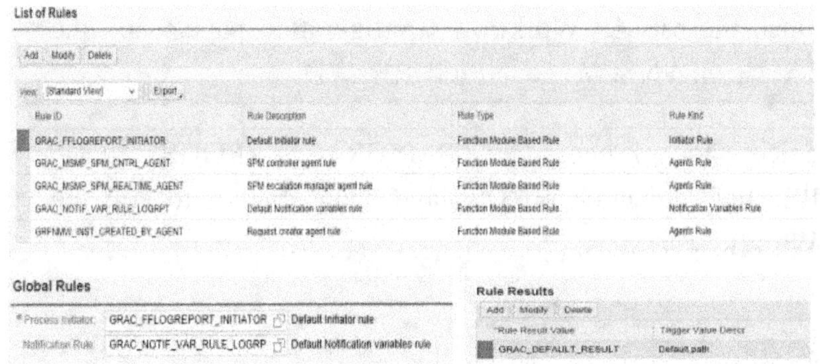

MAINTAIN AGENTS

In this step, you can maintain new Agents if required other than the standard Agents provided by SAP.

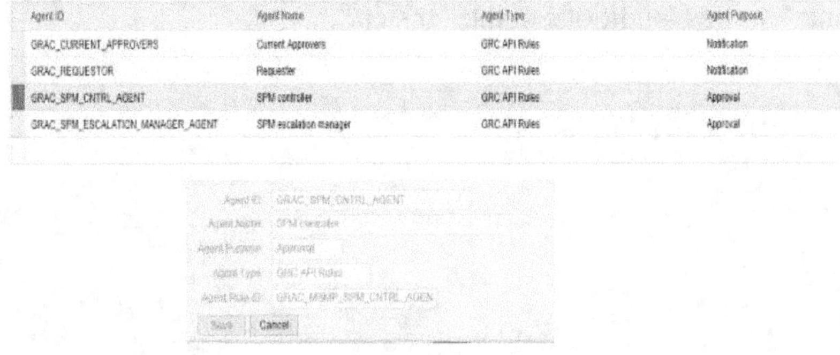

As per default Agents provided by SAP, Log Reviewer are the users who are maintained as FF Controller.

If the requirement is to have different criteria for agent identification, a new agent can be created.

MAINTAIN PATH

In this step, approval path and the stages would be configured. In the Standard Path provided by SAP, there is only one Stage for Log Report Approver (FF Controller Agent).

We can create multiple stages in the path or create a new path.

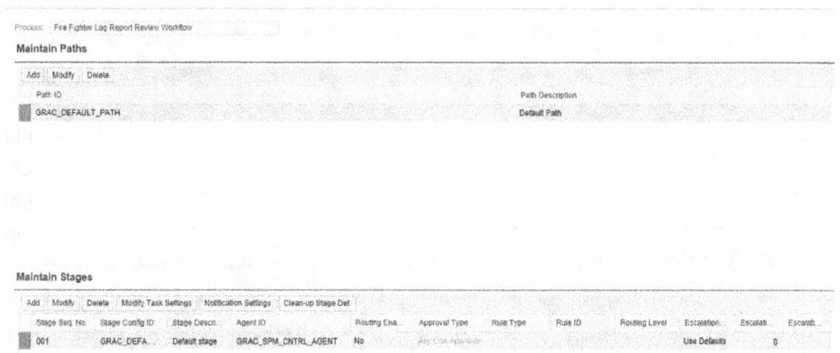

Process: Fire Fighter Log Report Review Workflow

Maintain Paths

Add   Modify   Delete

Path ID	Path Description
GRAC_DEFAULT_PATH	Default Path

Maintain Stages

Add   Modify   Delete   Modify Task Settings   Notification Settings   Clean-up Stage Def.

Stage Seq. No.	Stage Config ID	Stage Descr.	Agent ID	Routing Ena.	Approval Type	Rule Type	Rule ID	Routing Level	Escalation.	Escalati.	Escalati.
001	GRAC_DEFA.	Default stage	GRAC_SPM_CNTRL_AGENT	No	Any One Approver				Use Defaults	0	

MAINTAIN ROUTE MAPPING

In this step, Map the Initiator or Routing Rules and Result Values to Workflow Path.

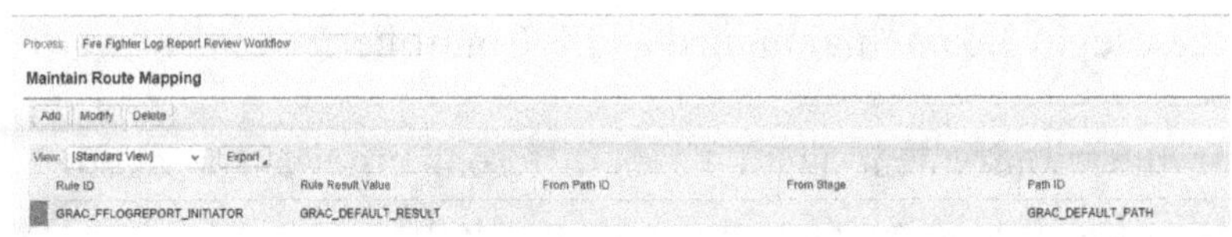

GENERATE VERSIONS

Save the changes and Activate the Version.

BRF RULE

If new Rule needs to be created based on different Line Items, you can create a BRF Rule similar to steps mentioned in Access Request Process Id.

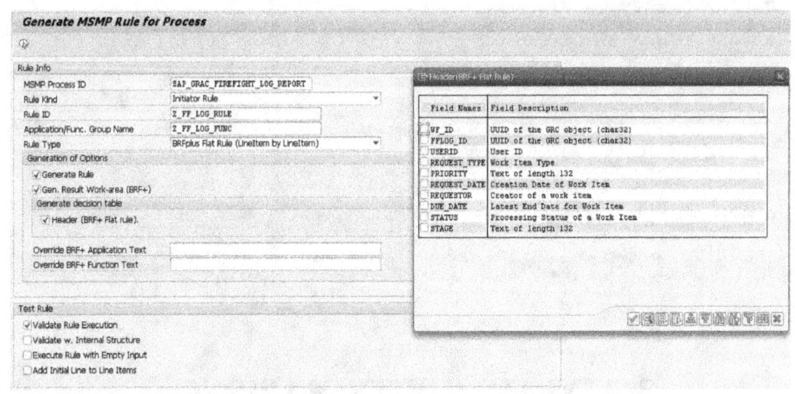

4. <u>FUNCTION APPROVAL WORKFLOW</u>

Using MSMP Workflow, we can Maintain the Workflow for the Approval of changes to Function.

Steps are mentioned as below:

Open the MSMP Workflow Configuration page using the T-code GRFNMW_ CONFIGURE_WD

Select the Process Id SAP_GRAC_FUNC_APPR and click on Display/Change button to edit the Workflow settings.

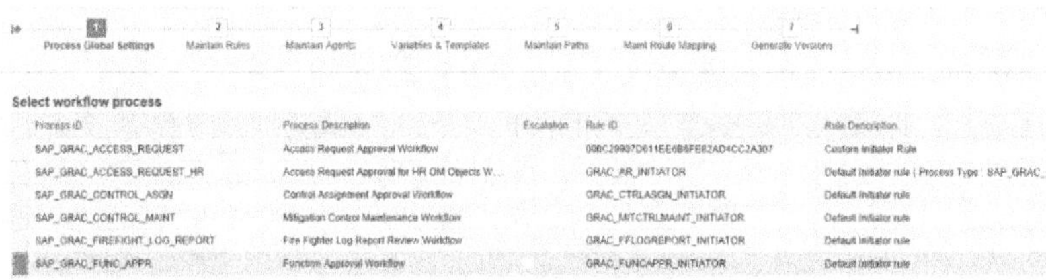

Maintain Process Global Settings, Notification Templates and Escape Conditions in the 1st step.

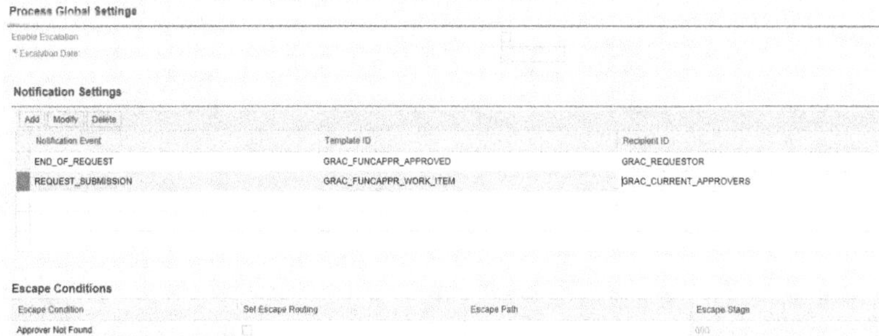

MAINTAIN RULES

In this step, you can maintain new Rules if created other than the standard Rules provided by SAP. Select the Process Initiator (Standard or Custom as required) and Notification Rule under Global Rules.

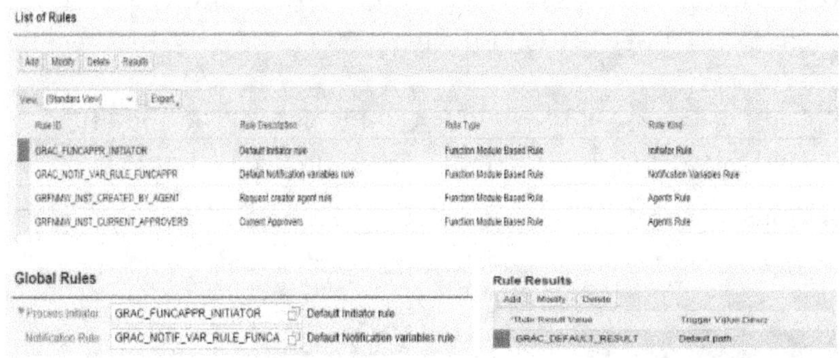

MAINTAIN AGENTS

In this step, you can maintain new Agents if required other than the standard Agents provided by SAP.

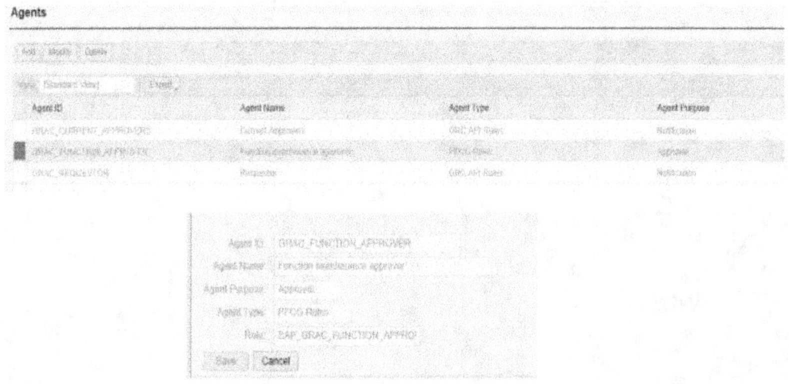

As per default Agents provided by SAP, Function Approver are the users who have been assigned the Role SAP_GRAC_FUNCTION_APPROVER in PFCG.

If the requirement is to have different criteria for agent identification, a new agent can be created.

MAINTAIN PATH

In this step, approval path and the stages would be configured. In the Standard Path provided by SAP, there is only one Stage for Function Approver.

We can create multiple stages in the path or create a new path.

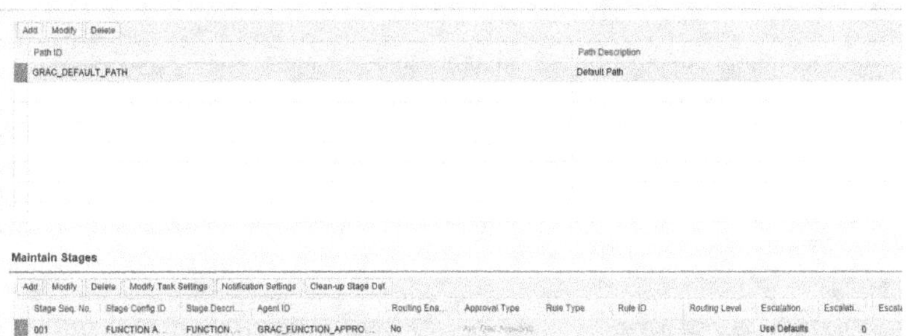

MAINTAIN ROUTE MAPPING

In this step, Map the Initiator or Routing Rules and Result Values to Workflow Path.

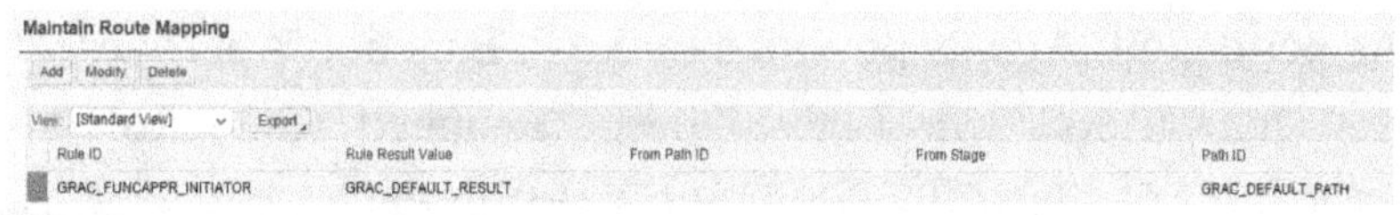

GENERATE VERSIONS

Save the changes and Activate the Version.

BRF RULE

If new Rule needs to be created based on different Line Items, you can create a BRF Rule similar to steps

mentioned in Access Request Process Id.

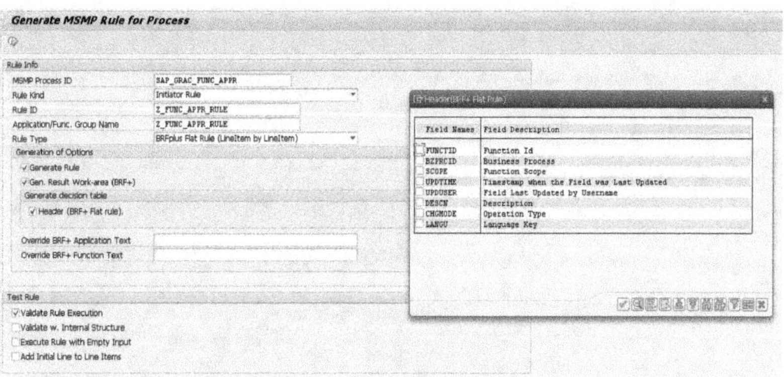

5. <u>RISK APPROVAL WORKFLOW</u>

Using MSMP Workflow, we can Maintain the Workflow for the Approval of changes to Risk.

Steps are mentioned as below:

Open the MSMP Workflow Configuration page using the T-code GRFNMW_ CONFIGURE_WD

Select the Process Id SAP_GRAC_RISK_APPR and click on Display/Change button to edit the Workflow settings.

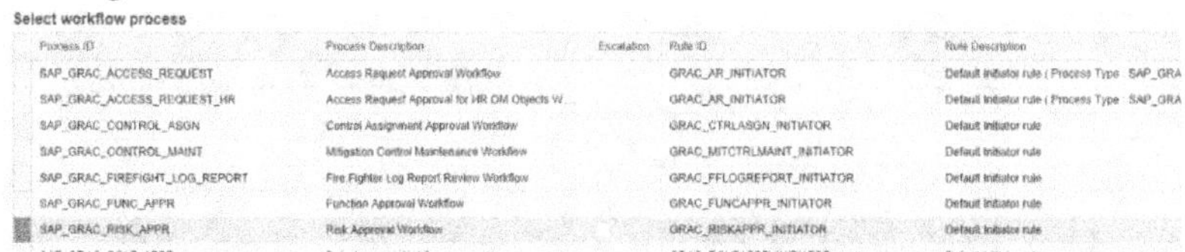

Maintain Process Global Settings, Notification Templates and Escape Conditions in the 1st step.

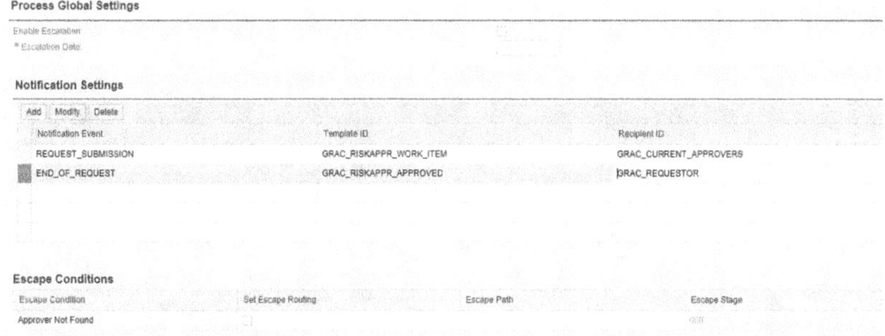

MAINTAIN RULES

In this step, you can maintain new Rules if created other than the standard Rules provided by SAP. Select the Process Initiator (Standard or Custom as required) and Notification Rule under Global Rules.

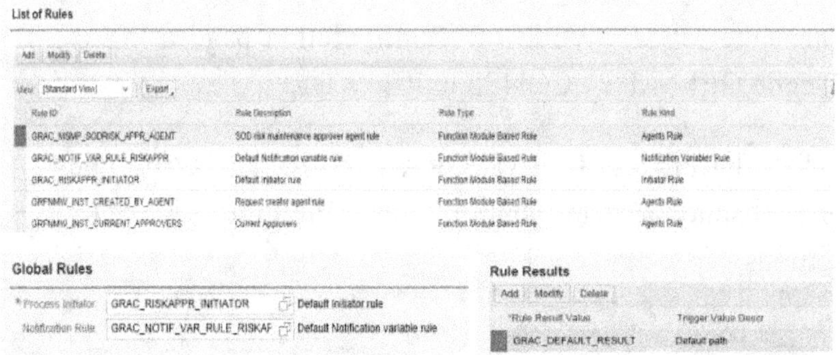

MAINTAIN AGENTS

In this step, you can maintain new Agents if required other than the standard Agents provided by SAP.

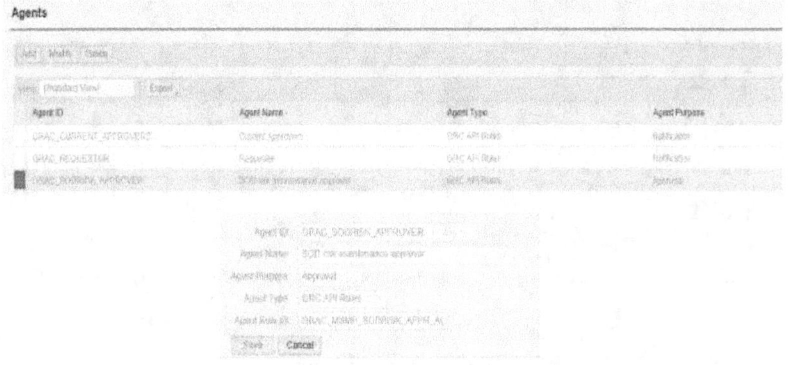

As per default Agents provided by SAP, Risk Approver are the users who have been assigned as the Risk Owner in Risk Definition.

If the requirement is to have different criteria for agent

identification, a new agent can be created.

MAINTAIN PATH

In this step, approval path and the stages would be configured. In the Standard Path provided by SAP, there is only one Stage for Risk Approver.

We can create multiple stages in the path or create a new path.

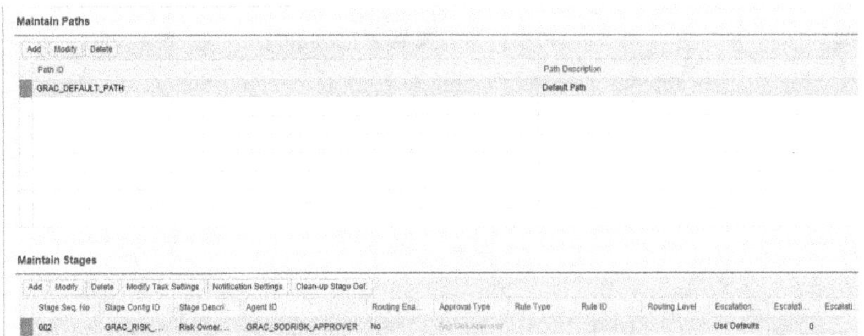

MAINTAIN ROUTE MAPPING

In this step, Map the Initiator or Routing Rules and Result Values to Workflow Path.

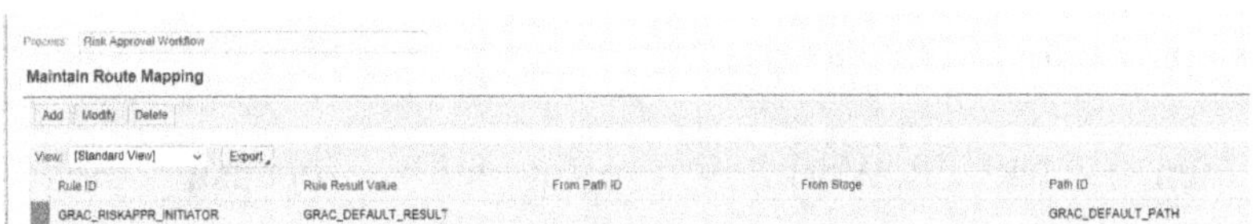

GENERATE VERSIONS

Save the changes and Activate the Version.

BRF RULE

If new Rule needs to be created based on different Line Items, you can create a BRF Rule similar to steps mentioned in Access Request Process Id.

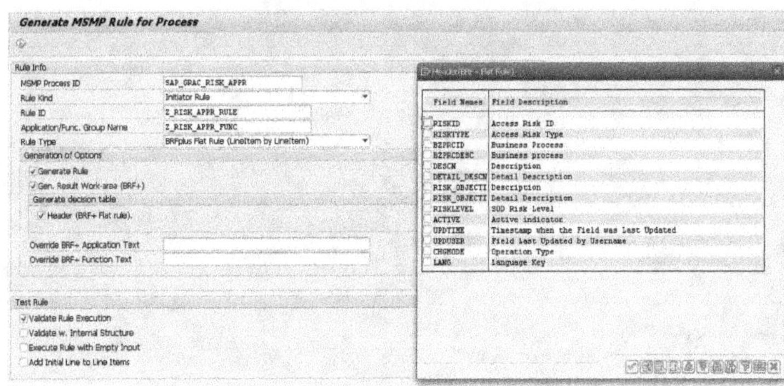

6. <u>SOD RISK REVIEW WORKFLOW</u>

Using MSMP Workflow, we can Maintain the Workflow for the SOD Risk Review.

Steps are mentioned as Below:

Open the MSMP Workflow Configuration page using the T-code GRFNMW_ CONFIGURE_WD

Select the Process Id SAP_GRAC_SOD_RISK_REVIEW

and click on Display/Change button to edit the Workflow settings.

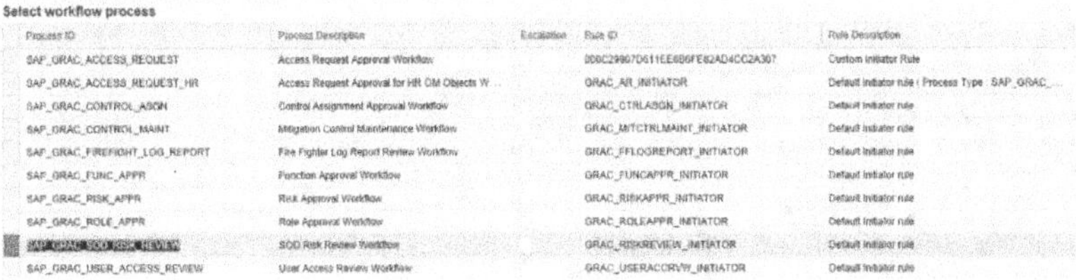

Select workflow process

Process ID	Process Description	Escalation	Rule ID	Rule Description
SAP_GRAC_ACCESS_REQUEST	Access Request Approval Workflow		008C29907D611EE6B6FE82AD4CC2A307	Custom Initiator Rule
SAP_GRAC_ACCESS_REQUEST_HR	Access Request Approval for HR OM Objects W...		GRAC_AR_INITIATOR	Default Initiator rule (Process Type : SAP_GRAC_...
SAP_GRAC_CONTROL_ASGN	Control Assignment Approval Workflow		GRAC_CTRLASGN_INITIATOR	Default Initiator rule
SAP_GRAC_CONTROL_MAINT	Mitigation Control Maintenance Workflow		GRAC_MITCTRLMAINT_INITIATOR	Default Initiator rule
SAP_GRAC_FIREFIGHT_LOG_REPORT	Fire Fighter Log Report Review Workflow		GRAC_FFLOGREPORT_INITIATOR	Default Initiator rule
SAP_GRAC_FUNC_APPR	Function Approval Workflow		GRAC_FUNCAPPR_INITIATOR	Default Initiator rule
SAP_GRAC_RISK_APPR	Risk Approval Workflow		GRAC_RISKAPPR_INITIATOR	Default Initiator rule
SAP_GRAC_ROLE_APPR	Role Approval Workflow		GRAC_ROLEAPPR_INITIATOR	Default Initiator rule
SAP_GRAC_SOD_RISK_REVIEW	SOD Risk Review Workflow		GRAC_RISKREVIEW_INITIATOR	Default Initiator rule
SAP_GRAC_USER_ACCESS_REVIEW	User Access Review Workflow		GRAC_USERACORVW_INITIATOR	Default Initiator rule

SOD RISK REVIEW

1. <u>OVERVIEW</u>

• The Segregation of Duties Review (SoD Review) feature automates and documents the periodic decentralized review of risk violations by business managers or risk owners.

• In the SoD Review process, the system checks periodically for any risk and violations associated with users and functions they are associated with.

• This feature can be used during the initial "clean-up" of risk violations as well as a long-term strategy to review and affirm previous mitigation assignments.

• Requests are generated automatically based on the company's internal control policy.

• The SoD Review provides a workflow-based review and approval process.

SOD REVIEW PROCESS

The high-level process for SoD reviews is as follows:

1. The SoD background jobs generate SoD review requests.

2. The system sends e-mail notifications to reviewers.

3. The reviewer reviews the request and chooses from the following options:

a. Reject request items.

b. Mitigate function risks by assigning controls.

c. Remove access for items that violate your company policies.

There are other optional steps involved in the SoD Review process such as performing Admin Review before sending requests to Reviewers

2. <u>PROCESS OPTIONS</u>

AC 12.X offers multiple process options that determine the approvers of SoD Review requests. This section describes the available process options.

• **Admin Review** : You have the option to enable an Admin Review which provides administrators an opportunity to validate request data after requests are generated (by the SoD Review Data job) but prior to generating workflow tasks (by the SoD Review Update Workflow job).

If any Reviewer information is incorrect or missing, administrators can modify that data prior to generating workflow tasks and notifications. The administrator can also delete requests as required.

• **Reviewer Stage** : You can specify whether the Reviewer stage is addressed by a user's manager or by the role owner, as appropriate.

• **Security Stage :** You can choose to include a security stage, if required.

3. <u>ROLES IN SOD REVIEW PROCESS</u>

SAP GRC 12.X includes the following roles that can appear in SoD Requests :

• **Administrator** – Administrators perform SoD Review-specific administration tasks such as performing an Admin Review before generating a workflow for the request.

• **Reviewer** - Reviewers are approvers at the Reviewer stage. A Reviewer can be a User's Manager or the Risk Owner.

• **User's Manager** – User's Manager is the direct manager of a particular user, as defined in the User Details Data Source.

• **Risk Owner** – Risk Owner is the owner specified in your Risk Analysis and Remediation (RAR) master data.

• **Coordinator** – Coordinators are users assigned to one or more Reviewers. Coordinators monitor the SoD Review process and coordinate activities to ensure that the process is completed in a timely manner.

4. CONFIGURATION SETTINGS

Below Configuration Settings needs to be defined in SPRO for SOD Risk Review:

Enable Offline Risk Analysis: Under Risk Analysis, parameter 1027 should be set to YES.

SOD REVIEW SPECIFIC CONFIGURATION:

SOD Review	2016	010	Request Type for SoD
SOD Review	2017	013	Default priority for SoD
SOD Review	2018	RISK OWNER	Who are the reviewers?
SOD Review	2019	YES	Admin. review required before sending tasks to reviewers
SOD Review	2020	9999	Number of unique line items per SOD request. (Maximum 9999)
SOD Review	2023	YES	Is actual removal of role allowed

1. **Request Type :** This is the request type that will be associated with SoD Review workflow requests. Request types can be reference points for initializing a workflow and determining the actions to be performed.

2. **Request Priority :** You can set a priority for a request to determine how quickly a request is to be approved. The request priority is also one of the workflow request attributes.

3. **Reviewers :** This term refers to the approver at the Reviewer stage. For the SoD Review, the Reviewer may be the user's Direct Manager or the Risk owner as maintained in the RAR master data.

4. **Admin Review :** This configuration option provides an opportunity for the administration to review the request data for completeness and consistency prior to sending

the request to Reviewers. If any manager or risk owner information is incorrect or missing, the administrator can modify the data prior to generating workflow tasks and notifications. The administrator can also cancel the requests. An Admin can perform SoD Review-specific administrator tasks, such as cancelling SoD Review requests and regenerating requests for rejected users.

If this Configuration Option is set to :

Yes : The administrator reviews the SoD Review requests prior to the generation of workflow tasks. The administrator can change the Reviewer and approval roles or cancel any unwanted SoD Review requests.

No : The administrator does not have an opportunity to Review SoD Review requests prior to sending the workflow notifications to Reviewers.

If there are users with no manager identified in the User Detail Data Source and the Reviewer is defined as the User's Manager, then Admin Review is required. This allows the administrator to maintain the missing data prior to sending workflow tasks to Reviewers.

5. **Removal of Roles :** In AC 10.0, Reviewers can remove a role if any risk is associated with any transaction(s) given to user(s) due to some role.

5. <u>SYNCHRONIZATION JOBS</u>

Before running the SoD Review data job, ensure that the Batch Risk Analysis job is executed and completed with the Management Report and that Risk Owners are assigned to risks.

Also make sure to run the following synchronization and action usage jobs as preconditions for performing SoD Reviews in GRC 12.X.

JOBS TO BE EXECUTED FOR SOD REVIEW:

1. Repository Sync : User, Profile and Role Sync

2. Batch Risk Analysis

3. Action Usage Sync

4. Role Usage Sync

6. <u>MANAGE COORDINATORS</u>

This Step describes how to manage Coordinators for requests.

Go to NWBC and Access Management Work center, Click on Manage Coordinators under Compliance Certification Reviews

To change a coordinator-to-reviewer mapping, choose the Open pushbutton. The Change Mapping screen appears. Modify the settings, as required, and choose the Save pushbutton.

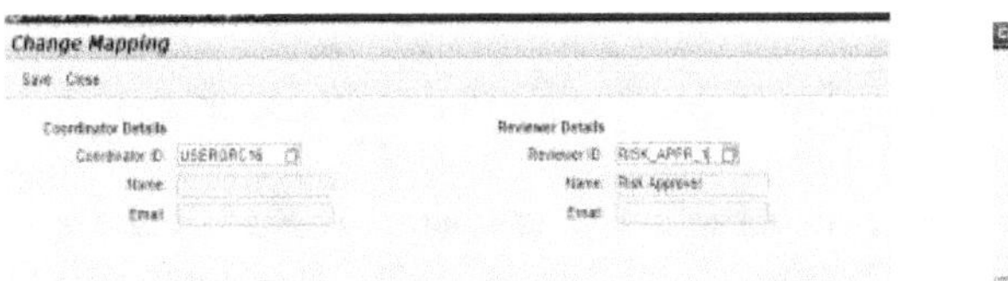

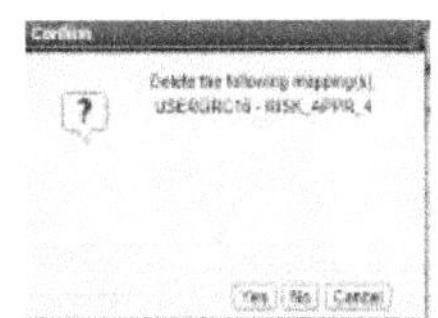

To delete a coordinator-to-reviewer mapping, select the mapping you want to delete, and choose the Delete pushbutton. A confirmation dialog box appears. Choose Yes.

To create a new coordinator-to-reviewer mapping, choose the Create pushbutton. The Create Mapping screen appears.

Enter the Coordinator and Reviewer Id and click on Save.

You can also Import the mapping by using Import Pushbutton from Manage Coordinators screen.

Template to be used for importing can be downloaded from Download Template Button.

7. <u>SOD REVIEW REQUEST</u>

This step describes how to generate data for SoD Review requests by creating a schedule using the Background Scheduler.

Go to NWBC, Access Management WorkCentre, click on Background Scheduler under Scheduling.

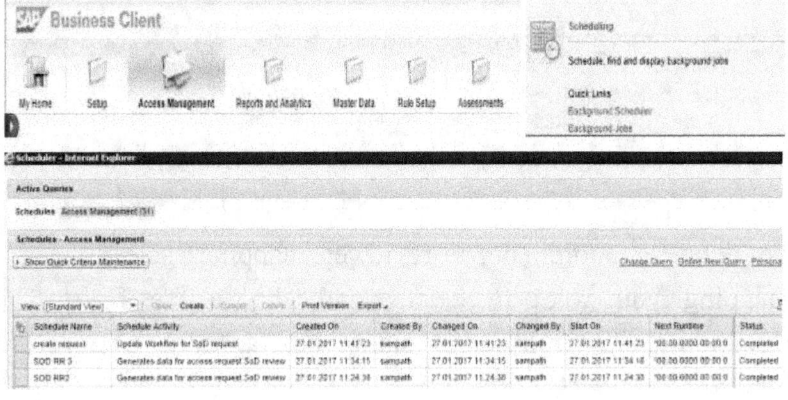

- Choose Create to create a new SoD Review Request background job. The Schedule Details step appears.

- In the Schedule Name field, enter the name for the SoD Review job.

- In the Schedule Activity field, select Generates data for access request SoD Review from the dropdown list.

- In the Recurring Plan field, choose YES or NO for whether to schedule the job to recur.

- If you select Yes, you need to specify the recurring date and time range, along with the frequency and recurrence interval.

- In the Start Immediately field, choose whether to start the job immediately.

- If you select Yes, the job will start immediately. If you select No, specify the date and time for the job to start in the Start Time field.

- Click on Next Button. Select Variant screen appears.

- Define the selection criteria for the background job by selecting a variant or entering the criteria, and then saving it as a new variant.

Review the summary, and then select FINISH.

The scheduled job appears in the table with one of the following statuses:

- **Planning :** The job is either currently working on the request or the job is scheduled to start later.

- **Completed :** The job has completed.

- **Terminated :** The job was terminated by the administrator.

- **Error :** An error was detected with the job.

Once the Job is completed, SoD Request data is Generated and sent for Admin Review if enabled Else the Workflow path is initiated.

8. <u>ADMIN REVIEW</u>

This step is only required if you have enabled the Admin

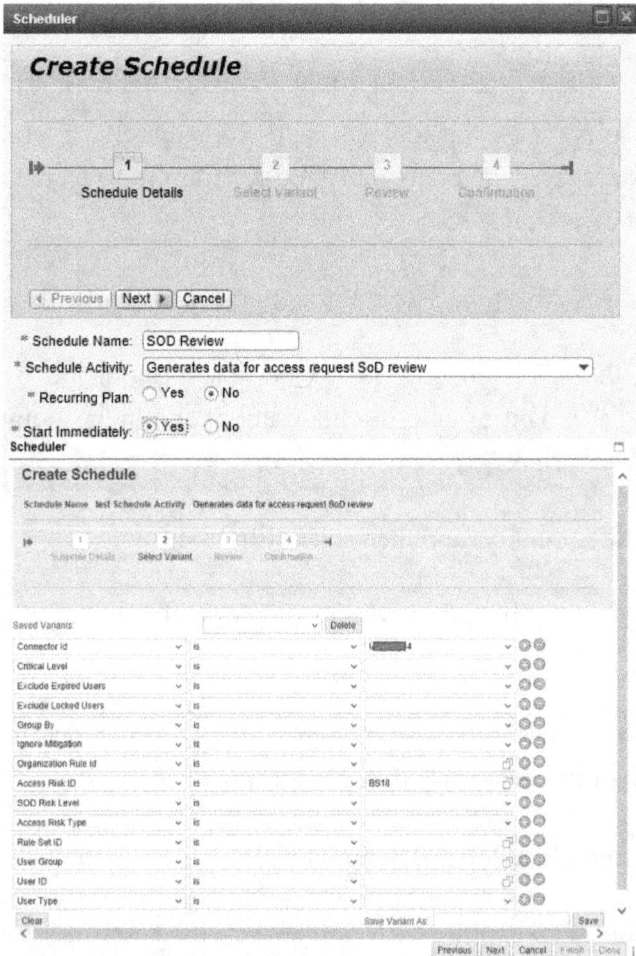

Review option. The administrator reviews the requests to ensure completeness and accuracy of the request information prior to sending to Reviewer.

Go to NWBC, Access Management WorkCentre, click on Request Review under Compliance Certification Review.

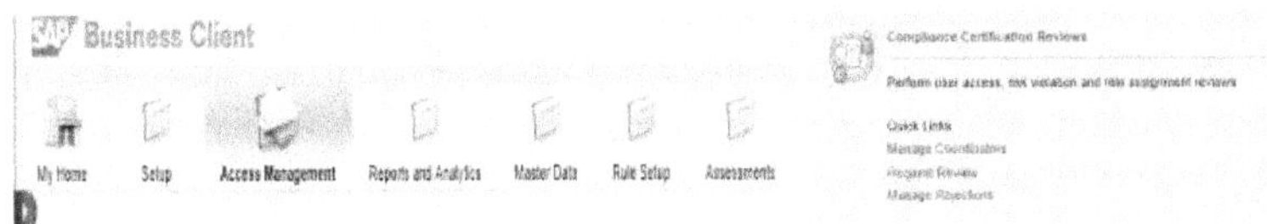

- On the Request Review screen, search for the SoD Review requests by selecting the SoD Risk Review Workflow and then review the data to confirm the Reviewer and Coordinator information is accurate.

- This is an intermediate stage (since YES was selected for the Admin Review) where all the requests come for the Administrator to work on them prior to being generated.

- On this screen you can enter information about the reviewer to the requests if not available.

- To enter Reviewer data, select the Request and choose the Change Reviewers pushbutton.

- Select Reviewers and Coordinators from the list.

- An Administrator can also cancel the request if SoD Reviews are not required or if there is incorrect data.

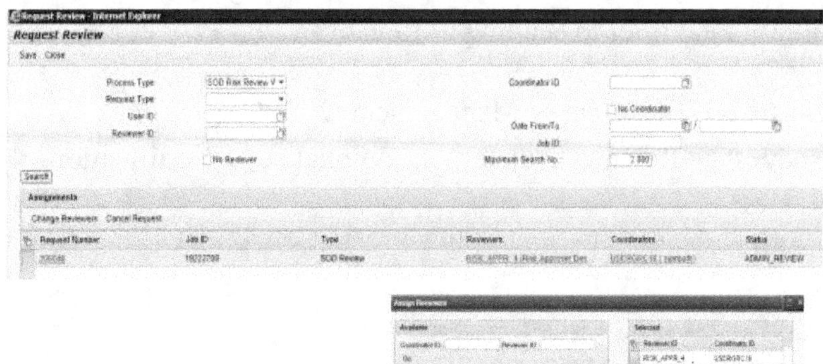

• To enter Reviewer data, select the Request and choose the Change Reviewers pushbutton.

• Select Reviewers and Coordinators from the list.

• An Administrator can also cancel the request if SoD Reviews are not required or if there is incorrect data.

9. <u>UPDATE WORKFLOW JOB</u>

This step is only required if you have enabled Admin Review and the Admin Review has been completed. Execute the SoD Review Update Workflow Job to push the workflow tasks to the Reviewers.

Go to NWBC, Access Management WorkCentre, click on Background Scheduler under Scheduling.

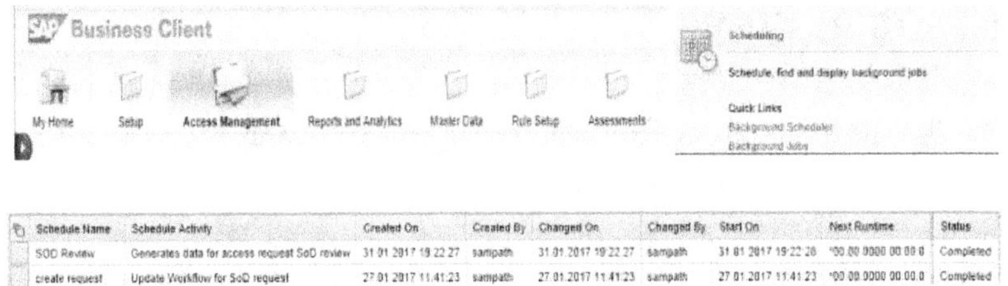

• From Schedule - Access Management Screen will appear, Choose Create to create a new request for Update Workflow.

• The Create Schedule screen will appear.

• Enter Schedule Name.

• Select Schedule Activity from the dropdown list. For SoD Requests, select Update Workflow for SoD Request.

• Choose Finish.

• After completing all the above-mentioned steps, the request(s) will now come to the Reviewer's Work Iop[Inbox (or Outlook) to work on it or to any other approver configured in MSMP workflow configured earlier.

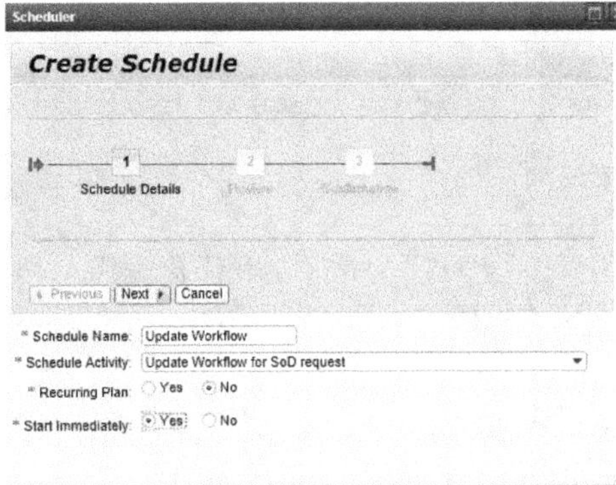

10. <u>SOD REVIEW</u>

After you update the request workflow, the request follows the workflow path and is routed to the appropriate reviewer.

After a request is generated, it is sent to the reviewer's Work Inbox.

Using Search Request link, view the Request created and the Audit Logs.

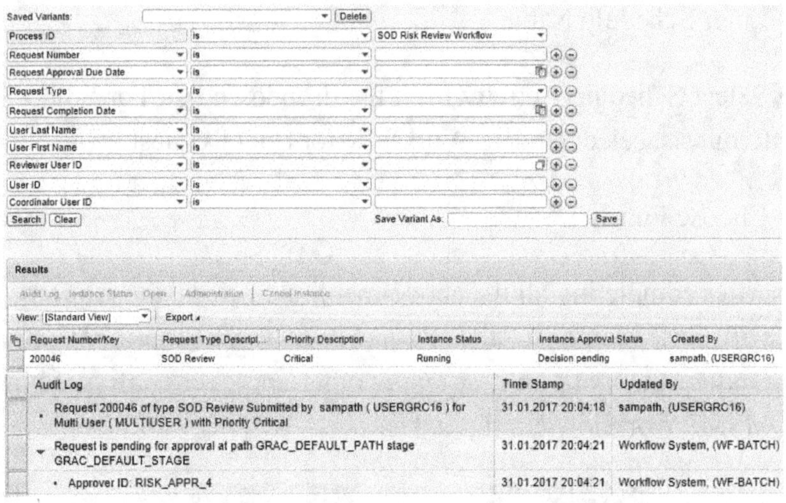

Request is sent to the reviewer based on the Risk Approver maintained.

Open NWBC using Reviewer's Id and go to Work Inbox under My Home Work Center.

In the Reviewer's Work Inbox, select the request you want to open by clicking on the selected request.

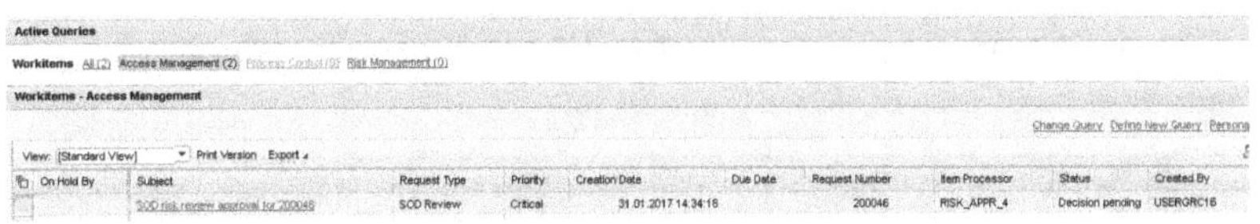

- You will see SoD Review Screen with the Request Number that you selected.

- If YES was selected for Actual removal of Roles during the configuration process, the ACTUAL REMOVAL pushbutton appears on the screen.

- If NO was selected, then the PROPOSE REMOVAL pushbutton appears instead.

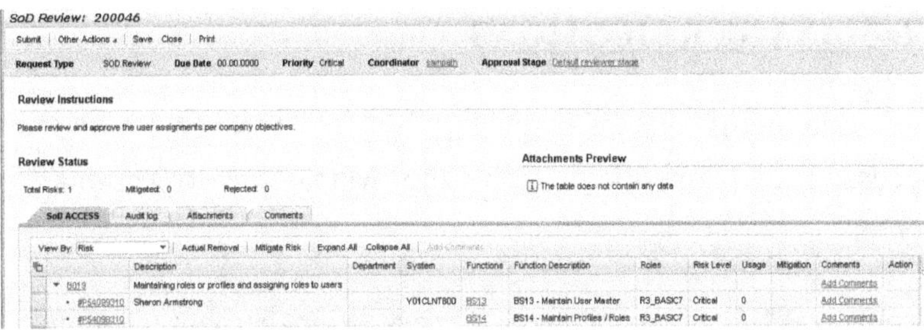

- By selecting Risk and then choosing the Actual Removal pushbutton, you can remove the actual role associated with this Risk.

- By choosing the Propose Removal pushbutton you can only propose the removal, no actual removal is done on any roles.

- Reviewer can mitigate the Risks by selecting the Mitigate Risk Pushbutton.

• Choose Submit to complete the Review process.

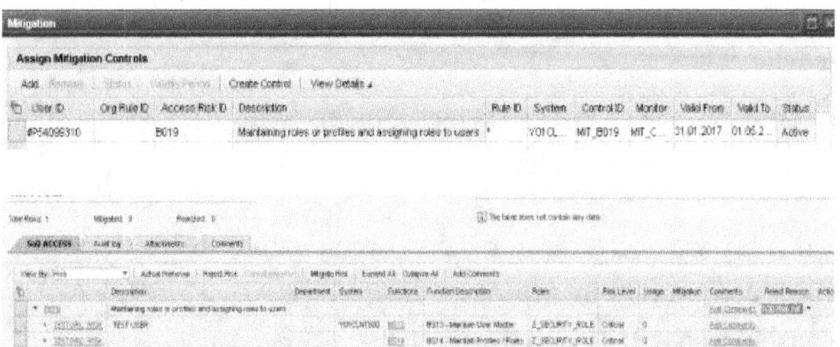

• You can also reject a Risk by selecting it and clicking on Reject Risk along with a Reject Reason from the dropdown.

11. <u>MANAGE REJECTIONS</u>

The line items that are rejected by an approver can be accessed and reworked from the Managing Rejections screen.

From NWBC, Navigate to Access Management, under Compliance Certification Reviews click on Manage Rejections.

The Manage Rejections screen appears.

Specify the search criteria and choose the Search pushbutton. The rejected Items appear in the Result table.

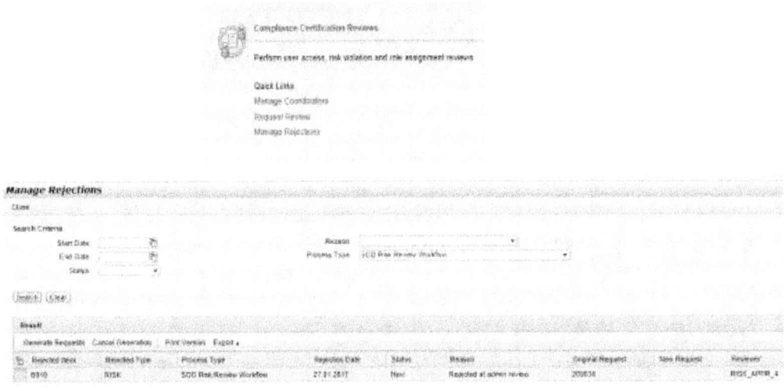

• Select the corresponding rejection and choose the Generate Requests pushbutton.

• This marks the request for inclusion in a new SoD Review request when the SoD Review Process Rejected background job is executed from Background scheduler.

• Similarly click on cancel generation to unmark the prevent the inclusion in new SoD Review request.

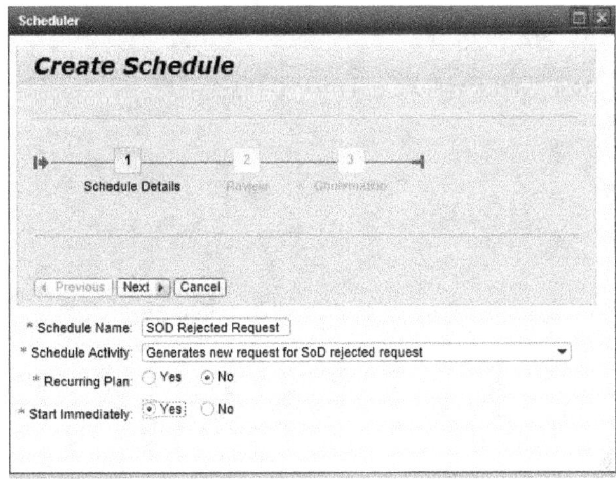

<u>USER ACCESS REVIEW</u>

1. Overview

2. Key Users for UAR

3. Configuration Settings

4. Synchronization Jobs

5. Manage Coordinators

6. User Access Review Request

7. Admin Review

8. Update Workflow Job

9. UAR Review

10. Manage Rejections

1. <u>OVERVIEW</u>

- The User Access Review (UAR) feature provides a workflow-based review and approval process for user access requests.

- The User Access Review feature automates and documents the periodic decentralized user access review by business managers or role owners.

- System automatically generates the requests based on the company's internal control policy.

- The reviewer assesses roles assigned to users and the frequency of use for that role by the user.

- The approver can approve, remove access or take different actions, such as forward, reroute or reject a request

2. <u>KEY USERS FOR UAR</u>

SAP GRC 12.X includes the following Users that can appear in UAR process :

- **Administrator** – This person has the Admin role assigned for Access Control. They can perform UAR- specific administrator tasks, such as cancelling UAR requests and regenerating requests for rejected users as well as Admin review before generating workflow for request.

- **Reviewer** - Reviewers are approvers at the Reviewer stage. A Reviewer can be a User's Manager or the Role Owner.

- **User's Manager** – User's Manager is the direct manager of a particular user, as defined in the User Details Data Source.

- **Role Owner** – Risk Owner is the owner specified in your ARM master data.

- **Coordinator** – Coordinators are users assigned to one or more Reviewers. Coordinators monitor the UAR process and coordinate activities to ensure that the process is completed in a timely manner.

3. <u>CONFIGURATION SETTINGS</u>

Below Configuration Settings needs to be defined in SPRO for User Access Review:

1. **Request Type :** This is the request type that will be associated with UAR requests. Request types can be reference points for initializing a workflow and determining the actions to be performed.

2. **Request Priority :** You can set a priority for a request to determine how quickly a request is to be approved. The request priority is also one of the workflow requests attributes.

3. **Reviewers :** This term refers to the approver at the

Reviewer stage. For the User Access Review, the Reviewer may be the user's Direct Manager or the Role owner as maintained in the BRM master data.

4. **Admin Review** : This configuration option provides an opportunity for the administration to review the request data for completeness and consistency prior to sending the request to Reviewers. If any manager or role owner information is incorrect or missing, the administrator can modify the data prior to generating workflow tasks and notifications. The administrator can also cancel the requests. An Admin can perform User Access Review-specific administrator tasks, such as cancelling UAR Review requests and regenerating requests for rejected users.

If this Configuration Option is set to:

Yes : The administrator reviews the User Access Review requests prior to the generation of workflow tasks. The administrator can change the Reviewer and approval roles or cancel any unwanted User Access Review requests.

No : The administrator does not have an opportunity to Review User Access Review requests prior to sending the workflow notifications to Reviewers.

NOTE : If the User does not have a manager or, the role owner does not have an owner, selecting No on Admin review will not generate workflow for request. And the role owner / manager must have a coordinator assigned to him. This mapping is defined in Manage Coordinator link under

Access management tab.

4. <u>SYNCHRONIZATION JOBS</u>

Before running the UAR Review data job, ensure that the appropriate jobs are executed and completed with the Management Report and that Role Approvers are assigned to Roles.

Also make sure to run the following synchronization and action usage jobs as preconditions for performing UAR Reviews in GRC 12.X.

Jobs to be executed for UAR Review.

1. Repository Sync: User, Profile and Role Sync

2. Action Usage Sync

3. Role Usage Sync

5. <u>MANAGE COORDINATORS</u>

This Step describes how to manage Coordinators for requests.

Go to NWBC and Access Management Work center, Click on Manage Coordinators under Compliance Certification Reviews

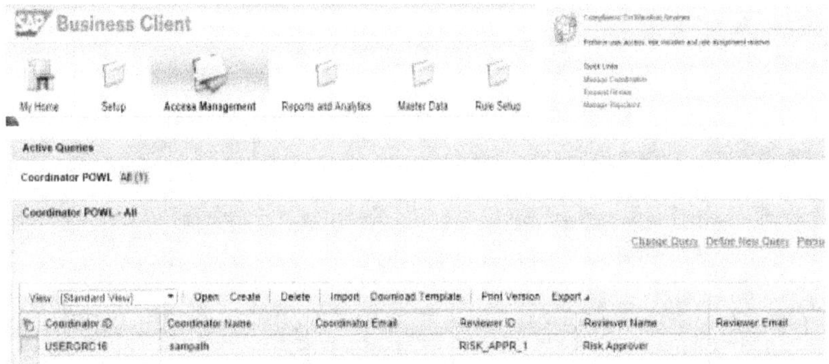

To change a coordinator-to-reviewer mapping, choose the Open pushbutton. The Change Mapping screen appears.

Modify the settings, as required, and choose the Save pushbutton.

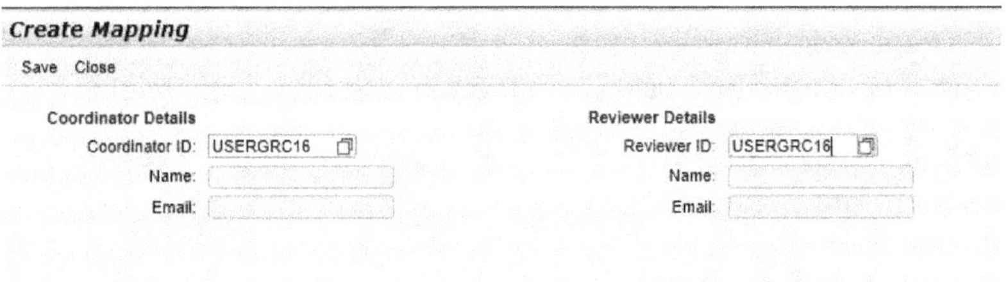

To delete a coordinator-to-reviewer mapping, select the mapping you want to delete, and choose the Delete pushbutton. A confirmation dialog box appears. Choose Yes.

To create a new coordinator-to-reviewer mapping, choose the Create pushbutton. The Create Mapping screen appears.

Enter the Coordinator and Reviewer Id and click on Save.

You can also Import the mapping by using Import Pushbutton from Manage Coordinators screen.

Template to be used for importing can be downloaded from Download Template Button.

6. <u>USER ACCESS REVIEW REQUEST</u>

This step describes how to generate data for User Access Review requests by creating a schedule using the Background Scheduler.

Go to NWBC, Access Management WorkCentre, click on Background Scheduler under Scheduling.

• Choose Create to create a new User Access Review Request background job. The Schedule Details step appears.

Scheduling

Schedule, find and display background jobs

Quick Links

▤ Background Scheduler

▤ Background Jobs

Active Queries

Schedules Access Management (194)

Schedules - Access Management

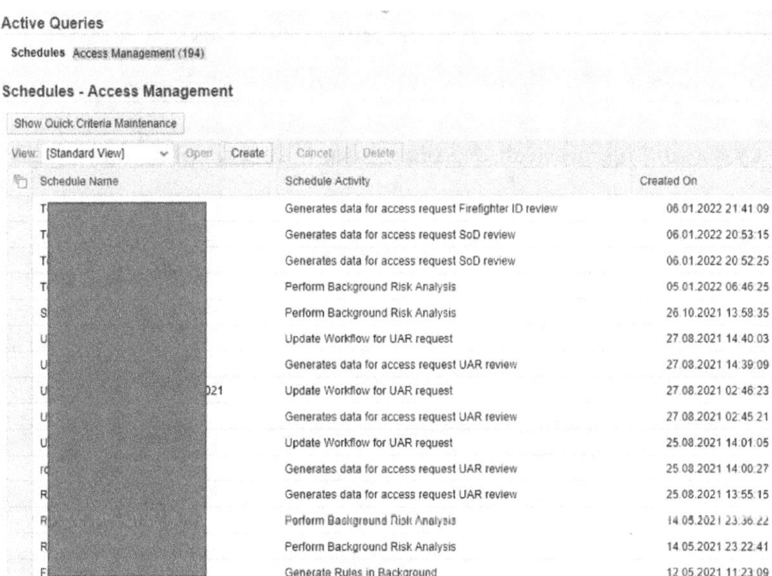

Schedule Name	Schedule Activity	Created On
T	Generates data for access request Firefighter ID review	06.01.2022 21:41:09
T	Generates data for access request SoD review	06.01.2022 20:53:15
T	Generates data for access request SoD review	06.01.2022 20:52:25
T	Perform Background Risk Analysis	05.01.2022 06:46:25
S	Perform Background Risk Analysis	26.10.2021 13:58:35
U	Update Workflow for UAR request	27.08.2021 14:40:03
U	Generates data for access request UAR review	27.08.2021 14:39:09
U	Update Workflow for UAR request	27.08.2021 02:46:23
U	Generates data for access request UAR review	27.08.2021 02:45:21
U	Update Workflow for UAR request	25.08.2021 14:01:05
r	Generates data for access request UAR review	25.08.2021 14:00:27
R	Generates data for access request UAR review	25.08.2021 13:55:15
R	Perform Background Risk Analysis	14.05.2021 23:36:22
R	Perform Background Risk Analysis	14.05.2021 23:22:41
F	Generate Rules in Background	12.05.2021 11:23:09

• In the Schedule Name field, enter the name for the User Access Review job.

• In the Schedule Activity field, select Generates data for access request UAR Review from the dropdown list.

• In the Recurring Plan field, choose YES or NO for whether to schedule the job to recur.

• If you select Yes, you need to specify the recurring date

and time range, along with the frequency and recurrence interval.

• In the Start Immediately field, choose whether to start the job immediately.

• If you select Yes, the job will start immediately. If you select No, specify the date and time for the job to start in the Start Time field.

• Check the Generate UAR for Business Roles checkbox if review is to be done for business Roles as well.

• Click on Next Button. Select Variant screen appears.

• Define the selection criteria for the background job by selecting a variant or entering the criteria, and then saving it as a new variant.

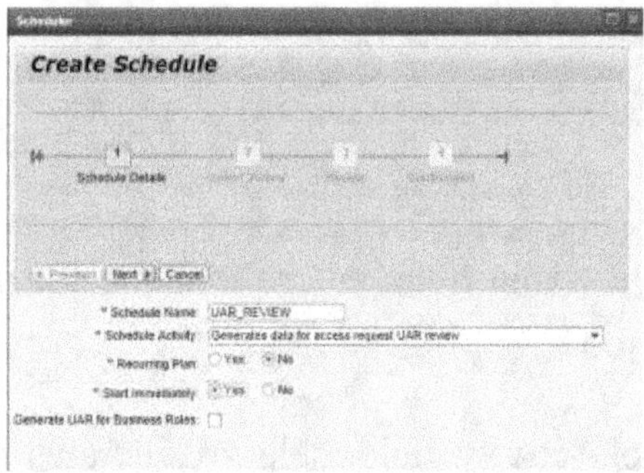

Review the summary, and then select FINISH.

The scheduled job appears in the table with one of the following statuses:

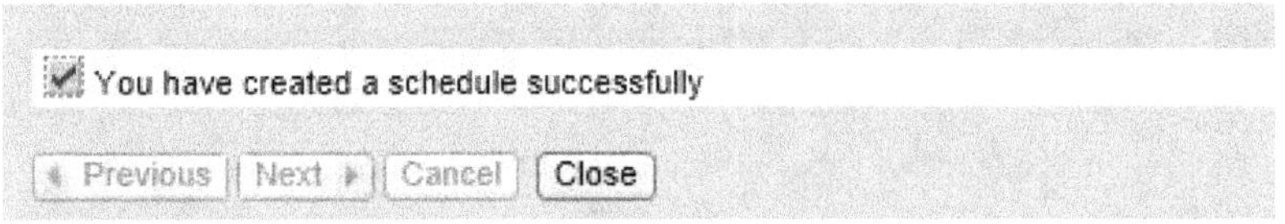

• **Planning :** The job is either currently working on the request or the job is scheduled to start later.

• **Completed :** The job has completed.

• **Terminated :** The job was terminated by the administrator.

• **Error :** An error was detected with the job.

Once the Job is completed, User Access Review Request data is Generated and sent for Admin Review if enabled Else the Workflow path is initiated.

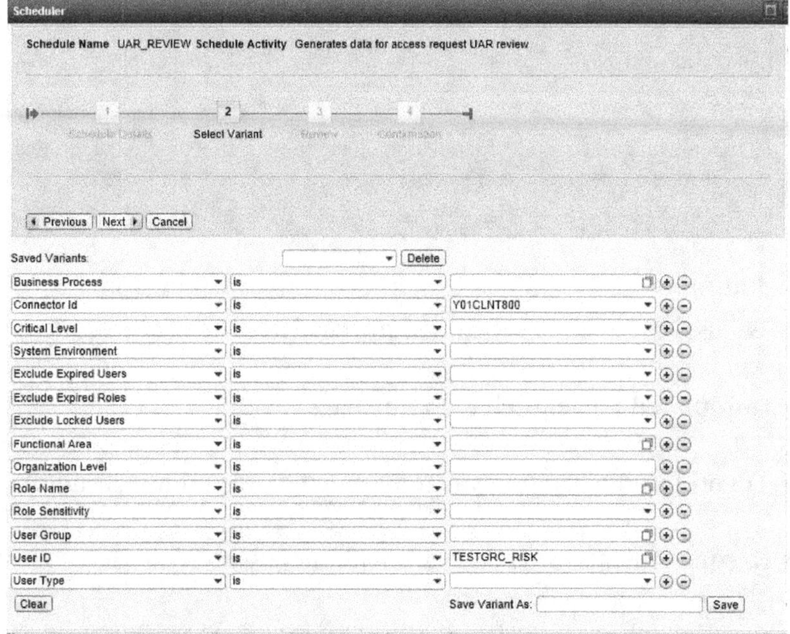

7. <u>ADMIN REVIEW</u>

This step is only required if you have enabled the Admin Review option. The administrator reviews the requests to ensure completeness and accuracy of the request information prior to sending to Reviewer.

Go to NWBC, Access Management WorkCentre, click on Request Review under Compliance Certification Review.

- On the Request Review screen, search for the User Access Review requests by selecting the User Access Review Workflow and then review the data to confirm the

Reviewer and Coordinator information is accurate.

• This is an intermediate stage (since YES was selected for the Admin Review) where all the requests come for the Administrator to work on them prior to being generated.

• On this screen you can enter information about the reviewer and coordinator to the requests if not available.

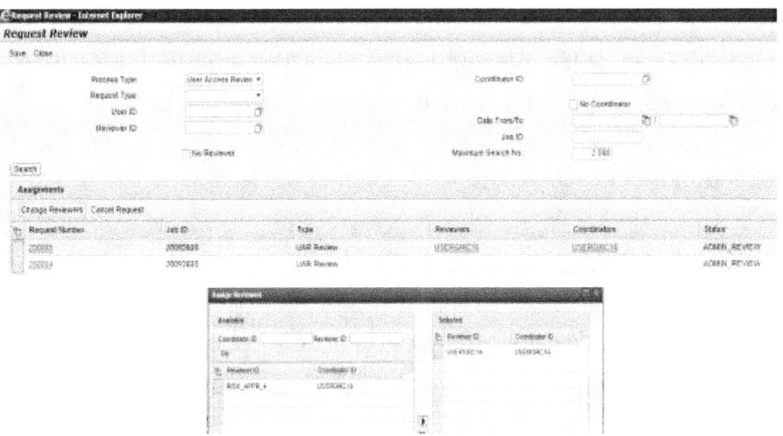

• To enter Reviewer data, select the Request and choose the Change Reviewers pushbutton.

• Select Reviewers and Coordinators from the list.

• An Administrator can also cancel the request if UAR Reviews are not required or if there is incorrect data.

• Click on Save to update the reviewers.

Click on a request no to view the Request Data. Add any comments if required for reviewer.

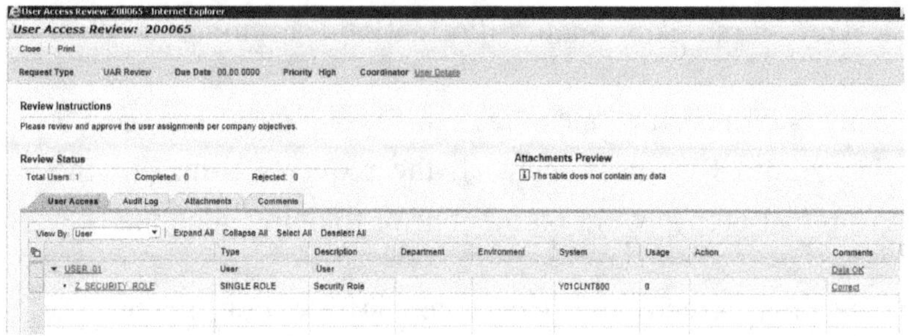

8. <u>UPDATE WORKFLOW JOB</u>

This step is only required if you have enabled Admin Review and the Admin Review has been completed.

Execute the UAR Review Update Workflow Job to push the workflow tasks to the Reviewers/any other approvers maintained in MSMP Workflow.

Go to NWBC, Access Management WorkCentre, click on Background Scheduler under Scheduling.

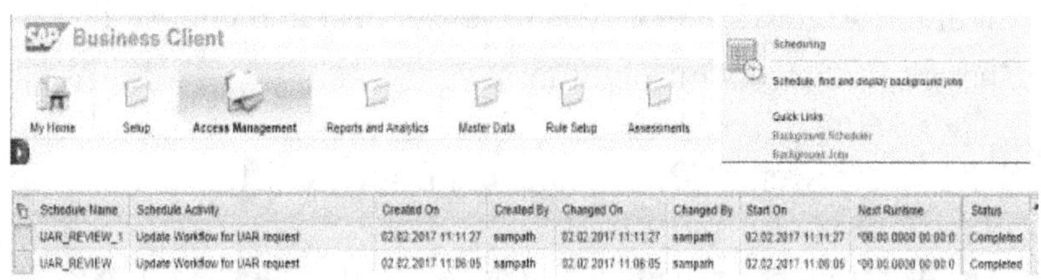

- From Schedule-Access Management Screen will appear, Choose Create to create a new request for Update Workflow.

- The Create Schedule screen will appear.

- Enter Schedule Name.

- Select Schedule Activity from the dropdown list. For UAR Requests, select Update Workflow for UAR Request.

- Choose Finish.

- After completing all of the above-mentioned steps, the request(s) will now come to the Reviewer's Work Inbox (or Outlook) to work on it or to any other approver configured in MSMP workflow earlier.

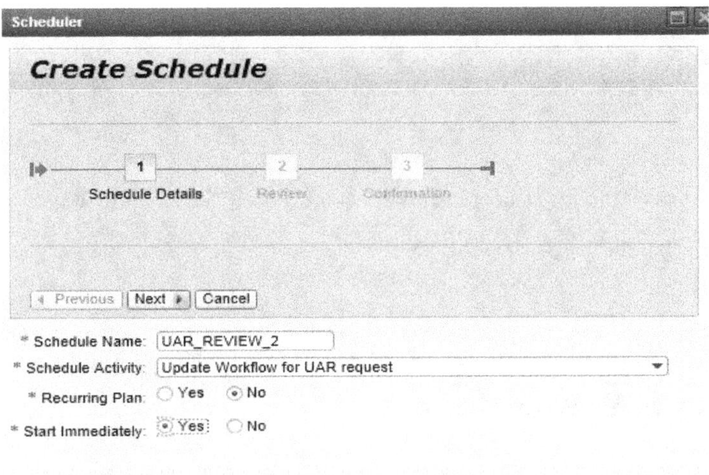

9. <u>UAR REVIEW</u>

After you update the request workflow, the request follows the workflow path and is routed to the appropriate reviewer.

After a request is generated, it is sent to the reviewer's Work Inbox. Using Search Request link, view the Request created and the Audit Logs.

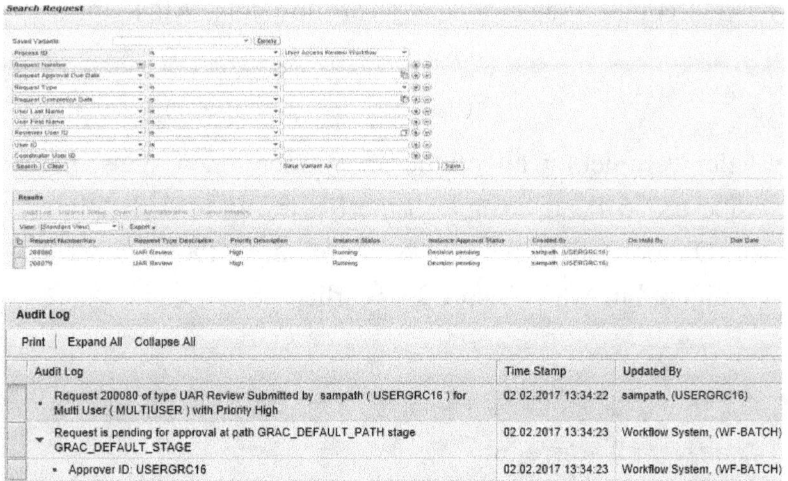

Request is sent to the reviewer based on the Reviewer (Manager/Role Approver/Reviewer updated by Admin) maintained.

Open NWBC using Reviewer's Id and go to Work Inbox under My Home Work Center.

In the Reviewer's Work Inbox, select the request you want to open by clicking on the selected request.

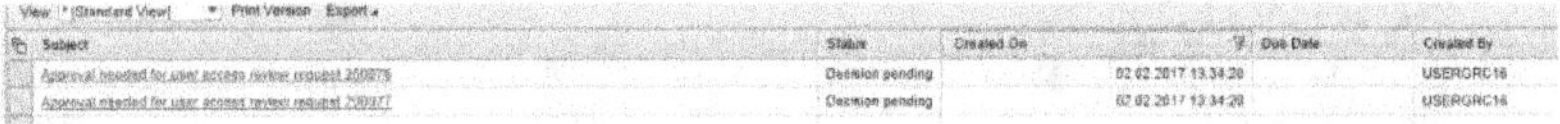

•You will see an UAR Review Screen with the Request Number that you selected.

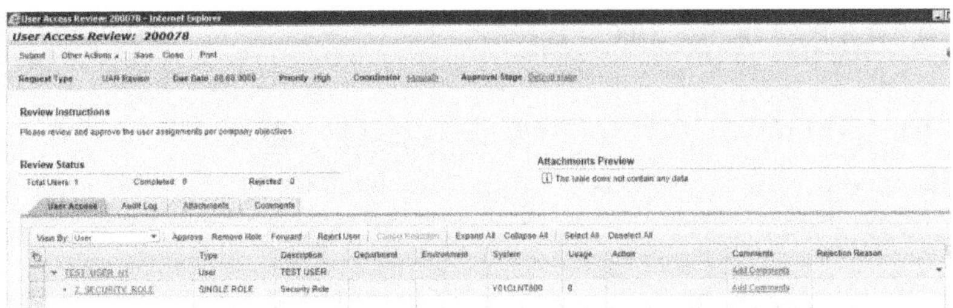

Select a user or Role and click on the available options as mentioned Below:

• **Approve** : You approve the request and the Role is not removed.

• **Remove Role** : Role is removed from the user.

• **Forward** : The request can be forwarded to another reviewer with a Note.

• **Reject User** : You reject to work on role for the user.

• **Reason** : Reason for rejection. Maintained in IMG under: T-Code: SPRO-> Governance, Risk, and Compliance-> User Provisioning-> Maintain Review Rejection Reasons

• **Add Comment** : Click Add Comment to add comment with the review request

• **Cancel Rejection** : You may cancel the rejected role/user prior submitting. ***Only applicable in rejected user view***

Once done click on Submit and then in next screen click on approve.

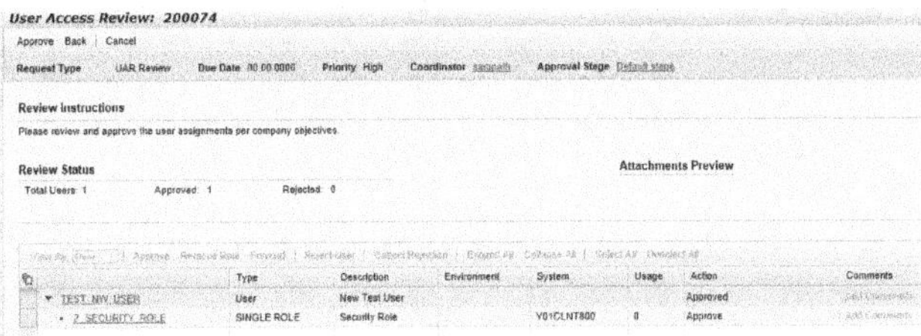

10. <u>MANAGE REJECTIONS</u>

The line items that are rejected by an approver can be accessed and reworked from the Managing Rejections screen.

From NWBC, Navigate to Access Management, under Compliance Certification Reviews click on Manage Rejections.

The Manage Rejections screen appears.

Specify the search criteria and choose the Search pushbutton. The rejected Items appear in the Result table.

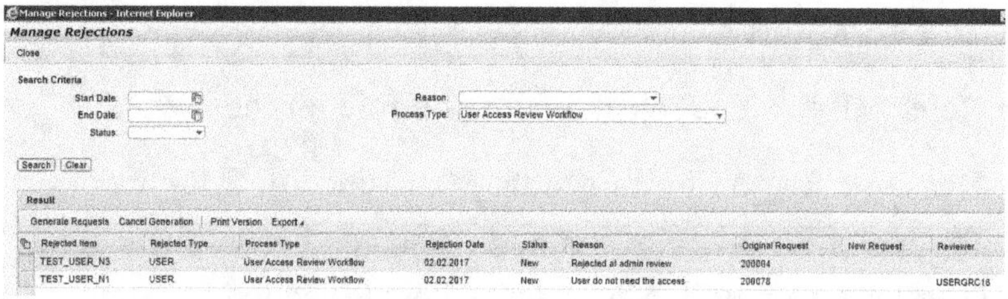

- Select the corresponding rejection and choose the Generate Requests pushbutton.

- This marks the request for inclusion in a new UAR Review request when the UAR Review Process Rejected background job is executed from Background scheduler.

- Similarly click on cancel generation to unmark the prevent the inclusion in new UAR Review request.

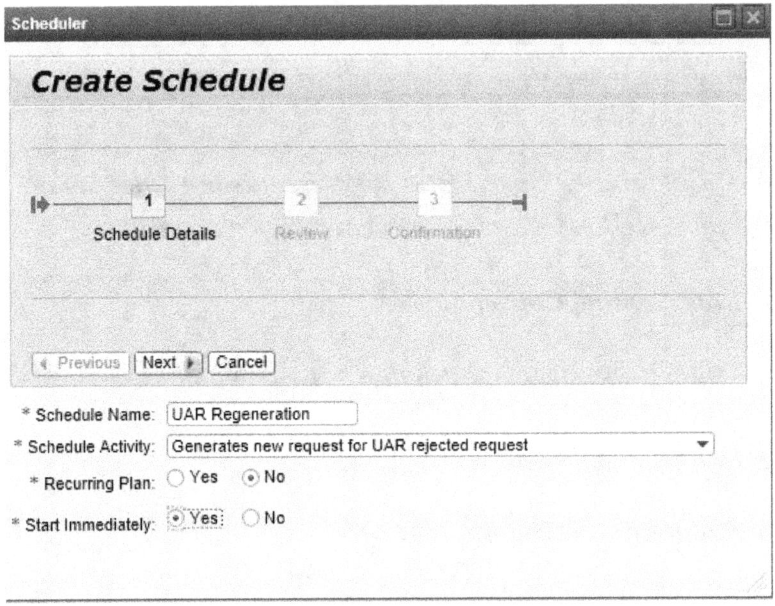

Scheduler
Create Schedule
1
Schedule Details
2
Review
3
Confirmation
Previous   Next   Cancel
* Schedule Name: UAR Regeneration
* Schedule Activity: Generates new request for UAR rejected request
* Recurring Plan: Yes   No
* Start Immediately: Yes   No

<u>BRM– BUSINESS ROLE MANAGEMENT</u>

1. Maintain Role Type Settings (Prerequisite : Integration scenario ROLMG needs to be activated for connector).

2. Role Naming Convention

3. Maintain Project and Product Release Name

4. Define Role Sensitivity

5. Maintain Role Status

6. Specify Critical Level

7. Define Companies

8. Maintain Functional Areas

9. Define Pre-Requisite Types

10. Define Role Prerequisites

11. Maintain Business Processes and Sub Processes

12. Role Methodology

1. <u>MAINTAIN ROLE TYPE SETTINGS</u>

This step provides the options to set various role types that can be designed in Business Role Manager.

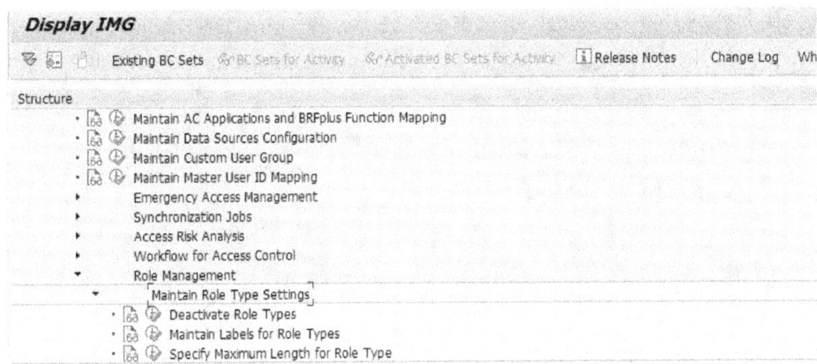

Call SPRO -->SAP Reference IMG --> Governance, Risk and Compliance --> Access Control --> Role Management -> Maintain Role Type Settings

Under Role Type Settings, complete the below configuration settings.

• Deactivate role types by selecting which aren't required for your environment (mandatory).

• Maintain labels for role types. This is an optional step if you want to create descriptions for role types.

• Define the maximum length for the role types per application type (optional).

DEACTIVATE ROLE TYPES

In this customizing activity, you can activate or deactivate role types. All role types are set as active by default

Call SPRO -->SAP Reference IMG --> Governance, Risk and Compliance --> Access Control --> Role

Management --> Maintain Role Type Settings --> Deactivate Role Types

The following role types are pre delivered:

• BUS - Business Role

• COM - Composite Role

• CUA - CUA Composite Role

• DRD – Derived Role

• GRP – Group (Enterprise Portal Group)

• PRF – Profile

• SIN – Single Role

• TPL – Template

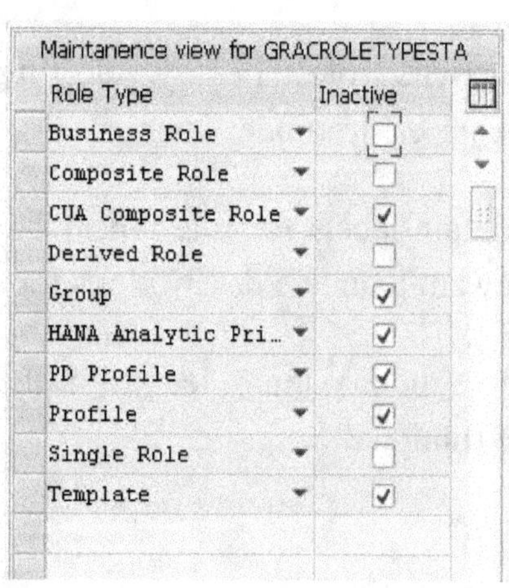

Check the inactive checkbox for the role types that you do not want to include in the role types definition

MAINTAIN LABELS FOR ROLE TYPES

In this customizing activity, you can maintain the description and language for the role types and is displayed on the role maintenance screen.

Call SPRO -->SAP Reference IMG --> Governance, Risk and Compliance --> Access Control --> Role Management ->

Maintain Role Type Settings --> Maintain Labels for Role Types

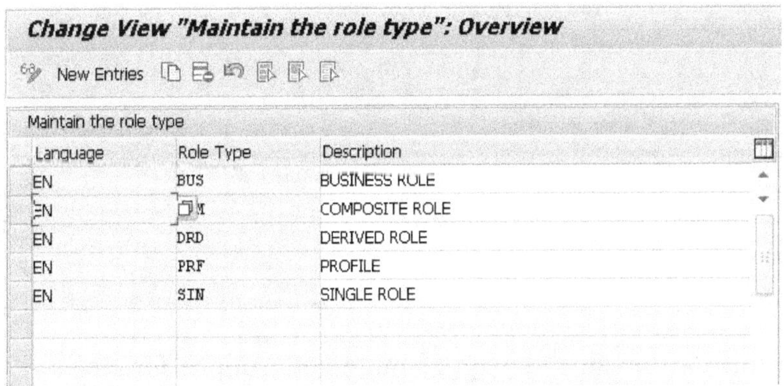

Language	Role Type	Description	
EN	BUS	BUSINESS ROLE	
EN	COM	COMPOSITE ROLE	
EN	DRD	DERIVED ROLE	
EN	PRF	PROFILE	
EN	SIN	SINGLE ROLE	

SPECIFY MAXIMUM LENGTH FOR ROLE TYPES

Call SPRO -->SAP Reference IMG --> Governance, Risk and Compliance --> Access Control --> Role Management

--> Maintain Role Type Settings --> Specify Maximum length for Role Types

In this customizing setting, you can specify the maximum length for the name of a role based on the role type.

Change View "Maintain the role name": Overview

New Entries

Maintain the role name

Role Type	Appl Type	Max Len
BUS	1	40
COM	1	32
DRD	1	36
SIN	1	34

2. <u>ROLE NAMING CONVENTION</u>

In this customizing setting, Naming conventions for Roles are maintained. This can be maintained for each of the Role Type defined earlier.

Call SPRO -->SAP Reference IMG --> Governance, Risk and Compliance --> Access Control --> Role Management

--> Specify Naming Conventions

The following Role Attributes are available for configuring the role naming convention:

- **BPROC** : Get information from Business Process attribute

- **BSUBPROC** : Get information from Business Sub-process attribute

- **CONNECTOR_GRP** : Get information from Connector Group Attribute

- **FREE_TEXT** : Free text entry. No Restrictions

- **PRJREL** : Get information from Project and Product Release attribute

- **ROLE_TYPE** : Get information Role Type attribute

- **STATIC_TEXT** : Use the text as provided by you.

Click on New Entries to create a Naming convention.

The attributes that can be maintained for a naming convention are position, description, role type and connector group.

Position is the sequence no of Naming convention.

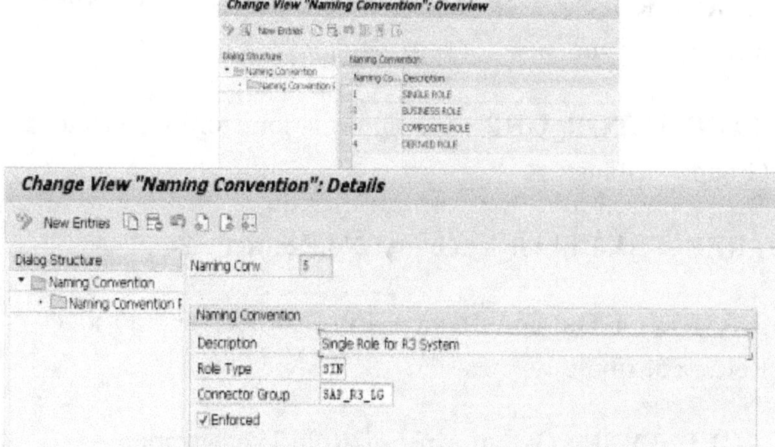

Click on Naming Convention Position to provide the contents of the Role Name.

The attributes to be maintained is the sequence no, Length, Role attribute and the static text.

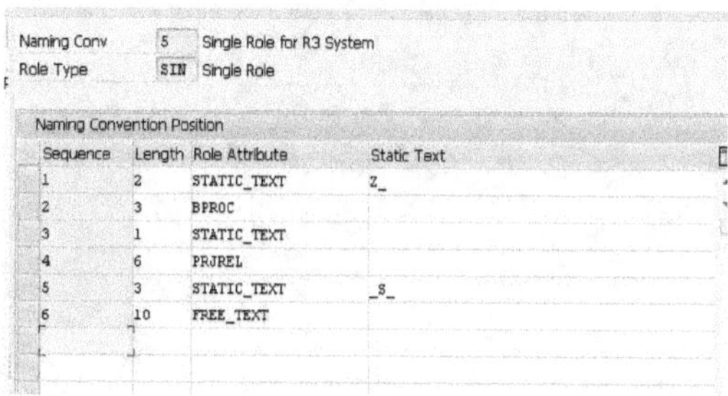

Sequence	Length	Role Attribute	Static Text
1	2	STATIC_TEXT	Z_
2	3	BPROC	
3	1	STATIC_TEXT	
4	6	PRJREL	
5	3	STATIC_TEXT	_S_
6	10	FREE_TEXT	

Based on above Naming convention, the role name will be displayed as: Z_<BPROC>_<PRJREL>_S_<FreeText> on the role maintenance screen if the role type is Single Role and the Group is SAP_R3_LG.

3. <u>MAINTAIN PROJECT AND PRODUCT RELEASE</u>

In this Customizing activity, you can create and edit the list of available projects and product releases.

Call SPRO -->SAP Reference IMG --> Governance, Risk and Compliance --> Access Control --> Role Management

--> Maintain Project and Product Release Name

• Projects are major undertakings planned by organizations.

• Some organizations may refer to projects by its product release name or version, for example, Customer Relation Manager 1.0

• In the application, the names for the projects and product release are attributes that you can assign to specific roles.

• They are available in a dropdown list in the role management screens.

• You can use the attribute to specify that a role is relevant for a specific project or product release.

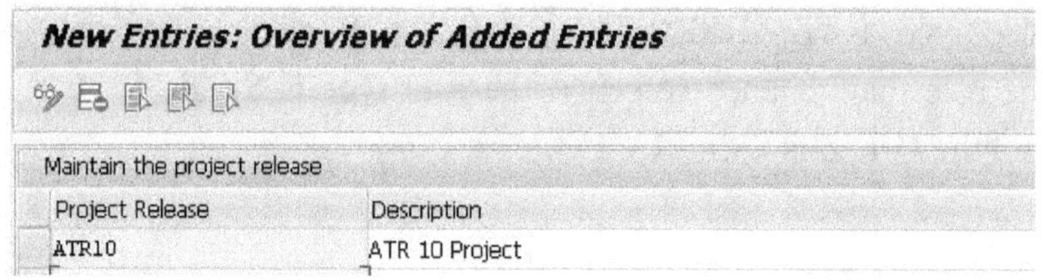

4. <u>DEFINE ROLE SENSITIVITY</u>

In this Customizing activity, you can create and edit the available role sensitivity values.

Call SPRO -->SAP Reference IMG --> Governance, Risk and Compliance --> Access Control --> Role Management

--> Define Role Sensitivity

Available entries are populated from the BC Set GRAC_ROLE_MGMT_SENTIVITY

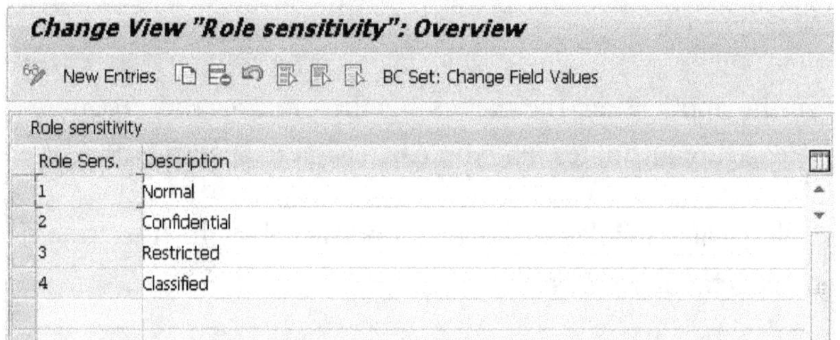

5. <u>MAINTAIN ROLE STATUS</u>

In this Customizing activity, you can create and edit the list of role status, and then choose one as the production status

Call SPRO -->SAP Reference IMG --> Governance, Risk and Compliance --> Access Control --> Role Management -> Maintain Role Status

Only roles with the status Production are available for provisioning.

The attribute is available in a dropdown list on the Role Management screen

Available entries are populated from the BC Set

GRAC_ROLE_MGMT_ROLE_STATUS

Change View "Maintain the role status": Overview		
New Entries ☐ ☐ ☐ ☐ ☐ ☐ BC Set: Change Field Values		

Maintain the role status		
Role Status	Productio...	Role Status
DEV	☐	Development
PRD	☑	Production
TST	☐	Testing

6. <u>SPECIFY CRITICAL LEVEL</u>

In this Customizing activity, you can create and edit the list of available critical levels.

Call SPRO -->SAP Reference IMG --> Governance, Risk

and Compliance --> Access Control --> Role Management -
-> Specify Critical Level

This is an attribute that you assign to roles.

You can use critical level to label as to how essential a role
for your company. Click on New Entries to add a critical
level.

Change View "Maintenance view for critical level": Overview

New Entries

Maintenance view for critical level

Critical Level	Critical Level
001	High
002	Meduim
003	Critical
004	Low

7. DEFINE COMPANIES

In this Customizing activity, you can create and edit the list
of available companies.

Call SPRO -->SAP Reference IMG --> Governance, Risk
and Compliance --> Access Control --> Role Management -
-> Define Companies

• This is an attribute that you assign to roles.

• It allows your organization to divide its divisions or
  groups by companies.

• This attribute is available in a dropdown list on the Role
  Management screen of the application Click on New

Entries to add a new company.

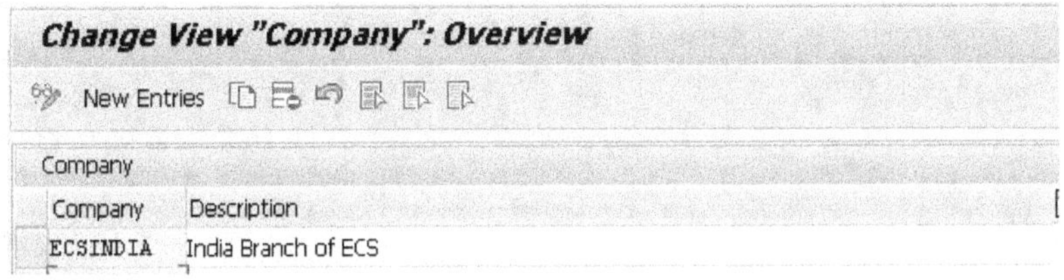

8. <u>MAINTAIN FUNCTIONAL AREAS</u>

In this Customizing activity, you can create and edit the list of available functional areas.

Call SPRO -->SAP Reference IMG --> Governance, Risk and Compliance --> Access Control --> Role Management -> Maintain Functional Areas

- A functional area is a group or department in a company that performs a specific task or function, such as engineering.

- In the application, function area is an attribute that you assign to roles.

- This attribute is available in a dropdown list on the Role Management screen of the application.

Click on New Entries to add a new functional Area.

Change View "Maintain functional areas": Overview

New Entries

Maintain functional areas

Funct Area	Description	Abbr	Company
FA01	Finance		HCL
HR	Human Resource		CTS
MM	MM	MM	ACCENTURE

9. DEFINE PREREQUISITES TYPES

In this Customizing activity, you can Define Role Prerequisites that are required to be validated before granting access to a user

Call SPRO -->SAP Reference IMG --> Governance, Risk and Compliance --> Access Control --> Role Management

--> Define Prerequisite types

Available entries are populated from the BC Set: GRAC_ROLE_MGMT_PRE_REQ_TYPE

You can create a new Requisite type by clicking on New Entries.

Change View "Prerequisite type": Overview

New Entries   BC Set: Change Field Values

Prerequisite type

Prereq Typ	Prerequisite Type
CERTIF	Certification
COURSE	Course Taken
HRS	Hours Worked
NDA	Non-disclosure Agreement
POINTS	Points Accumulated
TRAINING	Training

10. **DEFINE ROLE PREREQUISITES**

In this Customizing activity, you can create and maintain role prerequisite.

Call SPRO -->SAP Reference IMG --> Governance, Risk and Compliance --> Access Control --> Role Management --> Define Role Prerequisites

• You use this activity to specify whether the application must validate if a user has completed the requirements before being granted access.

• These Prerequisites are associated with a Role in NWBC Role Management screen by clicking on Prerequisite tab.

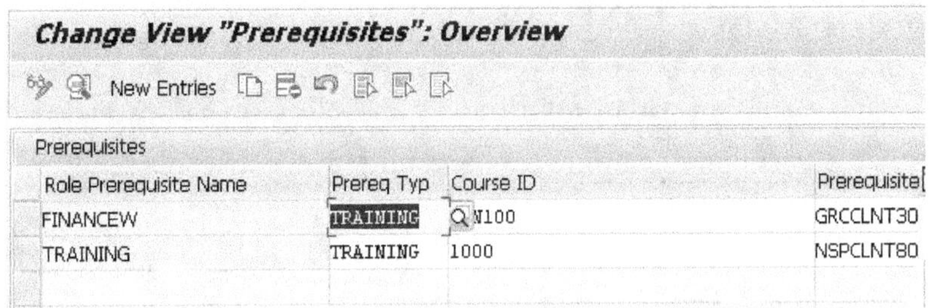

11. **MAINTAIN BUSINESS PROCESS AND SUB - PROCESS**

In this Customizing activity, you can create and edit the list of available businesses processes and subprocesses.

Call SPRO -->SAP Reference IMG --> Governance, Risk and Compliance --> Access Control --> Maintain Business

Processes and Subprocesses

• Business processes and subprocesses are the activities defined by your organization to meet its objectives.

• In the application, business processes and subprocesses are attributes that you can assign to specific roles.

• If the business process does not have a subprocess, then you must create a subprocess with the same name as the business process.

• As an example Finance is a Process and Accounts Receivable is a subprocess with Finance Business Process.

These are loaded as part of the activation of BC Set: GRAC_RA_RULESET_COMMON.

You can select a Business Process and click on Subprocess to view associated Subprocess and add new entries as well.

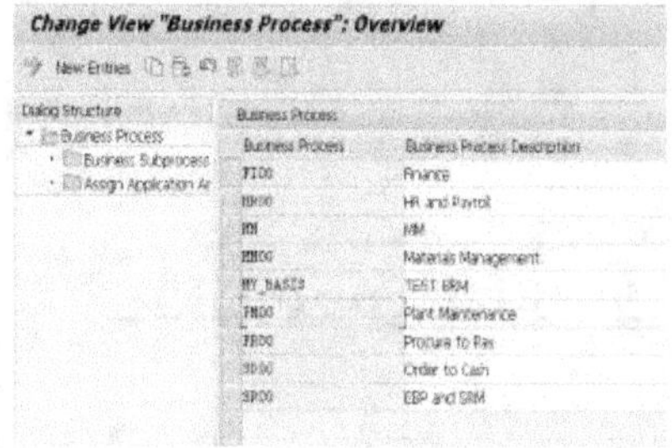

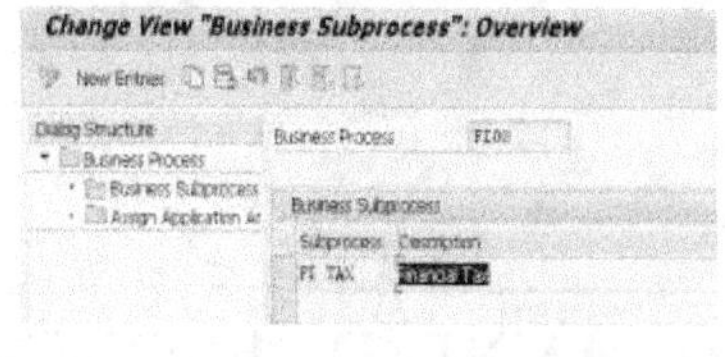

ROLE METHODOLOGY

1. Overview

2. Create BRF+ Rule

3. Assign Condition Group Type to BRF+ Application and Function

4. Define Role Methodology Process and Steps

5. Associate Role Methodology Process to Condition Group

1. OVERVIEW

- Role Methodology is the process followed for role creation and maintenance operation.

- The well-defined role management process that aligns with the Organization policies of an Organization can be configured in the Role Methodology.

- The Methodology customizing steps like "BRF+ Rule Creation" and "Methodology Process Definition" are not necessary when the default methodology process is used for role creation.

• These steps are required while creating customized methodology process

• BRF+ Rule Creation: Business Rules Framework plus (BRF plus) provides a comprehensive application programming interface (API) and user interface (UI) for defining and processing business rules.

• BRF+ is the rule engine that evaluated the various attributes of the role.

• Condition Groups link the BRF+ rules and the Role Methodology

2. <u>CREATE BRF+ RULE</u>

Call SPRO -->SAP Reference IMG --> Governance, Risk and Compliance --> Access Control --> Role Management -> Generate BRFplus Applications, Approvers, and Methodology Functions

Program Name: GRAC_GENERATE_ERM_BRFRULE

Define the BRF+ Application by giving Application name, Methodology Rule ID and Approvers Rule ID.

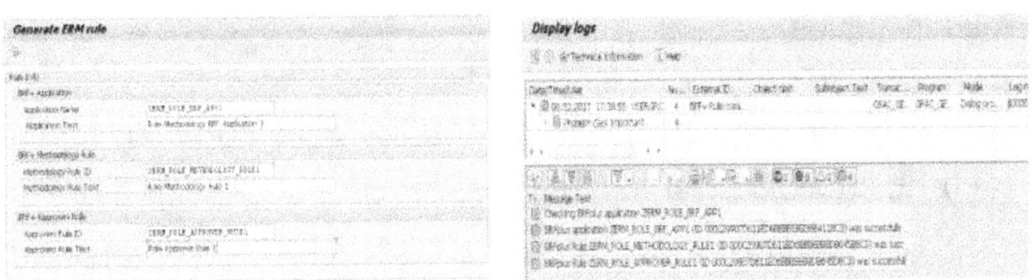

After executing the program verify the log for any errors. If errors are present, then they need to be fixed before proceeding to next step.

• Execute the TCODE: BRF+

• Select My Applications and search for the application that was just created.

• Expand the Application and Function Node

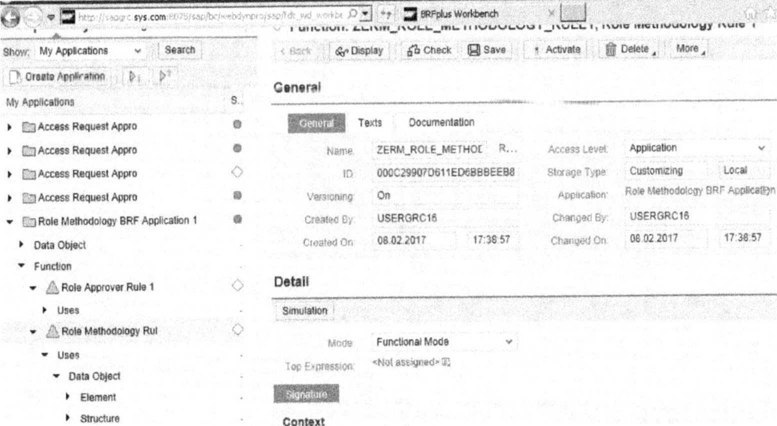

+DECISION TABLE

- Create a Decision Table by entering name and other related attributes.

- The decision table provides the rule for evaluation so, for each function a decision table is required

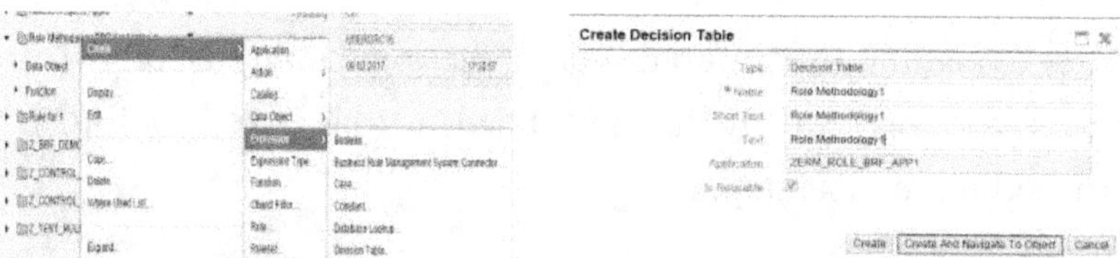

- Create Condition Columns for the Decision Table.

- Click Insert Column button and select From Context Data Objects.

Select the conditions that need to be evaluate. In this example, We will use Role Type to make decision.

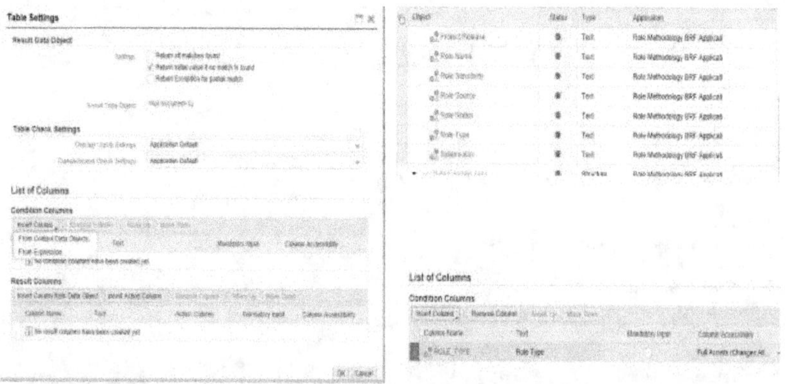

- Create Result Columns by clicking Insert Column from Data Object.

• Search for Result Column.

• Select Condition Group (GRAC_CNDGP) object from the search result

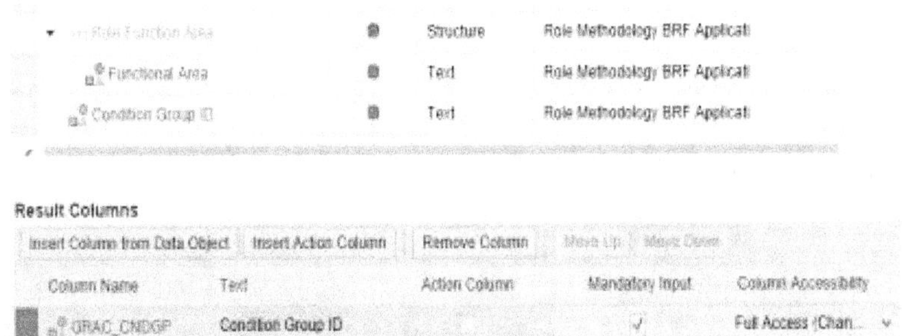

• Review the conditions and results

• Click OK to confirm the definition

• By Defining the Conditions and Results the definition of the Decision Table is complete.

Once the values for the Condition and Result Columns are defined, enter values for the Decision table used for rule execution.

• Click Insert New Row to create the values; enter values for the columns.

• Select Direct Value Input.

• Enter Value for the columns.

• Activate the Decision Table

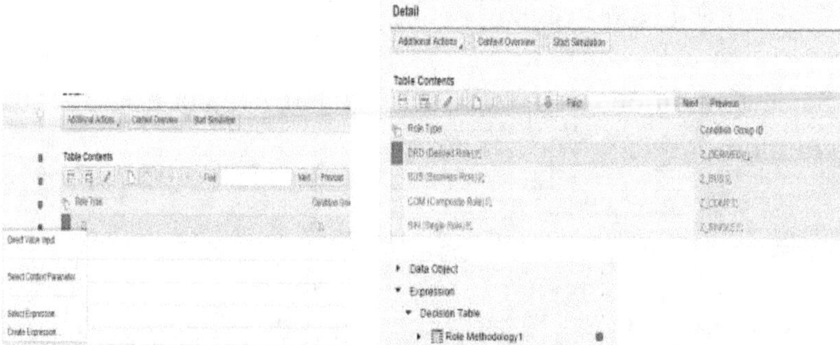

- Associate the Decision Table to Function by selecting it in the Top Expression of Function.

- Activate the function.

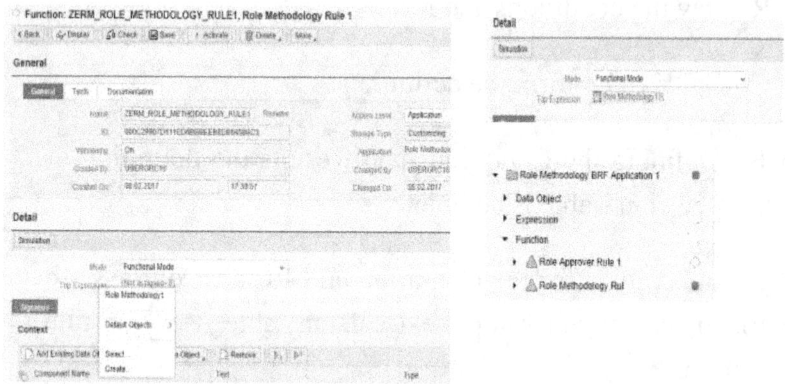

3. ASSIGN CONDITION GROUP TYPE

In this Customizing activity, you can assign the two delivered condition group types (methodology and approver) to the BRFplus applications and the BRFplus functions.

Call SPRO --> SAP Reference IMG --> Governance, Risk and Compliance --> Access Control --> Role Management --> Assign Condition Groups to BRFplus Functions

In this screen, select Condition Group and maintain the BRF+ application and relevant rule ID or function name. Two different condition groups are available: APPROVER and METHODOLOGY.

Change View "Condition group type to BRFplus assgnment": Overview

New Entries

Condition group type to BRFplus assgnment

Condition Group	BRFplus Application Name	BRFplus Function Name
APPROVER	ZERM_ROLE_BRF_APP1	ZERM_ROLE_APPROVER_RULE1
METHODOLOGY	ZERM_ROLE_BRF_APP1	ZERM_ROLE_METHODOLOGY_RULE1

4. <u>ROLE METHODOLOGY PROCESS AND STEPS</u>

• In this Customizing activity, you define the methodology processes and steps for role maintenance.

• The application provides a set of actions that can be used for role maintenance, such as definition, generation, and so on.

• You can select which actions to use, the order, and the frequency. This is called your methodology.

Call SPRO --> SAP Reference IMG --> Governance, Risk and Compliance --> Access Control --> Role Management -> Define Methodology Processes and Steps

DEFINING A STEP

• SAP provides a set of actions that you can perform for role maintenance.

• When you define a step, you select which actions to use and assign a name that in line with your companyguidelines.

• For example, you can select delivered action and Permissions, and name its phase as Maintain Authorizations per your company guidelines

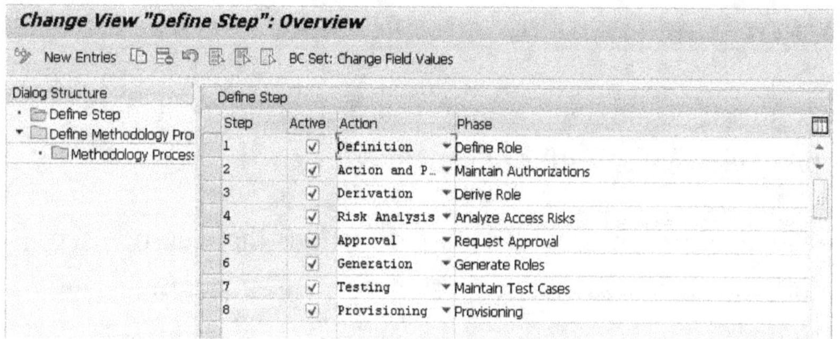

DEFINING A METHODOLOGY PROCESS

• You create the methodology processes as a framework to attach the methodology steps.

• You can create as many methodology processes as you needed.

• For example, you may want to have one methodology for finance role requests, and another for office administration role requests.

• Or you can create different methodology (set of steps) for single Role, Business Role or composite Role.

• Define the methodology name and provide a description, status, and which methodology will be defaulted for role creation.

• The Default methodology steps will be used when the Role creation screen is opened.

• The Applicable methodology only comes in place once the define Role step is completed and saved.

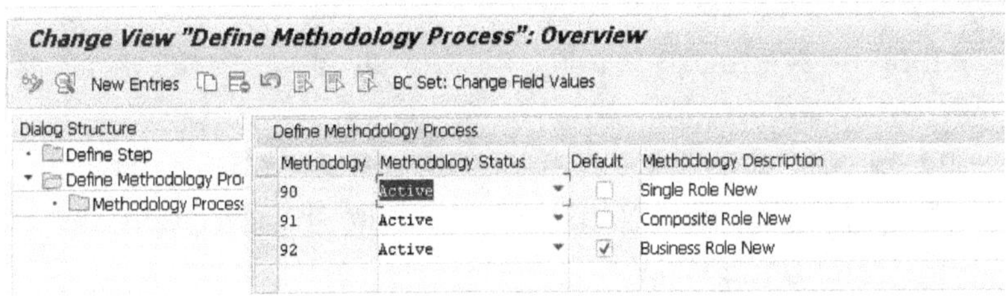

ADDING STEPS TO THE METHODOLOGY PROCESS

You assign the steps to the methodology processes and select the order of the steps. For example, for finance role requests, you may want to require several approval steps and risk analysis.

Define the step sequence or phases of the processes under this methodology that the role creation process will undergo.

Methodology Process Step		
Step Sequence	Step	Action
1	1	Definition
2	2	Action and Permis…
3	4	Risk Analysis
4	3	Derivation
5	5	Approval
6	6	Generation
7	7	Testing

5. <u>ASSOCIATE METHODOLOGY TO CONDITION GROUP</u>

• In this Customizing activity, you can associate the methodology processes to a condition group.

• The application uses this association to determine which methodology process to use based on the specified settings in the condition group.

Call SPRO --> SAP Reference IMG --> Governance, Risk and Compliance --> Access Control --> Role Management --> Associate Methodology Process to Condition Group

• Click on New Entries on the screen.

• Then you need to map the conditions groups created earlier to specific Role Methodology.

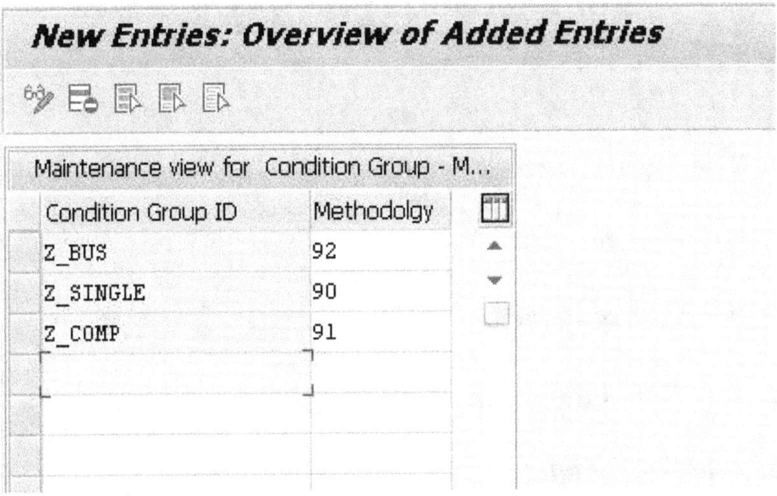

New Entries: Overview of Added Entries

Maintenance view for Condition Group - M...

Condition Group ID	Methodolgy
Z_BUS	92
Z_SINGLE	90
Z_COMP	91

<u>ROLE MASS MAINTENANCE</u>

1. Role Import

2. Role Update

3. Derived Org Value Update

4. Role Risk Analysis

5. Role Generation

6. Role Comparison

7. Role Usage Report

ROLE AFFIRMATION

• Role Reaffirm is used to reaffirm permissions and authorizations for selected roles that are due to expire. For example, over a period, employees may change employment positions within a company or leave the company. It is standard practice for companies to have their managers review   whether the authorizations and roles assigned to their employees is still relevant.

• On the Role Reaffirm screen, you can search for roles, and then choose from the following actions: Approve, Remove, or Hold.

The Role Reaffirmation option is similar to User Access Review with role approver with the exception of Role Reaffirmation entails configuring the reaffirm date on roles in Role Management.

Role reaffirm must be configured for the periods which the roles need to be reaffirmed with notification configuration that will send email reminders to the approvers. The approvers then can perform the role reaffirm action.

CONFIGURATION OF ROLE AFFIRMATION:

Go to Access Management > Role Management > Role Maintenance >Click on Role Maintenance>open the Role and go to properties to set up the Role Reaffirm period.

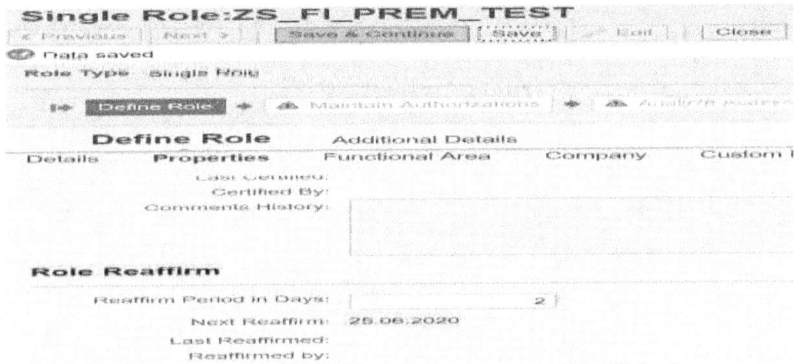

To do the Role reaffirmation, click on the below highlighted option in Role management and search the Role as per connector name.

Take the required decision to approve, remove or hold the Role assignment and click in Submit.

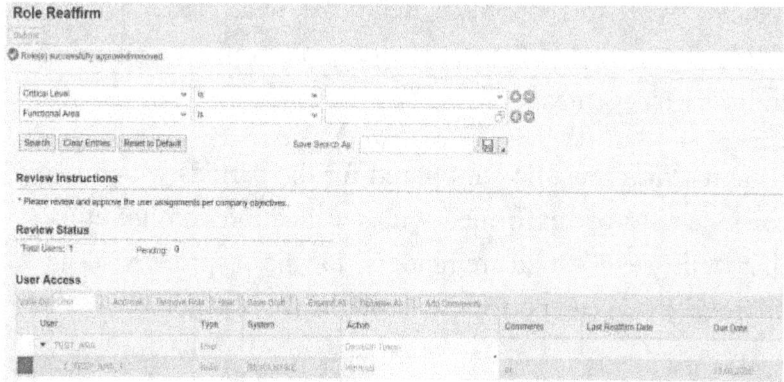

SAP GRC ACCESS CONTROL 12.0 END USER LOGON CONFIGURATION

Allows users who do not have direct access to SAP Access Control to perform the following services, providing the specific service is activated:

- ***Submit requests for access***

- ***Find the status of submitted requests***

- ***Register for Password Self Service***

- ***Change passwords***

- ***Execute a name change***

- ***View their profile***

Limitations of End User Logon: End User Logon is intended to allow users to request access to SAP Access Control without having a user ID in SAP Access Control and hence SSO is not supported.

Prerequisite to enable End User Login:

- Configure User Authentication Data Source and End user Verification.

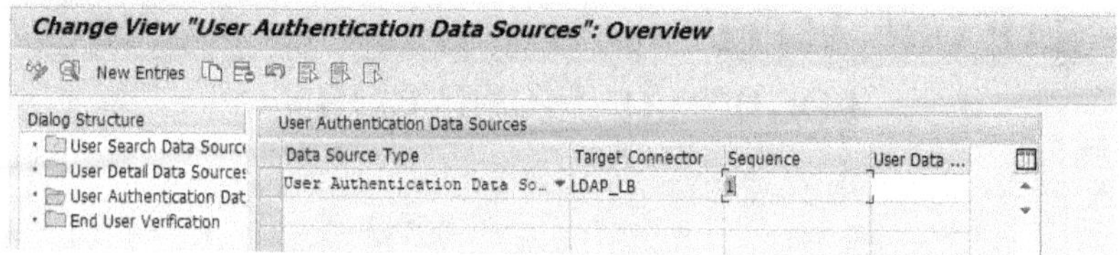

- Create a Guest user(Type-System) for SAP end user Logon Service with Role SAP_GRAC_END_USER

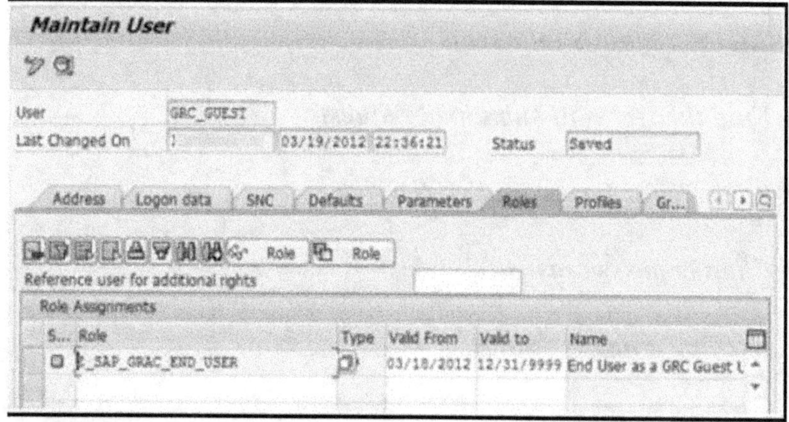

- Activate the SICF Service - GRAC_UIBB_END_ USER_LOGIN

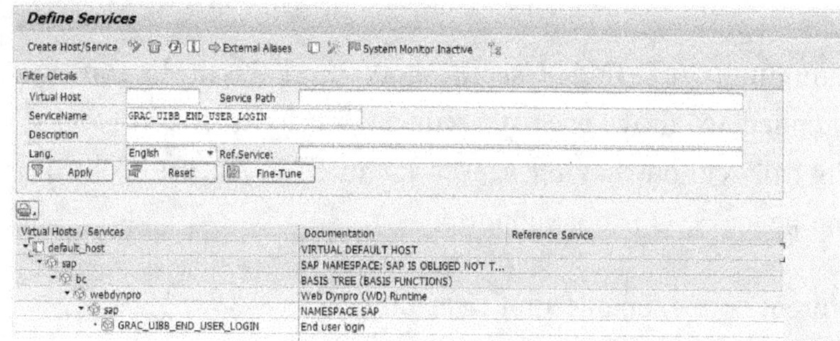

Modify Logon Data Information in change mode of Service.

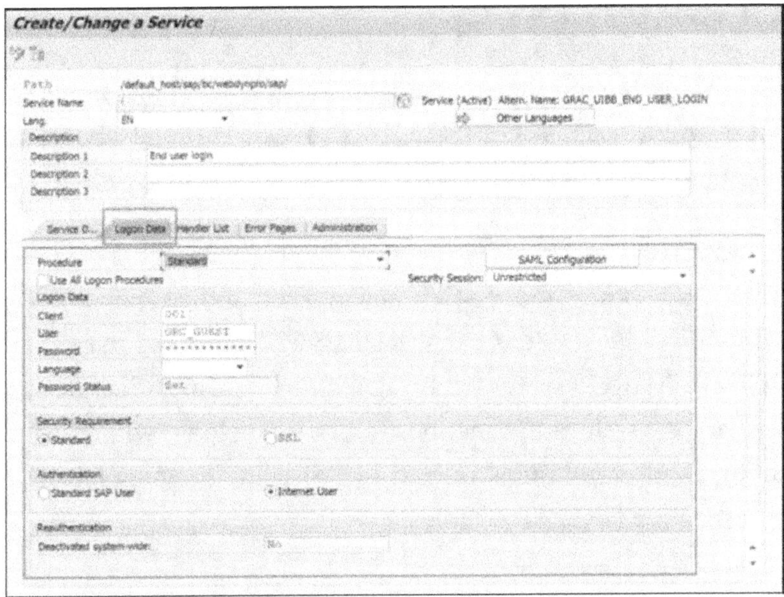

• Test the service again to access the End User Logon page.

• If authentication is set to NO, enter an ID that has been synchronized to the GRC system. b. If authentication is set to YES, use a valid ID and password from the authentication source. This should open the End User Home page.

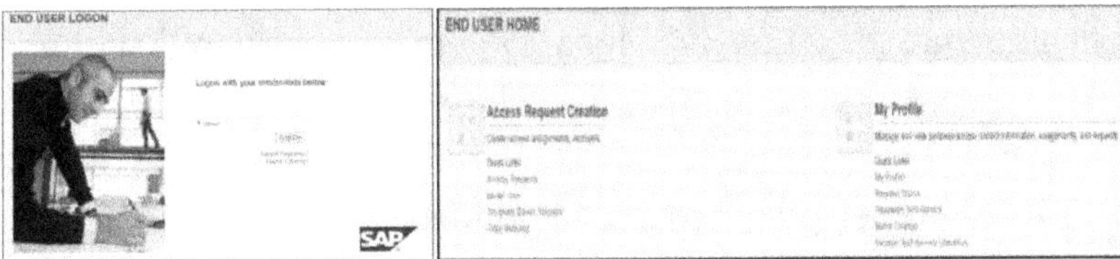

S/4 HANA FIORI RULESET

SAP has delivered the standard ruleset for S/4 Hana along with the Fiori apps with SAP GRC 10.1 SP20 and above versions (All SP levels > 20 for SAP GRC 10.1 and with all the SP levels of SAP GRC 12.0).

You may bring the S/4 Hana ruleset into action by activating the "GRAC_RA_RULESET_S4HANA_ALL" BC set in GRC system. Upon activating the specified BC set, all the relevant functions and risks along with the actions and permissions related to S/4 Hana get populated in respective GRC ARA tables.

Please follow below steps to activate the S/4 Hana ruleset.

- Ensure that you are on at least SP20 of SAP GRC 10.1 version or any SP level of SAP GRC 12.0

- Activate the GRAC_RA_RULESET_S4HANA_ALL and GRAC_RA_RULESET_COMMON BC sets using SCPR20 in GRC system

- Make sure that the S/4 Hana system is configured with GRC system for the intended purpose

- Modify the standard S/4 connector group created automatically during the BC activation to incorporate the S/4 connector in it (A new group can also be created depending upon the requirement)

- Generate the ruleset to ensure that the risk analysis is giving the results correctly for the updated connector group

DIFFERENT OPTIONS TO CONFIGURE THE FIORI APP INTO THE RULESET

There are two ways by which you may configure the Fiori app into Ruleset.

1. By adding Fiori app relevant O-data services

2. By adding Fiori app relevant Semantic Object and Action combination

Steps to add Fiori app relevant O-data services

- Identify the Fiori Apps that needs to be added to the rulebook

- Extract the leading O-data services details for the apps identified for the addition

- Identify the Function-Fiori app mapping (Fiori app can be either added to the existing function or new function can be created depending upon the functionality of the Fiori app)

- Identify the Function-Risk mapping in case new function in being added

- Select the appropriate connector group and add the Fiori app relevant services into respective functions identified for Fiori app addition by adding [SVC] prefix to it e.g. For Fiori App F0718, add [SVC]FAC_GL_DOCUMENT_POST_SRV as an action into relevant function

- Once the O-data service is added to the action tab, system will populate the permission details automatically

- Once the services addition activity is over, generate the ruleset again so that system will consider the recently added changes while running the risk analysis

DIFFERENT OPTIONS TO CONFIGURE THE FIORI APP INTO THE RULESET

Steps to add Fiori app relevant Semantic Object and Action combination

- Identify the Fiori Apps that needs to be added to the rulebook

- Extract the Semantic object and Action details for the apps identified for the addition

- Identify the Function-Fiori app mapping (Fiori app can be either added to the existing function or new function can be created depending upon the functionality of the Fiori app)

- Identify the Function-Risk mapping in case new function in being added

- Select the appropriate connector group and add the Fiori app relevant Semantic Object-Action combination into respective functions identified for Fiori app addition by adding [FAPP] prefix to it

e.g. For Fiori App F0718, "AccountingDocument" is a Semantic object and "postGLDocument" is a semantic action. Add, [FAPP]AccountingDocument-postGLDocument as an action into relevant function

- Once the O-data service is added to the action tab,

permission details need to be added manually

- Once the services addition activity is over, generate the ruleset again so that system will consider the recently added changes while running the risk analysis

<u>COMPARISON: O-DATA SERVICES VS SEMANTIC OBJECT-ACTION</u>

O-Data Service in a Function	Semantic Object-Action in a Function
[SVC] Prefix is added before the service name	[FAPP] Prefix is added before Semantic Object-Action
Once the service is added as an Action into "Actions" tab, Permission details are populated automatically in Permissions tab	As there is no provision to add SU24 details for Semantic Object-Action combination, permissions details need to be maintained manually
Risk analysis results won't consider whether the catalog/group access is provided/being provided in Gateway system or not (False positive risks)	Risk analysis results will consider whether the relevant catalog/group access is provided/being provided in Gateway system or not (Fiori connector need to be maintained as subsequent connector for S/4 Hana system)